Israel and the Persian Gulf

Florida A&M University, Tallahassee
Florida Atlantic University, Boca Raton
Florida Gulf Coast University, Ft. Myers
Florida International University, Miami
Florida State University, Tallahassee
University of Central Florida, Orlando
University of Florida, Gainesville
University of North Florida, Jacksonville
University of South Florida, Tampa
University of West Florida, Pensacola

Also by Gawdat Bahgat, from the University Press of Florida:

American Oil Diplomacy in the Persian Gulf and the Caspian Sea (2003)

Israel and the Persian Gulf

RETROSPECT AND PROSPECT

Gawdat Bahgat

UNIVERSITY PRESS OF FLORIDA

Gainesville   Tallahassee   Tampa   Boca Raton

Pensacola   Orlando   Miami   Jacksonville   Ft. Myers

Library of Congress Cataloging-in-Publication Data
Bahgat, Gawdat.
Israel and the Persian Gulf: restrospect and prospect / Gawdat Bahgat.
p. cm.
Includes bibliographical references and index.
ISBN 0-8130-2908-2 (alk. paper)
1. Israel—Foreign relations—Persian Gulf Region. 2. Persian Gulf Region—
Foreign relations—Israel. 3. Israel—Foreign relations—Arab countries.
4. Arab countries—Foreign relations—Israel. I. Title.
DS119.6.B325 2005   327.5694053—dc22

The University Press of Florida is the scholarly publishing agency
for the State University System of Florida, comprising Florida A&M University,
Florida Atlantic University, Florida Gulf Coast University, Florida International University,
Florida State University, University of Central Florida, University of Florida, University
of North Florida, University of South Florida, and University of West Florida.

University Press of Florida
15 Northwest 15th Street
Gainesville, FL 32611-2079
http://www.upf.com

Contents

Preface

For decades, the Middle East has played a central role in world affairs. In the Levant, the creation of Israel in 1948 and the subsequent series of Arab-Israeli wars have drastically and permanently altered the landscape. In the Persian Gulf, the toppling of the monarchy in Iraq in 1958 was followed by a number of leftist and radical-nationalist regimes that created chaos and instability not only in Iraq but throughout the Gulf region. These upheavals included an eight-year war with neighboring Iran and an invasion of another neighbor, Kuwait. Finally, an American-led international coalition overthrew the regime and opened a new chapter in Iraqi history in 2003. The toppling of the Pahlavi regime in 1979 and the drastic shift in Iran's domestic and foreign policy represented a turning point in Iran's and the region's policy. Finally, changes in oil prices and policies have contributed to the emergence of Saudi Arabia and the other Gulf monarchies as prominent players on both the regional and international scenes.

These extraordinary developments have attracted the attention of many analysts and students of Middle Eastern policy. Ironically, very few analysts have sought to establish the connection between the two Middle Eastern subsystems—the Levant and the Persian Gulf. This volume is an attempt to fill this void. The main argument in this book is that the Levant and the Persian Gulf are interrelated; developments in one region are echoed in the other. I first tried to establish this connection in a paper presented at a conference in Copenhagen in 1999, sponsored by the Ford Foundation. "Israel and Iran: Prospects for Détente" later appeared as a chapter in a book edited by Bjorn Moller, *Oil and Water: Cooperative Security in the Persian Gulf*. I have continued and expanded my research on the interactions between the two regions.

No attempt is made in this book to analyze the foreign policy of Israel or the Gulf states. Rather, I examine all major episodes between Israel and the eight Gulf states (Bahrain, Iran, Iraq, Kuwait, Oman, Qatar, Saudi Arabia, and the United Arab Emirates). The experience and lessons learned from these episodes help to shed light on the potential course they are likely to take toward each other in the foreseeable future. At the end of each chapter I take the risk of providing some guidelines on future relations between Israel and the Gulf states. The main conclusion and policy implication of the analysis in this volume is that a comprehensive peace in the Middle East has to address sources of instability in the Levant and the Persian Gulf simultaneously.

This study is addressed primarily to university students concentrating on the Middle East, to foreign-service officers and government officials dealing with the region, and more broadly, to educated laymen interested in international relations. The time span expands from the creation of Israel in 1948 until the death of Yasser Arafat in November 2004. The analysis is based exclusively on Arabic, Iranian, Israeli, and Western open sources available to researchers and the public.

Many people helped me in writing this book. Most notably, Amy Gorelick, editor at University Press of Florida, gave substantial help and support at different stages. I am very grateful to her. I also would like to thank Sandra and Pat Dickson, Beth and Steven Sims, Helen and Gene Hooker, Anthony McDermott, Dorothea El Mallakh, Theresa McDevitt, Tami Hughes, and Michele Reynolds. Without their inspiration, this work would not have been completed. Despite all the assistance I have received in the course of preparing this book, all errors of fact or judgment are mine alone.

Abbreviations

AMAL	Battalions of the Lebanese Resistance
EU	European Union
IAEA	International Atomic Energy Agency
ICO	Islamic Conference Organization
KDP	Kurdish Democratic Party
NPT	Treaty on the Non-Proliferation of Nuclear Weapons
OPEC	Organization of Petroleum Exporting Countries
PLO	Palestine Liberation Organization
WMD	Weapons of Mass Destruction

1

Introduction

For a long time two persistent themes—oil and Israel—have shaped the contemporary Middle East. The discovery of huge hydrocarbon resources and the accumulation of massive oil revenues have intensified regional and international interests and conflicts in the Persian Gulf since the early twentieth century. Equally important, the creation of Israel in 1948 in the midst of the Arab and Muslim Levant has led to several major military conflicts between the Jewish state and its Arab neighbors.

Most students of Middle Eastern policy and policy makers in Europe and the United States have addressed these two Middle East subsystems—the Persian Gulf and the Levant—separately. The underlying assumption is that developments in one area are independent of changes in the other region. Despite growing literature on the Persian Gulf and the Arab-Israeli conflict, very few analysts have sought to establish the connection between the two regions. This study seeks to bridge this gap.

International, regional, and domestic developments in the past five years have underscored the strong links between the two regions, particularly the continuing violence between Israel and the Palestinians, the September 11 terrorist attacks on the United States, and the 2003 war in Iraq. The escalation of attacks and counterattacks in the West Bank and Gaza Strip has further deepened the need to reach a negotiated peace agreement. The death of Yasser Arafat in November 2004 was seen by many as an end of an era and an opportunity to aggressively pursue peace talks. This lack of meaningful peace and the deterioration of socioeconomic conditions have intensified the Palestinians' sense of desperation and contributed to an increase of attacks on military and civilian Israeli targets. Israeli military operations against Palestinian civilians have been shown on television screens throughout the Middle East. Many Arabs and Iranians see the Palestinian attacks on Israeli targets as a legitimate form of resistance against foreign occupation. Thus Hamas, Palestinian Islamic

Jihad, and the Lebanese Party of God (Hizbollah) drew a great deal of sympathy from Arabs and Iranians. These same groups are considered terrorist organizations by the United States, Israel, and some European countries.

The September 11 terrorist attacks on the United States and the ongoing war on terrorism have highlighted the differences between the United States and the Persian Gulf states on the definition of terrorism and have increased pressure on the latter to disassociate themselves from anyone Washington considers a terrorist. Iran and Saudi Arabia have emphasized that they provide humanitarian, not military, assistance to the Palestinian and Lebanese groups. In addition, Tehran has sought to use its leverage to restrain Hizbollah and prevent an escalation of violence by the Shi'ias either in Lebanon or in post-Saddam Iraq. Equally important, the Saudi leaders have renewed their efforts to reach a comprehensive peace in the Middle East in what is known as the Abdullah Peace Plan. This initiative, launched in 2002, was driven partly by the need to distance Saudi Arabia from terrorism and improve the kingdom's image in Washington and other Western capitals, and partly by the need to put an end to the bloodshed between the Palestinians and the Israelis.

The 2003 war in Iraq, probably more than any other development, has demonstrated the close links between the Gulf and the Levant. Shortly after the toppling of Saddam Hussein's regime, an Arab-Israeli peace plan known as the "Road Map" was introduced. This initiative is sponsored by the United States, the European Union, Russia, and the United Nations. This international effort to make peace between the Arabs and Israel in the aftermath of a major war in Iraq is not new. Following the 1991 Gulf War, the Madrid Peace Conference was held with the participation of all major parties of the conflict. In other words, the connections between the Arab-Israeli peace process and stability in the Persian Gulf are not coincidental. Furthermore, the war and its aftermath represent the peak of American intervention in the Middle East. This is the first time in the region's history that a U.S.-led international coalition toppled an Arab regime, arrested its leader, and occupied the entire country for a prolonged period of time.

To sum up, the Middle East is on the verge of a historic transformation. The world's only superpower—the United States—is heavily involved in shaping the future of a major Arab country—Iraq. The slow emergence of a post-Saddam Iraq will have a tremendous impact on neighboring states and the regional order. Will a stable Iraq, if and when it emerges, serve as a model for other countries in the Persian Gulf? What role will Iraq play in the Persian Gulf and the Arab-Israeli conflict? What kind of interaction, if any, will Iraq have with Tel Aviv? How will Tehran, Riyadh, and other Arab states respond to the changing dynamics of the regional order? Will a détente, or a rapprochement, emerge between the Persian Gulf states and Israel?

This volume seeks to provide tentative answers to these questions. Instead of speculating on what might happen, it examines major economic, political, and strategic interactions between Tehran, Baghdad, and Riyadh on one side and Tel Aviv on the other side. Attention is focused on the contribution of each of these Gulf states to the Arab-Israeli conflict/peace process. These contributions were either direct (Baghdad and Riyadh sending troops to fight in the wars against Israel) or indirect (Tehran and Riyadh supporting Lebanese and Palestinian groups in a proxy war against Israel). It is also important to point out that the Gulf states' attitude toward the Jewish state has not always been negative. The Pahlavi Iran had close relations with Israel. Similarly, Saudi Arabia proposed two peace plans with Israel.

In short, this study examines direct and indirect interactions between the Persian Gulf states and Israel. It sheds light on the main forces that shaped the Gulf states' attitude toward the Jewish state. Analysis suggests that ideological orientations (pan-Arabism and political Islam), as interpreted by the ruling elites, have hardened the stance toward Israel. On the other hand, economic and strategic interests have contributed to a more accommodative policy. Accordingly, the steady and slow decline of ideology and the relative predominance of national interests in formulating foreign policy in the region suggest that the future interaction between the Gulf states and Israel is likely to be less hostile than it was in the last half century. Indeed, assuming real progress in the Arab-Israeli peace process, prospects for cooperation between Tel Aviv and Tehran, Baghdad, and Riyadh should not be ruled out. Another significant policy implication of this study is that peace between the Arabs and the Israelis and stability in the Persian Gulf are intertwined and reinforce each other. The two subsystems should not be addressed separately. Developments in one region are echoed in the other. A détente between the Persian Gulf states and Israel is essential to reaching a lasting, comprehensive peace in the broad Middle East.

Framework for Analysis

An examination of the Persian Gulf states' attitude toward Israel over the past half century is so complicated that it defies analyses based on any one conceptual approach to foreign policy. Instead, this study employs a multidimensional approach to capture the complexity of the interactions between the two Middle Eastern subsystems. Specifically, six theoretical tools have been used in this study—international system, realism, geopolicy, ideology, minorities, and decision-making theory.

The International System

Given its strategic location, the Middle East has long been subject to competition from the global powers. The discovery of oil in the twentieth century—first in Iran, then Iraq, and later in the other Gulf monarchies—and the growing world dependence on this strategic commodity have further intensified global interests in the region. The creation of Israel in 1948 with its strong ties to foreign powers, particularly the United States, has added one more dimension to international involvement in the Middle East.

It is important to point out that the American support of Israel and Soviet support to the Arabs during the cold war did not immediately follow the birth of Israel. Seeking to win support from what were then the world's two superpowers, David Ben-Gurion, the first Israeli prime minister, deliberately adopted "a non-identification foreign policy stand."[1] Besides their status as superpowers, the United States and the former Soviet Union had the two largest Jewish communities in the world. They represented a significant manpower pool for the newly born state. Thus, Israel's involvement with the superpowers has been of extraordinary intensity since its creation. With the growing polarization of both the regional and international systems, Israel had to choose sides. Gradually the Soviet Union emerged as the main patron of revolutionary Arab states, and Tel Aviv consolidated its close relations with Washington.

This close cooperation between Israel and the United States had been a major source of contention in Washington's relations with Riyadh. American officials have long sought to separate their policy in the Arab-Israeli arena from that in the Persian Gulf. Many Arabs and Iranians see the two issues as inseparable. The Saudis have always sought to use their close relations with the United States to pressure it to adopt an evenhanded approach to the Arab-Israeli conflict. Mostly these efforts have been unsuccessful. Like the Islamic Republic of Iran and Iraq, Saudi Arabia does not recognize the state of Israel. However, the Saudi rhetoric is not as negative as that of Iran or Iraq (until the 2003 war). In 1981 and 2002 two Saudi crown princes proposed peace plans that included a diplomatic recognition of Israel. Thus it can be argued that the close relations between the United States, Saudi Arabia, Oman, and Qatar have contributed to a less hostile stand toward Israel by these three Gulf monarchies.

Similarly, it can be argued that the close relations the shah of Iran had with the United States played a role in his cooperation with Israel. Put differently, the top officials in the Pahlavi regime thought that good relations with Tel Aviv would improve Iran's image in Washington. The Islamic regime's declared hostility toward Israel is a major hurdle in any possible rapprochement with the United States. It is hard to imagine any improvement in American-Iranian relations without relaxation of Tehran's opposition to the Arab-Israeli peace process and some acceptance of the Jewish state.

Finally, the nationalist and leftist regimes that ruled Baghdad from 1958 until 2003 expressed strong opposition to the United States and Israel.[2] The drastic changes in Iraq since March 2003 and the heavy American involvement in rebuilding the "new Iraq" probably will not lead to immediate normalization of relations between Baghdad and Tel Aviv, but it is safe to predict that the post-Saddam Iraq, when it emerges, is likely to be less hostile toward Israel than the "old Iraq."

Realism

Realism is the traditionally dominant school of international relations theory. Some of its major themes are as follows: The state is the preeminent actor in the international and regional systems. Accordingly, the state is the major unit of analysis in realism. States are seen as unitary rational actors advancing their national interests, responding to external threats, and taking advantage of opportunities provided by the regional and international systems. These national interests are defined in terms of power. Power is viewed as the ability to induce another actor to behave in some desired fashion or to refrain from undesired behavior. This power is attained and maintained either by diplomatic means or by displaying force. Given the conflicting national interests and the fact that the increased security of one state actor is usually at the expense of another, the international system is inheritably unstable.[3] Finally, it is maintained that both the above assumptions accurately "characterize the perceptions and actions of foreign policy elites, and that these elites are able to formulate such policy independently of any significant pressures from their domestic political and economic systems."[4]

The Israeli raid on the Iraqi nuclear reactor Osiraq in 1981 seems to fit this model. Seeking to prevent a regional rival from obtaining and developing nuclear capabilities, Israel sent jets, in a preemptive strike, to destroy Baghdad's nuclear facilities. Despite the success of the Israeli raid, it can be argued that it provided incentives for the proliferation of other kinds of weapons of mass destruction. Some of Israel's regional rivals decided that, since the risks of developing nuclear capabilities were too high, the second best choice was to stockpile chemical and biological weapons. Moreover, the Israeli raid did not stop Saddam Hussein from trying to acquire nonconventional capabilities, including nuclear ones, in the late 1980s and early 1990s. In short, as realism argues, states pursuing their national interests, defined as power, contribute to anarchy in the regional and international systems.

Despite the validity of the realist theory in explaining some of the interactions between the Persian Gulf states and Israel, the model shows some significant drawbacks. Basically, realism "focuses upon the state's outward behavior but largely ignores its origins and its composition."[5] In other words, realist writers pay almost exclusive attention to the state's vulnerability to external powers and little attention to vulnerability of the ruling regime within the state. The Persian Gulf states' attitude toward Israel can be partially explained by transnational ideological orientations such as pan-Arabism and political Islam. In addition, it can be argued that hostility toward Israel has served as a legitimizing mechanism to some Arab regimes including Iraq, which does not share borders with the Jewish state. In short, in calculating their physical and political survival, policy makers often tend to use foreign policy as a tool to achieve domestic goals.

Geography

A state's geographical characteristics have a significant impact on the formulation of its foreign policy goals. As Hinnebusch and Ehteshami argue, "A state's capabilities, plus the strategic importance or vulnerability of its location, shape the main threats it faces and its likely ambitions."[6] These geographical characteristics include location, resource distribution, and population size and composition. Several components of the Persian Gulf states' attitude toward Israel can be explained by these geographical attributes. For example, the massive increase in military spending by the Gulf states in the 1970s can be attributed more to skyrocketing oil prices and revenues and less to the intense rivalry with Israel. The same can be said about the increase in Saudi and Kuwaiti financial aid to Egypt, Syria, Jordan, and the Palestinians following the 1973 Arab-Israeli war. Indeed, the Gulf monarchies' huge hydrocarbon resources combined with their small population have determined their contribution to the Arab-Israeli conflict. Their role has always been to provide financial assistance to the more populated Arab states. Militarily, their contribution has been largely symbolic. Finally, the Gulf states do not share borders with Israel, as do Egypt, Syria, Jordan, Lebanon, and the Palestinians.[7] The former actors have been able to adopt a more radical stand against Israel than the latter ones with less concern about paying a price. Being immediate neighbors to Israel, these "frontline" Arab states have to contain their rhetoric.

The most serious defect of the geopolitical model has been the failure to anticipate and accommodate technological and political changes. For example, the proliferation of missiles in several Persian Gulf states since the 1980s has significantly reduced the importance of the distinction between "frontline" states and other Middle Eastern states. During the Gulf War (1991) Iraq launched several missile attacks against Israel. Additionally, in the last several years some Israeli policy makers have threatened to launch a preemptive strike against Iranian nuclear facilities. Similarly, geographical theory cannot explain the change in Iran's attitude toward Israel in 1979. This shift in policy was fundamentally due to the toppling of the Pahlavi regime and the establishment of the Islamic Republic, which changed the ideological orientation of the decision makers. Finally, the model cannot explain the anticipated changes in Iraq's foreign policy following the 2003 war. The main force behind these changes is the American occupation of the country.

Ideological Orientation

The geographical characteristics of a state shape the potential goals it can aspire to achieve on the regional and international scenes. An important factor in determining and prioritizing these goals is the ideological orientation of the political elites. Unlike the geographical characteristics, which are relatively static or slow in change, ideological orientations are often altered, particularly following revolutions and major wars. The change in Iran's foreign policy since 1979 is a case in point.

As one of the oldest civilizations in the Middle East, the Iranians have always had a strong sense of nationalism. Even when the Iranians converted to Islam they maintained many of their pre-Islamic traditions. The country's foreign policy has always reflected an uneasy combination of Iranian nationalism and Islam. During the Pahlavi regime, nationalism had the upper hand but was replaced by Islam after the 1979 revolution. Indeed, since the toppling of the shah, Iran's role in the regional and global arenas has been shaped by the interpretation of the ruling clerics of Islam in general and Shi'ia jurisprudence in particular. Within this context, animosity toward Zionism has been one of the major principles of the Islamic Republic. Yet, despite revolutionary and ideological rhetoric, national interests continued to play a role in shaping the country's policy even under Ayatollah Khomeini, as was illustrated by secret arms deals with the United States and Israel in the mid-1980s, the so-called Iran-Contra affair.

As early as the late 1980s, Iran witnessed what can be called "de-ideologization," defined by Shireen Hunter as "the waning of ideological principles as the driving force in shaping foreign policy."[8] This can be seen as a result of the inevitable learning and adjustment process that revolutionary regimes undergo. It can also be explained by deteriorating economic conditions and the need to be integrated in the regional and global systems.

From its creation as a nation-state in 1921 until the overthrow of Saddam's regime in 2003, the Sunni minority dominated the Iraqi political establishment. In order to assert Sunni influence and power against the Shi'ia majority and the large Kurdish minority, the Sunni leaders sought to strengthen their ties with the broad Arab and Sunni population in neighboring countries. Thus, even under the monarchy, Arab nationalism was prominent in determining Iraq's foreign orientation. The Ba'ath Party regime (1968–2003) had further confirmed Baghdad's leading role in the Arab world and in fighting Israel. The Ba'ath doctrine considered Israel an "artificial Zionist entity" that was conceived by imperialistic powers to prevent the Arab nation from achieving its natural potentials. The toppling of Saddam Hussein's regime and the process of economic and political reconstruction will certainly change Baghdad's ideological orientation and foreign policy.

Finally, pan-Arabism and political Islam have dominated almost all aspects of social, economic, and political life in Saudi Arabia. The kingdom is the birthplace of both the Arab nation and Islam. However, unlike revolutionary Iran and Ba'athist Iraq, the Saudi government has sought to promote its version of pan-Arabism and political Islam more by consensus and less by violence. Saudi leaders view themselves as having a special responsibility to the entire Arab world and the global Islamic Umma "community."

Within this context, Saudi Arabia has seen Israel as occupying Arab and Muslim land. The hostility toward Israel was further intensified in 1967 as a result of the Israeli occupation of east Jerusalem, the site of al-Aqsa Mosque, Islam's third holiest place after Mecca and Medina. Instead of confronting Israel directly, Riyadh has financially supported Arab states and Palestinian organizations in their fights against Tel Aviv. Furthermore, Riyadh has sought to use its special relationship with Washington to put pressure on Israel to withdraw from the occupied Arab territories.

The closing decades of the twentieth century saw a gradual rise of national interests at the expense of ideological beliefs throughout the entire Middle

East.[9] As Gregory Gause put it, "Increased 'stateness' at the domestic level across the region may lead to decreased salience for transnational ideological challenges to the existing state system."[10] This slow "de-ideologization" of the region has facilitated the fundamental shift in the perception of the Arab-Israeli conflict from an ideological one (Arabs against Zionists or Muslims against Jews) to an interstate contest (Palestinians and Syrians against Israelis). This trend is likely to endure.

Minorities

According to Bengio and Ben-Dor, "Minorities are as varied as there are cleavages in any given society."[11] In the Middle East, two of the main cleavages are based on ethnicity and religion. The ethnic division has long represented a major challenge. Indeed, the Kurds are one of the largest ethnic groups in the world without a nation-state to represent them. The majority of Kurds are Sunni Muslims, like the majority of Arabs. However, the Kurds do not speak Arabic. They have their own language and reside in several countries, including Iraq, Iran, Turkey, and Syria. The attempts by several Iraqi regimes to "Arabize" the Kurdish population in northern Iraq have failed. It is not an exaggeration to state that the Kurdish question "has been the most violent issue in modern Iraq."[12]

The most important societal cleavage is based on religion. On the eve of the Muslim conquest in the seventh century, writes Philippe Fargues, "Most peoples in the Middle East were Christian, with Jewish communities scattered throughout the region and a sizeable Zoroastrian population in Iran (then called Persia)."[13] Islam recognizes three categories of peoples—Muslims, "People of the Book" (Ahl al-Kitab), encompassing Christians and Jews, and "polytheists or pagans, with whom there can be no compromise."[14] For centuries Muslim and Jewish communities lived side by side in peace in both the Ottoman Empire and Iran. For the most part, Jews enjoyed some degree of autonomy, particularly in conducting their personal and religious affairs such as marriage, divorce, and worship. Furthermore, some Jews (and Christians) rose to the top in the state administration and played a great part in commerce, finance, certain crafts, and the medical field. The status of religious minorities (mainly Christians and Jews) improved substantially in the nineteenth and twentieth centuries in response to growing European influence in the Middle East. The creation of Israel in 1948 represented a turning point for Jewish communities in Arab countries. The declaration of Israel as the homeland of the Jewish people and its desire to encourage, facilitate, and absorb Jews from various Arab and Muslim countries intensified a sense of apprehension. In some Arab countries the distinction between Jews and Israelis was blurred, if not eliminated.

This issue of ethnic and religious minorities is particularly important to understand foreign policy in the Middle East in general and the Persian Gulf states' attitude toward Israel in particular. The relatively late creation of some Middle Eastern states and the relative failure of assimilating minorities and reaching a consensus on a national identity have further intensified the debate on the role of minorities in formulating foreign policy in the region. In both the Levant and the Persian Gulf, ethnic and religious minorities are separated socially and politically if not physically from each other and from the majority. Albert Hourani describes the status of minorities in the region as follows: "On the whole, these groups formed closed communities. Each was a 'world' sufficient to its members and exacting their ultimate loyalty. The worlds touched but did not mingle with each other."[15]

The composition of Persian Gulf states' population has had a significant impact on formulating their foreign policy toward Israel. In interactions between the Levant and Persian Gulf subsystems, regional players used the plights of minorities to promote their national agenda. Two examples validate this proposition: the Israeli involvement in the Kurdish insurgency in northern Iraq in the early 1970s, and the Iranian active role in the Shi'ia community in southern Lebanon, particularly since the early 1980s. The Kurdish case suggests that "ethnic divisions within a state can be exploited by its rivals to weaken it and improve its security."[16] The Israelis (and the Iranians) were able to play the "Kurdish card" because the Kurds were highly mobilized against the Iraqi government. This was not the case with the Iranian Jews. When Israel was created in 1948, Jews in Iran had little incentive to immigrate to the newly born Jewish state. Finally, it is important to point out that attempts by an outside power (Israel) to champion the cause of a minority in a rival state (Iraq or Iran) is strongly resented and is often seen as a "Zionist" conspiracy. The Israeli government's role in facilitating the immigration of Iraqi Jews to Israel is a case in point.

Decision-Making Theory

Decision-making theory provides another important theoretical tool to understand Persian Gulf states' foreign policy toward Israel. Adherents to this model argue that it is difficult to give an operational meaning to the concept of "national interest," the core of realism. Furthermore, the state and other national institutions such as the executive are abstract terms that are hard to define. Instead, decision-making theorists seek to identify the person(s) or group(s) whose images of the operational environment shape decisions. According to this model, "decision making is the act of choosing among available alternatives about which uncertainty exists."[17] Accordingly, decision makers in any country try to reconcile demands by different domestic actors (foreign ministry, national security apparatus, religious establishment, factions within the royal family or the ruling party) with threats from and opportunities in the regional and international systems. This balancing process is filtered through decision makers' intellectual training, social background, and perception. Finally, in making choices in the foreign policy arena, decision makers pursue both national interests, as they define them, and their own individual interests. In other words, writes Raymond Hinnebusch, "Foreign policy is often used to legitimize the ruling regime. Accordingly, the personalities and perceptions of leaders are pivotal in determining choices."[18]

Decision-making theory is a useful tool for understanding the process of policy making, domestic and foreign, in both developed and developing countries. Given the relative lack of political institutionalization in the Persian Gulf states, the model is particularly important. The worldviews of such figures as the shah and Ayatollah Khomeini in Iran, Saddam Hussein in Iraq, King Fahd in Saudi Arabia, and Ben-Gurion in Israel substantially shaped the foreign policy of their respective states. Ayatollah Khomeini's perception of the United States as the "Great Satan" and Israel as the "Little Satan" was the major factor in the drastic shift in Iran's foreign policy since 1979. Saddam Hussein sought to legitimize his regime and build his image as the leader of the Arab world by championing the Palestinian cause and adopting a more radical stand than most Arab leaders—including some Palestinians. King Fahd and Crown Prince Abdullah of Saudi Arabia formulated their own peace initiatives to forge a comprehensive peace in the Middle East. Similarly, the low level of trade and diplomatic ties between Israel and both Oman and Qatar can be attributed, at least partly, to the personalities and perceptions of Sultan Qaboos and Emir Hamad Bin Khalifa al-Thani. Finally, Ben-Gurion played a pivotal role in formulating several Israeli policies. One of these policies, examined in some detail in this text, is the periphery doctrine of the 1950s.

These examples suggest that the role of political leadership in shaping foreign policy "varies from actor to actor, from issue to issue, and from time to time."[19] Understanding this role permits tentative predictions of probable responses to similar challenges in the future. Still, like any model, decision-making theory has its own limitations. For example, in the context of this study, analyzing Ayatollah Khomeini's rhetoric against the United States and Israel does not explain the secret arms deals in the Iran-Contra affair of the mid-1980s. This episode is better explained by the struggle for survival of the regime in Tehran.

Organization of the Book

This study is addressed primarily to university students concentrating on the Middle East, to foreign-service officers and government officials dealing with the region, and more broadly to educated laymen interested in international relations. The volume is divided into three parts. The first part examines the main interactions between Iran and Israel. These include the status of Iranian Jews, the periphery doctrine, the Iran-Contra affair, Tehran's stand on the Arab-Israeli conflict/peace process, Iranian support to Hizbollah, and nuclear proliferation. The second part analyzes Iraq's policy toward Israel. The focus in this part is on the massive immigration of Iraqi Jews to Israel in the late 1940s and early 1950s, Baghdad's contribution to the Arab-Israeli wars, Tel Aviv's stand on the Iran-Iraq War (1980–88), the first Gulf War (1991) and the second Gulf War (2003), Israel's involvement in the Kurdish rebellion in the early 1970s, and the Israeli preemptive raid on the Iraqi nuclear facilities in Osiraq in 1981. The third part deals with the Gulf monarchies' role in both the Arab-Israeli wars and the peace process. The use of oil as a political weapon and Saudi Arabia's peace initiatives are discussed in detail. The main focus in this part, and indeed in the entire volume, is on the three largest and most populated Gulf states—Iran, Iraq, and Saudi Arabia. However, the limited but significant diplomatic and trade ties between Bahrain, Kuwait, Oman, Qatar, and the United Arab Emirates are examined in the chapter on the Gulf monarchies.

The discussion in each chapter is preceded by an analysis of the main determinants of the Gulf states' policy toward Israel. Specifically, four variables are identified and examined in some detail: economic resources and performance, ideological orientations (political Islam and pan-Arabism), geopolitics, and relations with the United States. The concluding chapter seeks to predict the likely interactions between the Persian Gulf states and Israel in the aftermath of the 2003 war. The analysis in this volume suggests that the tense encounters that characterized the relations between the two Middle East subsystems in the last half century do not need to endure. The changing regional and international landscapes as well as evolving domestic, economic, and political forces, indicate that a détente is both desired and possible.

2

Iran and Israel

Iran is a major non-Arab state in the Middle East. Over the past half century, relations between Iran and Israel, another major non-Arab regional power, have experienced a dramatic shift. Whereas the Pahlavi regime granted the Jewish state a de facto recognition and established close economic and military cooperation with it, the destruction of Israel has been at the forefront of Iran's propaganda since the Islamic leaders took power in 1979. Tel Aviv, in turn, perceives Tehran as an archenemy and the main threat to regional security. Despite some arms transfers and other covert links in the 1980s, the relations between the two nations can be characterized as mutual hostility and mistrust since the ouster of the shah.

Iran started formulating its policy toward Israel even before Israel was established. Supporting the Arab position, in 1947 Iran voted for the minority plan, which envisaged a federated state of Palestine composed of two autonomous Jewish and Arab states, and "voted against the Palestine Partition Plan that led to the creation of Israel."[1] Furthermore, Iran voted against Israel's entry into the United Nations, but did not disguise its unwillingness to become actively involved in the Arab-Israeli conflict. Finally, unlike Turkey, a Muslim and Middle Eastern state that granted Israel full recognition, the Iranian cabinet decided in March 1950 to grant Israel a de facto recognition.

These seemingly contradictory moves by Tehran in its relations with the then newly born Israel have been described by R. K. Ramazani as "calculated ambivalence,"[2] reflecting the relative weight of all forces that shaped the Iranian policy in the late 1940s and early 1950s. First, the shah strongly believed that the major threat to Iran's national security interests was the Soviet Union. Soviet involvement in regional conflicts as well as Soviet interference in the internal affairs of Iran by supporting leftist movements such as Mojahedeen Khalgh and Fedayeen Khalgh and the Kurdish minority in Iran were considered serious challenges that needed to be dealt with. In the late 1940s, the

Soviet Union extended vital support to Israel. Moscow was a leading power behind the success of the UN resolution on the partition of Palestine and promoted Israel's admission to the United Nations.[3] This brief period of Soviet-Israeli cooperation, however, did not last long. In 1950, Israel voted at the United Nations to condemn North Korea's invasion of South Korea. This vote was seen as a step closer to the United States and away from the Soviet Union. Thus in the early 1950s relations between Tel Aviv and Moscow were severely deteriorated. The Soviets were shifting support from Israel to the Arab states, while Israel was increasingly growing dependent on the West. In other words, during the first few years after its establishment, Israel adopted a neutral and nonaligned approach in foreign policy. Since the mid-1950s the pro-Western orientation has prevailed. The shah saw that the cooperation with Israel would serve as a barrier to the increasing Soviet penetration of the Middle East and the growing tide of radical Arab nationalism, led by the Egyptian president Gamal Abd al-Nasser.

Second, attracting and facilitating Jewish immigrants (*aliyah*) to Israel has always been crucial to the survival and development of the Jewish state, particularly during its formative years. Then Iraqi Jews, who outnumbered Iranian Jews two to one, "were subject to persecution, arrests and trials that at times resulted in death sentences, after Zionism was legally declared a serious criminal felony."[4] Securing this large Jewish community and finding a way to get Jews safely to Israel became a major priority. Iran, with its long borders with Iraq, served as a transit point for many Iraqi Jews on their way to Israel. Within this context, Israeli officials were anxious to establish formal diplomatic relations with Tehran.

In addition to these two strategic reasons—Soviet threat and Iraqi Jews—other factors contributed to the slow and gradual establishment of relations between Iran and Israel in the late 1940s and early 1950s. These include the growing Iranian dependence on U.S. economic and military aid to contain and neutralize the Soviet threats. For many Iranian officials, granting some kind of recognition to Israel would enhance the country's image within Jewish organizations in the United States. These organizations, according to Tehran, could lobby the American administration and Congress to serve the Iranian interests in Washington. Besides, the shah viewed Israel's military and agricultural expertise with great admiration. By establishing good ties with the Jewish state, Iran was able to benefit from the Israeli experience. Finally, sensitivity to Arab official and public opinion as well as domestic opposition in Iran by religious circles and leftist groups restrained how far the shah could go in cooperating with Tel Aviv.

All these forces shaped the Iranian policy toward Israel shortly after Israel was born. The outcome has been a close cooperation that lacked any publicity. The Pahlavi regime was reluctant to shed light on its close alliance with the Jewish state.

The following sections examine the main forces that shaped Iran's attitude toward Israel. The list includes geopolitics, nationalism and Islam, economic conditions, pan-Arabism, and relations with the United States. This will be followed by an analysis of some of the most salient areas of conflict and/or cooperation between Tehran and Tel Aviv since 1948. These include Iranian Jewry, the periphery doctrine, the Iran-Contra affair, the Iranian stand on the Arab-Israeli conflict and the peace process, and Iran's role in supporting Hizbollah (Party of God) in its struggle against Israel. Finally, the issue of nuclear proliferation between Tehran and Tel Aviv is analyzed. Rhetoric aside, the chapter argues that the two states share important interests. Pragmatism and ideological considerations have guided their policy toward each other. Despite mutual public hostility, Tehran and Tel Aviv can work together in the future.

Determinants of Iran's Foreign Policy toward Israel

Iran has an extended history that in many ways distinguishes it from its neighbors. Most Iranians are Shi'ia Muslims, unlike the majority of people in the Middle East who are Sunni Muslims. Iran is a Middle Eastern state and has always had extensive ties with the Arab world, but it is not an Arab country. Iran has its own history, culture, language, and overall civilization. In short, Iran's historical experience and geographical traits are unique in the Middle East. The country's policy toward Israel has always been independent from the policy adopted by its Arab neighbors. This policy has been shaped by the following characteristics: geopolitics, nationalism and Islam, economic conditions, relations with the United States, and pan-Arabism.

Geopolitics

For centuries Iran's geographical traits have played a significant role in shaping the country's foreign policy. Iran borders Afghanistan and Pakistan to the east, Turkey and Iraq to the west, and the former Soviet Republics of Turkmenistan, Azerbaijan, and Armenia to the north. In addition, Iran has a long coastline on the Caspian Sea, which it shares with Azerbaijan, Kazakhstan, Russia, and Turkmenistan. Most important, the country's only connection to the high seas is the Persian Gulf. This is also where most of Iranian oil deposits are located. Given these geographical traits, several geopolitical characteristics can be identified.

First, Iran shares the Persian Gulf with seven Arab states: Bahrain, Iraq, Kuwait, Oman, Qatar, Saudi Arabia, and the United Arab Emirates. For centuries the two sides on the Gulf have forged strong cultural, religious, economic, and political ties. The significance of these historical ties cannot be overstated. Thus, the Arab world and the broader Middle East have always occupied a central stage in Iran's foreign policy.

Second, Iran is the largest and most populous country in the Persian Gulf and, along with Egypt and Turkey, has always played a leading role in the region's history and policy. In other words, given Iran's size, population, military, and economic resources, the leaders in Tehran, regardless of their political orientation (imperial or Islamic), have always perceived a special role for their country in shaping Middle Eastern economic, military, and political affairs.

Third, despite intense interactions with its Arab neighbors, Iran has its own separate cultural, ethnic, and sectarian identity. Whereas the great majority of Arabs are Sunni Muslims, most Iranians are Shi'ia Muslims. Iranians share a lot of their cultural heritage with their Arab neighbors, but they are not Arabs. Their ethnic and sectarian composition is different from the Arabs. Thus, in the long history of the Arab and Iranian civilizations, their interests have not always been identical. At different times, Tehran has perceived pan-Arabism as a threat and a challenge to its national interests and, accordingly, was receptive to cooperation with non-Arab actors (Turkey and Israel). Fourth, both religion and nationalism can, and do, unite Iran's numerous communities, but Iran remains ethnically and religiously diverse. According to the U.S. Central Intelligence Agency, Persians compose 51 percent of the country's total population. The rest are Azeris (24 percent), Gilakis and Mazandaranis (8 percent), Kurds (7 percent), Arabs (3 percent), Lurs (2 percent), Balochs (2 percent), Turkmens (2 percent), and others (1 percent). Iran is far more unified religiously: roughly 89 percent are Shi'ia Muslims, 10 percent are Sunni Muslims, and 1 percent are Zoroastrians, Jews, Christians, and Baha'is.[5] Iran has the largest Jewish community in the Middle East outside Israel. The presence and well-being of this Jewish minority have been an important consideration in the relations between Iran and Israel since the establishment of Israel in 1948.

Finally, Iran shares borders with Russia. According to Shireen Hunter, "The emergence of vastly superior powers in its vicinity during the nineteenth century, while Iran was steadily declining, worsened its security dilemmas."[6] It became the immediate neighbor of a great power (Russia/Soviet Union), with all that implies in terms of constraints on foreign policy choices of a contiguous small state. Thus in the early nineteenth century Iran lost trans-Caucasian territories to Russia, and during World War II the Soviet army occupied parts of Iran, and the Soviet Union supported two unsuccessful separatist attempts in Iran by the Azerbaijanis and the Kurds. The shah explained his country's concern about the ambitions of its powerful neighbor: "I have lived as neighbor to the masters of the Kremlin my whole adult life. In forty years I had never seen any wavering of Russia's political objectives: a relentless striving toward world domination."[7] The fear of Soviet and communist penetration of the Middle East had been a driving force in shaping Iranian policy during most of the imperial era.[8] In order to resist Soviet and communist expansion, which forged alliances with revolutionary Arab states such as Egypt and Iraq, Iran worked closely with pro-Western states, particularly Israel.

Nationalism and Islam

Iranian foreign policy has always reflected the relative weight of two significant trends in the country's psyche—nationalism and Shi'ia Islam. Shi'ism has been the state religion of Iran since the sixteenth century.[9] Hunter notes that the majority of Iranians do not perceive any contradiction between the two identities.[10] They can be loyal to both their country and their Islamic belief. Recent Iranian history, however, has witnessed tension between the two concepts. During the Pahlavi reign, the focus was more on Iranian nationalism and less on Shi'ia Islam. The shah's foreign policy was driven by the principle of "equilibrium." Under this principle, the government did not seek to challenge the premises of the international system. Rather, it accepted the structure and rules of the global policy and tried to protect and promote Iran's national interest by maintaining a balance of power and influence in relation with other states. Shortly after the Islamic revolution in 1979, the new regime questioned the legitimacy of the international system and sought to protect and promote Iran's Islamic interest by rejecting the dominance of both superpowers in the international system by exporting the revolution throughout the world.

At critical points, Shi'ia belief, leadership, and institutions have played crucial roles in Iranian politics. Shi'ism has been the main foundation of Iran's ideology since 1979. As R. K. Ramazani, a prominent analyst of Iranian policy, states, "The interest that guided Iran's foreign policy during the Khomeini era reflected, on balance, more the influence of his interpretation of Twelver Shi'ia Islam than the interest of Iran as a nation-state." According to this interpretation, "sovereignty belongs to God, to the Prophet, and to the 'infallible imams' (masumin), and by extension to the Faqih."[11] Accordingly, the constitution establishes direct clerical rule and guidance of the state. While accepting the doctrine of popular sovereignty, the constitution enshrines the principle of government of the jurist (velayat-e faqih). Ramazani has identified four basic principles in the formulation of Iran's foreign policy under Khomeini:

1. No dependence on East or West
2. The designation of the United States as the chief enemy
3. The struggle against the "Zionist enemy" and the liberation of Jerusalem
4. Support for all "oppressed peoples" everywhere, especially "oppressed" Muslims.[12]

Shortly after the establishment of the Islamic Republic, Iran sought to "Islamize" the Arab struggle against Israel. Instead of approaching the conflict as a struggle between the Arabs and the Israelis, the Iranian leadership saw it as a war to liberate holy Muslim sites and Muslim land. This perception is in line with statements Ayatollah Khomeini made before and after rising to power as well as by his successor, Ayatollah Khamenei. During his exile Khomeini supported all struggles against Israel throughout the world and accused the shah of allowing Israel a free hand in Islamic Iran. Indeed, the shah's close cooperation with Israel and the United States was a major theme of Khomeini's opposition to the Pahlavi regime. Khamenei followed the same line, arguing that the Palestinian question and the ultimate disposition of Israel were an Islamic matter on which all Muslims, not just Palestinians, must have a say. Furthermore, the Iranian support to the Shi'ias in Lebanon in their struggle against Israel is an illustration and embodiment of the Islamic ideology. Meanwhile, Israel has sought to portray itself as "the West's first line of defense against the threat of Islamic fundamentalism."[13]

Finally, it is important to point out that the definition of Iran's national interests even during Khomeini's reign was not completely separated from practical considerations. The Iranian leadership engaged in arms deals with the United States and Israel in the mid-1980s when the survival of the regime was in doubt. Since the late 1980s Iranian foreign policy has been driven more by pragmatic national interests and less by ideological ideals. This does not mean that ideology has become irrelevant. Rather, Islam and Islamic issues continue to play a major role in Iran's foreign policy formulation. This trend toward moderation is unlikely to be completely reversed. Deviation, however, is possible.

The Economy

Iranian leaders before and since the revolution have perceived a sound economic performance and strong economic growth as prerequisites to political independence and regional influence. Given the structure of the Iranian economy, oil revenues have been the driving force in achieving these goals. Iran's economy relies heavily on oil revenues—around 80 percent of total export earnings, 40–50 percent of the government budget, and 10–20 percent of the gross domestic product.[14] This prominent share of oil in the Iranian economy has had at least three direct impacts on the country's foreign policy. First, the more dependent Iran is on oil revenues, the more vulnerable it has become to the international forces that shape the global oil markets. Thus until 1979 Iran established close relations with major oil-consuming powers, particularly in Europe and the United States. This close cooperation has expanded to cover political and strategic interests as well as oil. Second, Iran is as vulnerable to oil price fluctuation as its Arab neighbors on the other side of the Persian Gulf. The two sides share the same interest in avoiding low oil prices and pushing for a sustainable rise. Accordingly, Iran in the mid-1970s worked closely with Saudi Arabia and other Arab Gulf states to raise oil prices. Similarly, in the late 1990s under President Khatami, Iran forged close cooperation with the other Gulf producers to overcome the 1997–98 collapse of oil prices. In short, Iran and its Arab neighbors share a common goal—stability of oil prices, preferably at a high level in order to maximize their oil revenues. Third, oil revenues influence Iran's military capability. The high oil prices of the 1970s led to a substantial increase in arms purchases and enhanced Iran's military capabilities.[15] Similarly, low oil prices usually are translated into shrinking military budgets.

For the first half of the twentieth century Iran received substantial foreign economic and military aid. This situation changed drastically in the 1960s and 1970s when Iran began to accumulate massive oil revenues. The shah was determined to use these revenues to modernize Iran and make it one of the greatest powers on earth. The shah had put the whole of his personal prestige, and indeed the institution of the monarchy itself, on an attempt to raise Iran from the ranks of the underdeveloped nations so as to enable it to join the ranks of the newly industrializing regions of Asia, such as South Korea, Hong Kong, and Taiwan. Iran was one of the first Middle Eastern countries to begin economic planning for development.[16]

The early 1960s marked the rise of intensive capitalist development in Iran. The shah's ambitious plans necessitated an expanded role for the state in the economy. The government played a dominant role as the main engine to accelerate economic development through institutional control and investment in social and economic infrastructure. Anoushiravan Ehteshami notes, "Since the state had a monopoly control over oil revenues, it attained a certain degree of autonomy in its operations."[17] The emphasis was on the rapid expansion of the domestic economy and the broadening of the country's industrial and manufacturing base through an intensive import substitution industrialization strategy. This ambitious strategy had further increased Iran's dependence on its hydrocarbon resources and was further complicated by an acceleration of foreign capital penetration of the Iranian market.

The fall of the Pahlavi regime opened the door for the new Islamic regime to reshape the structure of the economic system. In a short time most economic sectors such as manufacture, foreign trade, major minerals, banking, insurance, transportation, and irrigation were brought under state control. It should be stressed, however, that ideological factors played little part in this expansion of state control. According to Ehteshami, "It was, largely, pragmatic reasons (i.e., the war with Iraq 1980–88), which led the state to take over industries and enterprises, which had previously been in private hands."[18] Thus the Iranian economy in the 1980s can be characterized as a managed war economy rather than a centrally planned command economy of the Eastern European type. The new regime promised to reorient the economy to promote self-sufficiency and self-reliance and to reduce the country's dependency on foreign powers. The continuing war with Iraq and the collapse of oil prices in the mid-1980s, however, prevented any serious improvement in the economic structure and performance. The Islamic government's attention and energy were focused more on the war and less on the economy.

With the end of the Iran-Iraq War, Iran focused on economic development. The government's agenda included "reconstruction of the war-ravaged areas, structural adjustment of the economy, and a general improvement of the quality of life of the population."[19] It was against this background that planners have developed a series of five-year plans for economic, social, and cultural development since 1989. Ironically, the same priorities that had preoccupied the shah's last decade had reemerged to dominate the economic and political agenda of Iran's post-Khomeini leadership. These include the need for foreign capital and expertise, trade links, importance of expatriate resources, and the need to diversify the economy and reduce dependency on oil. Recent negotiations with the European Union to sign a trade and cooperation agreement are a good illustration of the continuing Iranian economic concerns.

There is no doubt that Iran is much poorer now than it was in the 1970s. Several factors have contributed to this decline in the standard of living, including economic mismanagement, rapid population growth, the eight-year war with Iraq, and U.S. economic sanctions. Indeed, the legitimacy of the Islamic Republic, like many other governments, is increasingly based on sound economic performance. These economic necessities have influenced the choices Iranian leaders make in foreign policy pushing for more integration in the international system and overall moderation in both domestic and foreign policies.

Relations with the United States

Iran's relations with the United States have a relatively short history, but this short history has witnessed dramatic swings in relations between the two nations. Since his accession to the throne in 1941, Muhammad Reza Pahlavi had favored close cooperation with the West, particularly the United States. With the bipolarization of international politics and the emergence of the cold war between the Soviet Union and the United States, writes R. K. Ramazani, "the choice became increasingly clear for the shah—Iran had to side with the United States."[20] The unofficial alliance between Washington and Tehran reached its peak in the 1970s in what is known as "twin-pillar strategy."[21] Under this doctrine, Iran played a dominant role in protecting oil resources in the Persian Gulf region and resisting Soviet penetration. In return, the United States permitted Iran to purchase, at its own discretion, any military system in the U.S. arsenal short of nuclear weapons.

The Israeli connection in the American-Iranian relations during the Pahlavi reign can be seen in two ways. First, the perception that Israel could improve the Iranian image and protect Tehran's interests in Washington was an underlying reason for Tehran's cultivation of closer ties to Tel Aviv throughout the shah's reign. Iranian officials believed that given Israel's "special links" with the United States, "ties to the Jewish state could gain Iran considerable mileage in Washington."[22] Second, Iranian intellectuals, clerics, and religious-minded laymen adopted an anti-American view due to the U.S. involvement in the Arab-Israeli conflict. Many Iranian intellectuals perceived Israel as the vanguard of the Western imperial powers. Accordingly, the principal supporter of Israel, the United States, was blamed for the miserable plight of the Palestinians and Arabs. This anti-American feeling was further intensified as Israel's involvement in Iranian affairs increased, particularly in such activities as intelligence-sharing and military training. According to E. A. Bayne, "Virtually every general officer in the shah's army had visited Israel, and hundreds of Iranian junior officers had undergone some aspects of Israeli training."[23]

The overthrow of the Iranian monarchy and its replacement with an Islamic Republic in 1979 was a stunning blow to the United States. Since then, Iran's ties to the United States have been clouded by ideology, nationalism, and (some would argue) paranoia. Postrevolution relations between Washington and Tehran are characterized by what Gary Sick calls "missed communications, mistaken signals, policy gaffes, and opportunities that were overlooked or mistakenly discarded."[24] Several episodes contributed to severe deterioration of relations between the two countries in the first decade of the revolution, particularly the taking of American diplomats as hostages (1979–81), the Iran-Iraq War in which Washington tilted toward Baghdad, and the reflagging of Kuwaiti tankers, which led to military confrontations between the American and Iranian navies in the Persian Gulf and the tragic downing of a commercial Iranian aircraft by the USS *Vincennes* in July 1988.

The Gulf War (1990–91) represented another missed opportunity for a rapprochement between Washington and Tehran. The Clinton administration initiated a new policy toward Iran called "dual containment."[25] This policy explicitly rejected the classic U.S. strategy of balancing Iran and Iraq against each other, arguing instead for the containment of both countries by broadening and intensifying economic sanctions. Some analysts argue that the inauguration of dual containment policy was in line with an Israeli policy that labels Iran as the main center for global terrorism and Islamic fundamentalism. The Iran-Libya Sanctions Act, passed in 1996 and renewed for another five years in 2001, was an important embodiment of this policy. The law authorizes the administration to impose sanctions on any foreign cooperation that invested $20 million or more in the Iranian oil and gas sector.[26] The elections of President Muhammad Khatami in 1997 and 2001 eased some of the tension between the two nations, but the essence of the rift remained unchanged. The American-led war on terrorism in Afghanistan in late 2001 provided an opportunity for Washington and Tehran to fight their mutual enemy, the Taliban. However, this short period of low-profile cooperation did not last. In January 2002 President George W. Bush labeled Iran a member in an "axis of evil" along with Iraq and North Korea. The removal of Saddam Hussein in 2003 turned out to be another missed opportunity to improve relations between Washington and Tehran. The two nations were united in their opposition to Saddam Hussein's regime. However, their visions of the post-Saddam Iraq seem incompatible. Since the 2003 war, several American officials have accused Tehran of "meddling through" in Iraq and fueling instability. Iran categorically denies such accusations.

A reconciliation between Washington and Tehran, when and if it happens, will have to address the concerns expressed by both sides. Iran calls on the United States to (a) lift direct and indirect economic sanctions, (b) end its opposition to an Iranian role in developing hydrocarbon resources in the Caspian Sea, including the construction of pipelines through Iran, (c) settle the claims for Iran's assets that were taken at the time of the revolution, and (d) stop intervening in Iran's domestic affairs. In turn, the United States demands that Iran change its policy in three areas: (a) opposition to the Arab-Israeli peace process, (b) sponsoring terrorism, particularly Tehran's support to Hizbollah (Party of God), Hamas, and Islamic Jihad, and (c) attempt to acquire and develop weapons of mass destruction and the missiles that carry them.

All these American concerns are shared with Israel. Thus Israel features prominently in any U.S.–Iranian rapprochement. Bluntly, any reconciliation between Washington and Tehran has to be preceded by a relaxation of the tension and understanding between Tehran and Tel Aviv that addresses the Arab-Israeli peace process, terrorism, and weapons of mass destruction. It is important to point out that Iran has already paid a considerable price with the United States for its high-profile rejection of the peace process. Not surprisingly, the Iranian leadership is under a certain degree of pressure internally to adopt a more pragmatic stand on the Arab-Israeli conflict. Occasionally, Iranian intellectuals argue that Iran should not adopt a more extremist position than the Palestinians themselves, who have already accepted the existence of Israel and a negotiated settlement for the conflict.

Pan-Arabism

One of the strongest incentives for Iran to seek close military and strategic co-operation with Israel during most of the 1950s and 1960s was the rise of Arab nationalism led by Egyptian president Gamal Abd al-Nasser. After toppling the monarchy in a bloodless military coup in 1952, Nasser championed the call for Arab unity. This policy led to a sharp division and polarization of the entire Middle East political system. The Egyptian leader proposed a collective Arab security system and adopted an anti-West and anti-Israel foreign policy. He perceived the West and Israel as obstructing Arab unity and development. A significant step in this direction was the signing of a huge arms deal with Czechoslovakia in 1955, which broke the Western monopoly over arms sales to the Middle East and opened the door for close cooperation with the Soviet

Union. The following year, Britain, France, and Israel launched the Suez War in an attempt to contain Nasser's growing popularity. Despite Egypt's military defeat, the Suez War enhanced Nasser's credentials as a nationalist Arab hero who stood against Western imperialistic powers and Israel.

Following the Suez episode, Nasser's vision of Arab nationalism inspired coups and movements against pro-Western regimes in several Arab countries, including Syria, Iraq, Yemen, and Sudan. Meanwhile, conservative Arab regimes were vulnerable to radical Arab propaganda and subversion. This wave of Arab nationalism incited Western powers to send military forces to protect conservative Arab regimes and stop the Soviet penetration of the Middle East. Thus in 1958 British paratroopers landed in Jordan and U.S. Marines invaded Lebanon to prevent these two governments from falling under the pressure of Nasserism. Similarly, in the 1960s Western countries worked closely with Saudi Arabia and Oman to contain the nationalistic/leftist threat.

In order to face the Israeli challenge, Nasser sought to mobilize the Arab masses against Western powers and their regional "reactionary" allies. Within this context, Nasserism viewed the Persian Gulf as a major battleground against both Western influence and the Gulf regimes, Arab and Iranian. Western domination, Nasser argued, had deprived the Arabs of the oil revenues that could have been used to accelerate economic development and improve military capability to fight Israel. As the largest Gulf state, the Pahlavi Iran with its close alliance with the United States was seen by Nasser and other Arab nationalists as the main obstacle to achieving these objectives.

For its part, Iran viewed Arab nationalism as a major threat to its own national security and as a window for the Soviet Union to penetrate the Middle East. Arab nationalism threatened vital Iranian security concerns particularly in the Persian Gulf, where most of the country's oil installations are located. The Arabs and Iranians have had territorial disputes over Bahrain, the three Persian Gulf islands of Abu Musa, Greater and Lesser Tunbs, and the Iranian province of Khuzistan. The Bahrain dispute was settled in 1970 when Iran relinquished its claim. By contrast, Iran and the United Arab Emirates have yet to reach a settlement for their claims and counterclaims over the three Gulf islands.[27] Finally, the Arabs' claim to Khuzistan has never been clearly settled. Some Arabs call Khuzistan Arabistan and view it as historically and demographically Arab. Based on these claims, the problems of Arabistan and Palestine are similar, the argument goes, because "the Arabs in the two regions are living under a colonialist rule, which has occupied their homeland without any legal or regional foundation, namely, Zionist occupation and Iranian occupation."[28] The dispute has not been completely settled. Occasionally some Arab leaders raise the issue of Khuzistan and demand some concessions from Iran, particularly when relations are tense.

These threats reinforced the shah's determination to seek non-Arab regional allies. From the mid-1950s through the early 1970s, radical Arab nationalism had brought Iran and Israel into a close unofficial alliance. The two non-Arab Middle Eastern nations had found a common enemy in the anti-Western and pro-Soviet Arab nationalism, particularly the Moscow-Cairo axis. This relationship, based on the view that the enemy of my enemy is my friend, gave Tehran and Tel Aviv a useful regional counterweight in their conflicts with Cairo. Thus the shah's decision in 1955 to join the Baghdad Pact "ran counter to the declared Egyptian crusade against the pact as a 'Zionist plot.'"[29] The hostility between Egypt and Iran over the shah's cooperation with Israel prompted Nasser to sever diplomatic relations with him in 1960.[30] Iran and Israel then further consolidated their economic, military, and strategic cooperation, particularly in agriculture, aviation, oil sales, and military training.

The role of pan-Arabism in consolidating Israeli-Iranian cooperation has drastically changed since the late 1960s. The huge Arab defeat in the 1967 war with Israel dealt a heavy blow to radical Arab nationalism led by Nasser. The Arab-Israeli conflict has witnessed two significant, gradual, and long-term outcomes. First, the oil monarchies' accumulation of substantial oil revenues has decisively shifted the balance of power away from Egypt and in favor of conservative, pro-West Arab states, particularly Saudi Arabia. Second, rhetoric aside, the 1967 Arab defeat represented a dramatic shift from "liberating Palestine" to accepting the fact that the Jewish state is here to stay and legitimizing Israel as part of the Middle East state-system. In other words, for many Arabs the conflict with Israel has gradually shifted from eliminating it to liberating the Arab territories occupied in the 1967 war.

In addition to these regional changes, the shah had grown confident of his economic and military power. The massive oil revenues Iran had accumulated and the huge military capabilities it had built in the early 1970s made the Pahlavi regime more confident and less dependent on Israel than a decade ago. As a result, the shah repaired relations with Egypt and developed close personal rapport with Nasser's successor, Anwar al-Sadat. The shah worked closely with Saudi Arabia and other Gulf states to raise oil prices and manage global oil markets. Furthermore, the shah signed an agreement with Saddam Hussein in 1975 that temporarily ended their border dispute over Shat al-Arab (Arvand Rud in Farsi). In short, the role of pan-Arabism in consolidating

Israeli-Iranian cooperation had largely faded by the early 1970s. Still, the shah maintained close relations with Israel until the collapse of his regime in 1979. Since then, mutual antagonism has characterized the relations between Tehran and Tel Aviv.

To sum up, Iran's attitude toward Israel has been shaped by both internal and external forces. Ideological orientations of decision makers in Tehran guided its foreign policy toward the Jewish state. Concern about pan-Arabism and Soviet penetration of the Middle East were important reasons for the Pahlavi regime's cooperation with Tel Aviv. Similarly, political Islam, as interpreted by Ayatollah Khomeini and his followers, was, and still is, a major force in the shift in Tehran's foreign policy. In addition, Iran's geographical traits have shaped its regional role. Finally, Tehran's relations with Washington before and after the 1979 revolution played a role in shaping the Iranian attitude toward Israel.

Iranian Jewry

In its long history, Iran has always consisted of multiethnic and multireligious groups living side by side. In addition to the slight majority of Persians, other ethnic groups include "the Azeri in the northwest, the Kurds in the west, the Arabs in the southwest, the Baluchs in the southeast, and the Turkomans in the northeast."[31] Meanwhile, most Iranians are Muslims (mostly Shi'ias), with small religious minorities—mainly Jews, Armenians, and Zoroastrians.[32] Iranian Jews are among the oldest inhabitants of Iran. Indeed, the relationship between Iranians and Jews is an old story dating back to ancient times. For the most part, these historical ties between Jews and Iranians have been good. Walter Fischel, an authority on Jewish culture in Iran, describes the relations between the two peoples as follows,

> The history of Persia from its very beginning until today, from Cyrus the Great to Riza Khan Pahlavi—a history covering twenty-five centuries equally divided by the Arab conquest of the year 642 into a pre-Islamic and an Islamic period—has seen an uninterrupted and continuous association between Iran and Israel. Israel has been living on Iran's soil from the dawn of the first Persian Empire on, as an inseparable part of Iran's national destiny and development. Jews were the eyewitnesses of all the historical events in Persia under every dynasty—the Achamenids, Parthians and Sassanids, the Omayyads and the Abbassids, the Seljuks, Mongols, Safavids, and Qajars, under every ruler, Caliph, Sultan, Il-Khan, emir or shah.[33]

One of the earliest episodes between Iranians and Jews goes back to 597 B.C. when Nebuchadnezzar of Babylon sacked Jerusalem and took thousands of upper-class Jews back to Babylon with him. Robert Reppa writes, "In 538 Cyrus the Great, the first Achaemenian emperor and founder of Persia, defeated Babylon and its empire and liberated the Jews. Cyrus permitted the Jews and their descendants to return to Jerusalem."[34] Some of them preferred to remain in the diaspora. Gradually the Babylonian communities expanded to the provinces and cities of Persia. The tolerance of the Persian rulers enabled many Jews to rise to prominent positions at the royal court. Thus prosperous Jewish communities flourished and enjoyed religious and legal autonomy. According to Nicholas De Lange, "Only during the centuries of Sassanid rule (224–651) and with the intervention of Zoroastrian priests in affairs of government did the situation of Persian Jews begin to deteriorate." In the mid-seventh century, inspired by their religion, Muslims invaded modern-day Persia. The Persian state became a province of the Arab-Muslim empire. The Arab conquest replaced one state religion with another, but for the Jews this was a change for the better. As dhimmis, the non-Muslim minorities, they were treated not quite equally to the Muslim majority, but were protected by the rulers. Economically, they were free to engage in any occupation. Persian Jews were active as artisans, shopkeepers, merchants, and manufacturers. Adds De Lange, "The growing urbanization of the Muslim empire and the growth of international commerce led to the emergence of a wealthy class of merchants and bankers in the large cities of Ahwaz, Isfahan, and Shiraz."[35]

The Mongol conquest in 1258 ended the Abbasid caliphate. Under the Mongol leader Hulagu, the status of the dhimmi was abolished and all religions were acknowledged as equal. Once again non-Muslims were employed in the government institutions and a substantial Judeo-Persian literature emerged. This was a golden age for Persian Jews, who became more involved than ever in the economic and political life of the empire. The next major change came with the Safavids in the sixteenth century. Shi'ism was adopted as the state religion, and a religious hierarchy was established with unlimited power and influence in every sphere of life. Jews, Christians, and Zoroastrians were subjected to the harsh treatments, and Sunnis suffered the most. Segregation became a reality for all minorities, and Jewish ghettos were reinforced. Additional taxes and other forms of economic and social discrimination were imposed on religious minorities. These oppressive social and legal practices were relaxed under the warrior Nadir Shah (1736–47),[36] only to be vigorously revived during the Qajar dynasty (1794–1925). Indeed, Jewish chronicles report the Qajar period as one of the worst in their history in Persia.[37]

Given these deteriorating conditions, European powers and some Western Jewish organizations pressured the Iranian government to improve treatment of its Jewish citizens. In response some modern schools were opened in the early twentieth century. This step represented the beginning of fundamental changes in Iran in general and in the status of the Iranian Jewry in particular. Iranian Jews, along with other minorities, participated in the political movement, which produced the 1906 constitution. Jews, Christians, Zoroastrians, and Baha'i fought hard to form a national majlis (parliament). They succeeded in their efforts to ratify laws that gave equality to Muslim and non-Muslim citizens. Accordingly, Jews, Christians, and Zoroastrians were granted civil rights, including the right to elect one delegate each to the Majlis.[38]

Following World War I, the American-sponsored Joint Distribution Committee entered Iran, introducing a wide range of welfare activities. Writes Marvin Weinbaum, "These and other ties to Western Jewry gave Iranian Jews the kind of patronage and intervention that had earlier eased the lives of the country's Christians."[39] The accession of the Pahlavi dynasty in 1925 changed the course of Iranian history. The policy and reforms introduced by Reza Shah and his son Muhammad were all directed at bringing westernization and secularization to Iran and reinforcing an all-Iranian nationalism, similar to what took place in neighboring Turkey following the end of World War I. In line with this policy, the Pahlavi dynasty ended discriminatory laws against Jews and other minorities, closed down foreign and confessional schools to bring everyone under one national curriculum and language, and even encouraged minorities as a counterweight to overzealous Shi'ias. Despite the fact that Reza Shah was an admirer of Hitler, he did not share Hitler's hatred of the Jews. Rather, "Reza Shah showed respect to the Jews by praying to the Torah and bowing in front of it, when visiting the Jewish community of Isfahan."[40]

The Pahlavis' reign marked a golden age for Iranian Jewry. Thanks to the relationship between Tehran and Tel Aviv, and the fact that no restrictions were placed upon them, hundreds of Iranian Jews attained the highest levels of influence and power in both government and private business. Political, social, and economic conditions in Iran were so good that many Iranian Jews who had emigrated to Israel returned to Iran a few years later.

According to Eli Barnavi, "Shortly after the creation of Israel, the Iranian Jewry, which numbered nearly 100,000 in a total population of 16.5 million, represented great immigration potential in the Jewish Agency estimation."[41] This never materialized, however. The majority of these Iranian Jews lived in Tehran, Shiraz, and Isfahan. Most of them refused to emigrate to Israel, except for the poorer members of the community. The attractions of the new state failed to influence the thousands of educated and affluent Jews who controlled the carpet, gold, jewelry, textile, and pharmaceutical trades. Furthermore, after Israel's establishment and the war of 1948, the fact that the Iranian authorities did not harm the local Jewish population or hinder the activities of Israeli agents in Iran "mitigated any sense of urgency in efforts promoting Aliyah from Iran."[42] This approach was significantly reinforced by the fact that in other Middle Eastern countries the issue of Aliyah did bear urgency involving questions of life and death.

When the Islamic revolution broke out in 1978, hundreds of wealthy and professional Iranian Jews left Iran. Most went to the United States, where they formed a large and wealthy community, especially in California. Meanwhile, upon his return to Iran in February 1979, Ayatollah Khomeini sought to assure Iranian Jews that they had nothing to worry about from the Islamic revolution. Khomeini mentioned that although he wanted no political relations with Israel, he guaranteed that Iranian Jews could live and worship in Iran in a much better manner than under the shah. In other words, he made a distinction between Judaism as a religion and Zionism as a political movement. Since 1979, however, this distinction has occasionally been blurred.

To sum up, despite Khomeini's revolutionary ideology, the founder of the Islamic Republic adopted a moderate stand toward his country's Jewish citizens. The Islamic constitution recognizes Jews as a religious minority, allows them a representative in the Majlis, and accepts Jewish laws on burial and divorce. In Tehran, synagogues and Jewish schools flourish and the Jewish hospital is among the city's most respected. Not surprisingly, the Iranian Jewry is the largest Jewish community outside Israel in the Middle East. This practical moderation is reinforced by two factors. First, Jews do not pose any political threat to the regime in Tehran. On the contrary, they have proved loyal to the Iranian nation and the Islamic Republic. Second, Khomeini was trained as a jurist and sought to base all his policies on Islamic law. His relationship with the religious minorities was "undoubtedly shaped by the Islamic code of law, which prescribes tolerance toward monotheistic religious minority groups."[43] After the 1979 revolution, a few leading Jews were executed, but hundreds of Muslims were executed as well. So this is not as large a discriminatory point as it might seem. Rather, the arrest of thirteen Jews in early 1999 and charging them of spying for Israel created a big controversy.

In March 1999, thirteen Jews from Shiran and Isfahan in southern province of Fars were arrested and accused of spying for the "Zionist regime" and "world arrogance," references to Israel and the United States respectively, in Iranian terminology. The arrests were disclosed three months later. The Iranian government strongly denied that the group had been arrested because of their religion. President Muhammad Khatami stated that he was responsible for every single member of every religious persuasion who lived in Iran. Still, the arrest sparked grave concern in many Western countries, especially the United States. In separate statements, both Washington and Tel Aviv denied any connection to these thirteen Iranian Jews.[44] After the initial public protests over the arrests, Israel decided to focus its rescue efforts on secret contacts via Russia and European states that have open channels to Iran.[45] In July 2000 ten of the Iranian Jews were convicted of spying for Israel and sentenced to prison terms of four to thirteen years; the three others were acquitted. An Iranian appeals court later reduced the sentences, and in October 2002 Ayatollah Khamenei pardoned the remaining prisoners.

Based on open and unclassified sources, one cannot substantiate the claims and counterclaims made by the Iranian and Israeli authorities. This episode, however, seems to be less about espionage and more about internal rift within the Jewish community in Iran and rivalry within the religious/political establishment in Tehran. According to an account in the Israeli newspaper *Ha'aretz* confirmed by the Israeli government, "In recent years the Shiraz community underwent a distinct process of 'Haredization,' making contact with ultra-Orthodox groups in the United States. Jews in Tehran were afraid that this would complicate life for other Jews in Iran, and decided to draw the authorities' attention to what was afoot. The Israeli source says that the Tehran community did not contend that fellow Jews in Shiraz were engaged in espionage; rather, the authorities aggravated the charge, perhaps due to the rivalry between moderates and conservatives, with the aim of entangling the moderates in a confrontation with the West."[46]

Several conclusions can be drawn from this brief review of the Iranian Jewry. First, the large Iranian Jewish community is concentrated in urban centers, particularly in Tehran and Shiraz, and is represented in bazaar crafts and trade as well as in more modern middle-class positions. Under the Islamic Republic, the Iranian Jews do not enjoy the same privileges they had under the Pahlavi regime. Still, most of them lead a comfortable life with no official prejudice or harassment. Second, as David Menashri argues, "It has been a common practice in modern Iran that in times of crisis, when the central government seems weak, the ethnic minority groups are the first to contest it. Living on the periphery and possessing independent military strength, they regard such times as opportunities to change their status. On the other hand, the largely urban and virtually defenseless religious minority groups have always been dependent on the regime and sought its protection in order to maintain their status."[47] This explains why under the Islamic Republic the Jewish community enjoys relative tolerance. Third, this large and ancient Jewish community in Iran has always featured in the relations between Tehran and Tel Aviv. Both under the Pahlavi regime and the Islamic Republic, Israel has been concerned about the safety and well-being of the Iranian Jewry. This will continue to be a constant factor in shaping Israeli foreign policy toward Iran as demonstrated by the two countries' unofficial alliance, the peripheral pact, in the mid-1950s.

The Periphery Doctrine

One of the earliest attempts to create a strategic partnership between Iran and Israel was designed by Prime Minister David Ben-Gurion in the mid-1950s. The periphery doctrine was derived from the perception that Israel was surrounded by a wall of radical Arab states led by President Gamal Abd al-Nasser of Egypt. These Arab states had facilitated the Soviet penetration of the Middle East and sought the total destruction of Israel. In response, the Israeli leaders articulated a plan for a peripheral pact situated on the periphery of the Middle East and connected to Israel in a "triangle" with Turkey and Iran (both are non-Arab but Muslim states) in the north and Ethiopia (non-Arab Christian state) in the south. The common denominator of these states was expressed mainly in their political aspiration to halt Soviet influence and resist radical Arab nationalism. Furthermore, the unwritten pact had a clear implication for the West. The United States was concerned about the Soviet penetration of the Middle East. The Eisenhower Doctrine did not succeed in arresting the deterioration of the situation.[48] Thus Israel sensed that it had something to offer the United States. This was a bloc of states whose population exceeded the number of Arabs in the Middle East and which was prepared for far-reaching cooperation with the Americans in opposing Soviet ambition in the region. This periphery doctrine was one of the pillars of Israeli foreign and defense policy for about three decades.

The articulation of this strategic partnership between Israel and the other non-Arab Middle Eastern states was largely in response to the challenge of radical Arab nationalism in several states (Lebanon, Jordan, and Iraq among others) in the late 1950s and early 1960s. In May 1958, civil war erupted in Lebanon between the Christian groups and nationalist groups supported by Nasser. The deteriorating conditions led the United States to send military units to prevent the fall of Lebanon under Nasser's control. Similar developments took place in Jordan and led to British military intervention to protect the monarchy.

When the situation in Jordan worsened and the throne was endangered, the Iraqi government sent help in the form of a motorized division under General Abd al-Karim Qasim. But halfway, Qasim ordered his troops to turn back and instead carried out a speedy military coup and took power. King Faisal II was shot while pleading for his life, and the heir to the throne, Abdullah, was murdered in his palace. The prime minister, Nuri al-Said, fled, disguised as a woman, but was recognized and killed. Qasim vowed to fight imperialism and to formulate a popular republic. This was a major blow to Western powers and their allies in the Middle East. Iraq was considered a major link in the Northern Tier, which the West had set up against the Soviet Union. Iran's fears seemed to be realized almost immediately. Qasim's regime initiated several policies that were seen as threatening to Iranian national interests. The new regime in Baghdad initially allied itself with Nasser and established diplomatic relations with the Soviet Union and other countries of the Soviet bloc. Qasim also declared that the 1937 treaty between Iraq and Iran concerning the Shat al-Arab waterway was unacceptable to his government, and he laid claim to the entire river separating the two countries. Finally, Qasim invited Mullah Mustafa Barazani, a prominent Kurdish leader who fought against the Iranians in the 1940s, back to Iraq and provided him and his troops with arms. Although Barazani's alliance with Qasim was short-lived, Sohrab Sobhani argues that "the perception inside Iran that Iraq was a sworn enemy was reinforced and entered into the shah's strategic calculus."[49] Iran and Turkey, which both share borders with Iraq, sensed that the Soviet arms were gradually tightening around them. Ethiopia, the third county in the peripheral pact, shared the same sentiments.

Ethiopia, a pro-Western Christian country in the Horn of Africa, was particularly concerned about Nasser's pan-Arabism, pan-African, and anti-Western policies. Sharing the same concerns about the plight of Ethiopian Jews, Israel sought to establish and consolidate economic and strategic ties with Addis Ababa. For most of his reign, Emperor Haile Selassie remained a close ally to the West and Israel.

The developments in Syria in the late 1950s were seen as a direct threat to Turkey's national security and can be seen as the background for increasing cooperation between Turkey and Israel. Damascus witnessed several coups d'etat, which contributed to economic and political instability and radicalization of Syrian domestic and foreign policies. Syria consolidated its strategy and allied itself with Egypt's Nasser and the Soviet Union. In 1958 Egypt and Syria were united under Nasser's leadership into a new state called the United Arab Republic. This development was seen as a threat to both Israel and Turkey, and the two countries worked closely to face this challenge.

Iran also hoped to halt the Nasserist and Soviet influence in the Middle East. The growing appeal of Arab unity, the collapse of the monarchy in Baghdad, and warming of Iraqi-Soviet relations all contributed to Iran's sense of isolation and insecurity. The shah saw that one way to counter these challenges was to consolidate his ties with Israel. Such relations not only would help him with the "Jewish lobby" in the United States but also would ensure Israeli cooperation in the spheres of agriculture, water resources, and military training. In addition, a close cooperation that amounted to an unwritten and unofficial alliance with the pro-West Turkey and Israel would help in resisting Soviet penetration of the Middle East. Washington, in turn, supported this strategic pro-West and anti-Soviet Union alliance of the three states.

To sum up, the strategic partnership between the three non-Arab Middle Eastern states—Israel, Turkey, and Iran—was one of the main pillars of power configuration in the region for most of the 1950s, 1960s, and early 1970s. Changes in the Arab world following the 1973 war with Israel had weakened the foundations for the peripheral pact. The appeal of pan-Arabism faded, and Egypt broke ties with the Soviet Union, adopted a pro-West orientation, and made peace with Israel. Meanwhile, Iran was growing unstable, and eventually the shah's regime was overthrown and replaced by the Islamic Republic with its strong anti-Israel stand. In other words, by the late 1970s, as Joseph Alpher argues, "the foundations of the peripheral policy had become considerably less viable, as the Arab core and the non-Arab periphery of the Middle East in many ways exchanged roles."[50] The peripheral doctrine, however, has not completely faded away from Israeli foreign policy. Israel's continuing cooperation with Turkey is an embodiment of this strategy. Furthermore, the peripheral doctrine partly explains the Israeli military cooperation with elements within the Khomeini regime in the early 1980s.

The Iran-Contra Affair

The shah's departure and Khomeini's rise to power drastically altered the parameters of relations between Tehran and Tel Aviv. Iranian secular and Western-oriented elites were replaced by Shi'ia clerics who perceived the United States and Israel as their main enemies. While the shah granted Israel a de facto recognition and established close economic and strategic relations with it, Khomeini denied Israel the right to exist. However, a close examination of relations between the two countries in the early 1980s suggests a different configuration. Rhetoric aside, some officials in both Israel and Islamic Iran were convinced that the regime change in Tehran should not weaken the fundamentals that have connected Jews and Iranians for centuries. This conviction was further reinforced with the breakout of the Iran-Iraq War in September 1980. In an attempt to take advantage of the political upheaval that followed the 1979 revolution, Saddam Hussein launched a massive attack on his larger and more populous neighbor, Iran. Initially, the Iraqi army made significant advances in Iran. These early Iraqi military advances underscored Iran's vulnerability and threatened the survival of the Islamic Republic. The Iranians turned to their old Israeli friends, who were more than willing to help. Israeli arms sales to the Khomeini regime began in early 1980s and reached a significant stage in 1985–86 in the so-called Iran-Contra affair. During this episode there was a convergence of interests between Tehran, Washington, and Tel Aviv. Still, each nation had its own reasons to get involved in these secret arms sales.

In the early 1980s, Iran was almost entirely isolated from the international system, while Iraq received different types of assistance from regional and international powers. The United States and the Soviet Union supported Baghdad. Besides, Iraq received enormous military and technological aid from France and technical assistance from Jordan, Morocco, and Egypt. Arab Gulf states, particularly Saudi Arabia and Kuwait, provided generous economic aid. With the exception of Syria and the partial exceptions of Libya and Algeria, Iran found itself quite alone. This international isolation, along with the accumulated pressure of the war and the alarming Soviet occupation of Afghanistan (started in December 1979), led some elements within the political/religious establishment in Iran to secretly negotiate arms deals with the United States and Israel.

Early in the Iran-Iraq War, the United States adhered to a position of strict neutrality. However, confronted with the successful Iranian military campaigns of 1982 and the subsequent offenses against Iraq, Washington gradually tilted toward Iraq. Despite growing support for Iraq, some officials in the Reagan administration decided to negotiate arms deals with Iran. Their desire to approach Iran in 1985 was driven by three goals. First, the U.S. government anxiously sought the release of several U.S. citizens abducted in Beirut, Lebanon, in separate incidents between March 1984 and June 1985. One of those abducted was William F. Buckley, CIA station chief in Beirut. Available intelligence suggested that most, if not all, of the Americans were held hostage by members of Hizbollah. The Iranians did not entirely control Hizbollah, but they had, and still have, tremendous influence on its policy. For humanitarian and political reasons, Ronald Reagan was deeply concerned about the hostages.

Second, few in the U.S. government doubted Iran's strategic importance. Iran, under Khomeini, did not choose sides in the cold war rivalry. Under tremendous pressure from the war with Iraq, there was growing concern that the Iranian government might collapse and the country might disintegrate. To complicate things further, Khomeini's age and deteriorating health opened the door for a potential succession crisis. With its long borders with Iran and its occupation of Afghanistan on Iran's eastern borders, the Soviet Union was in the position to take advantage of these circumstances and expand its influence in Iran. By approaching Iran, the United States would prevent this strategic country from falling into the Soviet camp.

Third, since the Islamic revolution, the United States and other Western countries had virtually abandoned Iran. Isolating Iran contributed to its radicalization, both internally and externally.[51] Reagan sought to develop a line of communication with Iran and cultivate moderate elements within its leadership.[52] It is important to point out that the Reagan administration lacked any consensus over contacts with Iran. The Defense Department and the State Department were not enthusiastic, and indeed they expressed reservations about approaching Iran. Meanwhile, top officials in the National Security Council and the CIA sought a dialogue with Tehran that potentially would serve American national interests. Israel, for its own reasons, sought to facilitate a rapprochement between Washington and Tehran.

Some of Israel's motives to supply spare parts and arms to the Islamic Republic in the 1980s overlapped with those of the United States. Still, others are peculiar to Israel's strategic national interests. First, supplying arms to Iran prevented an Iranian military collapse and a decisive Iraqi victory. It contributed to and maintained a fragile balance of power between the two sides, which helped to prolong the conflict and deny victory to either party. This served Israel's national security tremendously. Two of Israel's sworn enemies were exhausting each other's military capabilities. Iran effectively removed the threat of the Arab Eastern front against Israel and kept Baghdad distracted from the anti-Israel resistance front. Effectively, Iraq was out of the equation of any possible military Arab-Israeli confrontation.

Second, a main theme of Israeli foreign policy toward Iran since 1979 has been the distinction between Iran as a geopolitical entity and the religious/political leadership in Tehran. Some Israeli officials believe that the historical rivalry between Iranians and Arabs and between Shi'ias and Sunnis will always separate Iran from Arab states and bring it close to Israel. According to this line of thinking, the Khomeini regime should be seen as a temporary setback in the long-term warm relations between Jews and Iranians. Tel Aviv should, the argument goes, establish and maintain lines of communication with moderate pro-Western Iranians, who would either overthrow Khomeini or succeed him. In the mid-1980s, the Israeli government identified three groups who were jockeying for power in Tehran. A hard-line radical fanatical group adopted an extremist stand in both foreign and domestic policies. This group called for a policy of exporting Iran's Islamic revolution to neighboring Arab countries, together with a wide-ranging policy of nationalization. A less conservative, or centrist, group was radical in foreign policy, but more pro-reform in domestic affairs. A liberal group believed in free trade, the guarantee of personal wealth, and the protection of private investment. Liberals were totally against the Soviet Union and communism and wanted better relations with the West and with Islamic governments throughout the world. They did not support the export of the revolution either by force or through political influence.[53] The Israeli government was eager to cooperate with this last group.

Third, some Israeli officials viewed Iraq as extremely hostile without a realistic hope for change. Unlike Tehran, Baghdad had participated in the Arab-Israeli wars and led the opposition against Egypt's peace initiative with Israel. Thus, writes Alpher, "An alliance with Iran might ultimately be better for Israel than the doubtful vicissitudes of a vague détente with Iraq."[54] Fourth, in the early 1980s, Israel and the United States were involved in the Lebanese civil war and came to direct military confrontation with Lebanese Shi'ia organizations, particularly Hizbollah. Given the close association between Hizbollah and Iran, some Israeli policy makers thought selling arms to Iran might prompt it to restrain Hizbollah. Fifth, shortly before and after the 1979 revolution, thousands of Iranian Jews left the country. Some went to Israel, whereas others chose to go to the United States. Still, tens of thousands stayed in Iran. The welfare of this large Jewish community in the Islamic Republic has been a major concern for Israel and played a role in Tel Aviv's desire to negotiate arms deals with Tehran. Sixth, Israel's arms exports play a significant role in the country's economy. Notes John Tower, "In 1985 Israel made three arms deliveries to Iran. The price charged to Iran was far in excess of what was paid to the U.S. Department of Defense for the arms."[55] In other words, despite the fact that the bulk of the profit went to arm the contras, Israel's military industry shared part of this profit.

Seventh, after the revolution, the United States stopped selling arms to Iran, and during the war with Iraq, Washington urged other countries to follow suit. This policy provided an opportunity to the Soviet Union and other countries to take advantage of Iran's security concerns. Instead of letting the Soviets, or other hostile powers, extend their influence in Tehran, Israel decided to sell arms and spare parts to Iran.[56] Thus Israel would maintain a foothold in Iran and neutralize a hostile Soviet penetration of the Islamic Republic. Finally, some policy makers in Israel wanted the United States involved for its own sake so as to "distance Washington from the Arab world and ultimately to establish Israel as the only real strategic partner of the United States in the region."[57]

Given all these incentives, Israel not only played a leading role in the Iran-Contra affair but also supplied Iran with various weaponry systems from the beginning of the Iran-Iraq War. In 1983, rumors persisted of ongoing supplies from Israel. In 1984, reports referred to Israeli plans for delivering badly needed supplies of antitank weapons. These sources estimated that "Israeli aid since the outbreak of the fighting may have amounted to nearly half a billion dollars by the end of 1983."[58] Based on open sources, the accuracy of such reports and the extent of Israeli help cannot be verified. It is certain, however, that Israeli arms were meant to prevent an Iranian collapse without providing it with the military means for a breakthrough. These Israeli arms supplies to Iran reached a significant level in 1985–86 when Israeli officials worked with American counterparts to sell arms and spare parts to Iran in return for the release of American hostages held in Beirut by Hizbollah in what became known as the Iran-Contra affair.

The Iran-Contra affair is a complex and emotional episode in the American-Israeli-Iranian relations. The affair engendered two investigations. One was conducted by the President's Special Review Board composed of former secretary of state Edmund Muskie, retired National Security advisor Brent Scowcroft, and ex-senator John Tower as chairman. On February 26, 1987, it published a report in which the essential facts of the dealings with Iran were represented. Later, a joint congressional committee held lengthy hearings and in turn published its own report. The latter, though more detailed in certain respects, did not bring any new major revelations.

According to the *Tower Commission Report*, the formulation, development, and implementation of the Iran-Contra affair passed through seven distinct stages. These stages underscore that top officials in the U.S. National Security Council (NSC), mainly Robert McFarlane, Michael Ledeen, John M. Poindexter, and Lt. Col. Oliver L. North, worked closely with Israeli officials, including David Kimche, director general of the Foreign Ministry, Yaacov Nimrodi, private Israeli arms dealer with contacts throughout the Middle East, and Amiram Nir, an advisor to Prime Minister Shimon Perez on counterterrorism.[59] Together they decided to change long-standing American policy of imposing embargo on all arms shipments to Iran and opposing making any concessions to terrorists in exchange for the release of hostages. William Quandt summarizes this twist in American policy: "The Reagan administration authorized the sale of American arms to Iran, and Israel was to serve as the conduit."[60] Israel made three arms deliveries to Iran in 1985, and the United States directly managed four arms deliveries in 1986. The most important arms in these shipments were TOW, a tube-launched, optically tracked, wire-guided antitank missile, and HAWK, a type of ground-launched antiaircraft missile.

These shipments ceased in November 1986 when a Beirut magazine, *al-Shiraa*, published an account of the U.S.-Israeli-Iranian transactions. This led to indictments against McFarlane, Poindexter, and North. These indictments confirm that the whole affair was contradictory to stated American foreign policy practices. George Lenczowski states that "the whole chain of transactions had originated in Israel and conformed more to Israel's national interest as perceived by its government than to the stated goals of United States foreign policy."[61] The *Tower Commission Report* reaches a similar conclusion: "Israel's objectives and interests in this initiative were different from, and in some respects in conflict with, those of the United States."[62]

The United States, Israel, and Iran came out of this delicate dance with different outcomes. The United States appeared a clear loser in the whole affair. James Bill explains the reasons for this failure: "The methodology of the plan to establish communication with Iran was poorly, clumsily, and unprofessionally conceived. It involved the wrong people, advised by the wrong 'experts,' supported by the wrong allies, they went to the wrong place at the wrong time, carrying the wrong tactical plan."[63] As a result, the controversy threatened a crisis of confidence in the role played by the National Security Council staff.

To the extent to which Israel viewed the arming of Iran as desirable, it also scored some success. It is important to emphasize that there was no consensus within Israel on arming Iran. Indeed, some Israelis advocated "a hands-off policy toward the Islamic Republic, arguing that Israel's arms sales to Iran were based on an obsolete strategic doctrine, namely, the peripheral policy."[64] According to this argument, in the 1980s the peripheral state, Iran, had become more hostile to Israel than the core Arab states (Egypt, Syria, and Iraq).

Iran emerged as a clear winner because it achieved its main purpose of acquiring badly needed arms without changing its basic foreign policies or modifying its form of government. Also, the controversy showed a clearly pragmatic side of the Iranian leadership. When the survival of the state was at stake, ideological considerations took a back seat to national interests. This switch back and forth between Islamic ideology and Iranian national interests characterizes Tehran's stand on two crucial issues with Israel: the Arab-Israeli conflict and support to Hizbollah.

Arab-Israeli Conflict

Since the 1979 revolution, the leaders of the Islamic Republic have perceived Israel as an archenemy. Tehran does not recognize the state of Israel and views it as an illegitimate identity that has to be eradicated. This radical stand, however, should not be seen as a complete departure from the stand adopted by the Pahlavi regime. True, the shah established economic and strategic ties with the Jewish state and granted it a de facto recognition, but his policies were not completely against Arabs. Indeed, Muhammad Reza Shah supported the Arab side in all Arab-Israeli wars and called on Israel to withdraw from occupied Arab lands after the 1967 war.

In numerous United Nations resolutions following the 1948 Arab-Israeli war, the imperial Iran affirmed the rights of the Palestinians to a choice between compensation or repatriation into Israel. In the Suez crisis of 1956, Iran condemned Israel and supported Egypt's right to nationalize the canal and opposed the use of force against Cairo. Sohrab Sobhani writes, "Tehran was deeply concerned about ensuring freedom of navigation in the canal, through which some 75 percent of its imports and exports passed."[65] This condemnation of Israel and support to Egypt did not restrain a growing cooperation between Tehran and Tel Aviv. Following the 1956 war, Nasser managed to transfer his military defeat into a political victory. The tide of Arab nationalism in alliance with the Soviet Union was on the rise. In order to neutralize this threat to regional stability and to Iran's national security, the shah expanded and consolidated his cooperation with Israel particularly in modernizing the Imperial Iranian Armed Forces.

The big Israeli victory and the stunning Arab defeat in the 1967 war caused a dramatic shift in the parameters of regional stability and the Iranian role in the Arab-Israeli conflict. Specifically, three outcomes of the war with far-reaching political implications can be identified. First, Israel took control of the entire city of Jerusalem, including the Muslim holy sites. This step was strongly resented by the majority of Muslims all over the world, including Iran. Second, the tide of radical Arab nationalism, led by Nasser, was shattered. Rhetoric aside, the center of gravity in Arab policy started to move gradually away from Cairo to Riyadh and the other conservative Arab states. Third, despite the initial increase in Soviet influence in Egypt particularly during the so-called War of Attrition between Cairo and Tel Aviv in the late 1960s, there were growing signs that the Egyptian leadership was warming up to improve relations with the United States and paying close attention to peace proposals coming out of Washington. Indeed, it was no coincidence that in the same year, 1970, that President Nasser accepted the American peace initiative, he was able to resume the diplomatic relations with Iran that he himself had broken ten years earlier. In line with these outcomes of the 1967 war, the shah adjusted his stand on the Arab-Israeli conflict both during and after the fighting. According to Bernard Reich, "The Red Lion and Sun, the Iranian version of the Red Cross, dispatched medical aid to Jordan and Iraq."[66] More important, Iran demanded that the Israelis withdraw from occupied territory and rejected Israeli control of the Muslim holy places in Jerusalem.

The shah maintained his opposition to Israeli occupation of Arab lands until his ouster from power in 1979. The deterioration of Egyptian-Soviet relations in the early 1970s further reinforced the shah's tilt toward the Arab side in the conflict with Israel. Although Egypt's ties with the Soviet Union were seemingly strengthened by a fifteen-year treaty signed in May 1971, they were in fact becoming strained because of Soviet reluctance to supply Anwar al-Sadat, Nasser's successor, with offensive weapons for use against Israel. In 1972, Sadat ordered all Soviet advisors and technicians to leave Egypt. This deterioration of Egyptian-Soviet relations paved the road for open and concrete Iranian support to the Arabs. Thus, during the 1973 war, Tehran "provided medical assistance to the Arab states and sent pilots and planes to Saudi Arabia to help with logistical problems" and "permitted the over-flight of Soviet civilian planes carrying military equipment to Arab states. At the same time, Iran refused to permit volunteers traveling to Israel from Australia to use Tehran as a transfer point."[67] Although Iran did not participate in the Arab oil-production reductions and the embargo imposed on the United States and other states friendly to Israel, it took the lead in increasing oil prices, which multiplied the effect of the Arab oil weapon. Despite some differences over optimal pricing and over the use of oil as a political weapon, Iran and the Arab oil producers worked together within the Organization of Petroleum Exporting Countries (OPEC) to the joint benefit of both.[68] On the other side, Israel continued to receive substantial oil supplies from Iran during and after the fighting.

The 1973 war opened the door for a significant breakthrough in finding a peaceful solution to the Arab-Israeli conflict. Sadat visited Israel in 1977 and spoke before the Israeli Knesset (parliament). This unprecedented move led to the signing of the first Arab-Israeli peace treaty in 1979. The shah strongly endorsed Sadat's peace initiative and expressed his reservations on and opposition to the hard-line positions of the Israeli rightist government led by Menachem Begin. The concern was that a breakdown of the Egyptian-Israeli negotiations would lead to another war and would radicalize and polarize the Middle East and revive and strengthen the Soviet influence.

The shah adopted this moderate stand on the Arab-Israeli conflict, and his close cooperation with Israel and the United States made him and his regime a principal enemy of several Palestinian organizations. Members of Iranian leftist opposition groups such as Tudeh, Mojahedeen Khalgh, and Fedayeen Khalgh received guerrilla war training in the Palestinian Liberation Organization (PLO) camps. These leftist Iranian opposition movements and the Palestinian organizations shared a similar ideological orientation, close ties with the Soviet Union, and resentment toward the United States and Israel. On the other side, the Israeli and Iranian internal security services (Mossad and Savak) exchanged intelligence information and collaborated to face their common enemies. To some degree the hostility between the Pahlavi regime and the PLO was contained in the mid-1970s when the shah called on Israel to withdraw from occupied Arab territories. Iran under the shah accepted the notion that the PLO was the sole and legitimate representative of the Palestinian people and that its participation in the peace process was essential. Still, "the shah refused requests by the PLO to establish offices in Tehran and other Iranian cities."[69]

The overthrow of the Pahlavi regime caused a fundamental change in Iranian-Israeli relations and Tehran's overall perception of its role in the Arab-Israeli conflict. When he was in exile, Ayatollah Khomeini charged that the shah opened Islamic Iran to Israeli (and American) influence and products and failed to support the oppressed Muslims of Palestine. Thus one of the main priorities of the Islamic Republic shortly after the revolution was to bury the shah's legacy of the Iranian-Israeli alliance, distance itself from Tel Aviv, and establish itself as a leading supporter of Palestinian rights. The Islamic Republic took the position that Israel has no right to exist and should be eradicated. This hostile stand was best demonstrated only a few days after Khomeini returned to Iran in February 1979. Palestinian leader Yasser Arafat was the first foreign dignitary to visit Iran after the revolution, and the PLO was allowed to establish its representative office in the very building that had housed the Israeli diplomatic mission.

This Iranian-PLO honeymoon, however, proved to be a short one. In the early 1980s, several developments contributed to a severe deterioration of the relations between the two sides. First, the Iran-Iraq War had disastrous consequences for the Palestinian struggle against Israel. Two of Israel's most powerful enemies were destroying each other's military and economic resources. Furthermore, the war led to further deepening of divisions within the Arab world. The PLO viewed the war as a "deflection of regional and international attention away from the conflict with Israel."[70] Second, despite unsuccessful attempts to mediate between Iran and Iraq, Arafat, like most Arab leaders, took the Iraqi side against Iran. Third, shortly after the revolution, Iran substantially increased its military and financial assistance to the Shi'ias in Lebanon. The deterioration in the Lebanese Shi'ias' relations with the Palestinians was reflected in Iranian-PLO relations. Fourth, when differences arose between Yasser Arafat and Syrian president Hafiz al-Assad, Palestinian-Iranian relations also suffered because of Iran's alliance with Syria.

The disagreement between Iran and the PLO proved to be long and deep. Despite a few meetings between top officials, suspicion continues to dominate the Iranian-PLO relations. Two conclusions can be drawn from this brief discussion of the relations between Tehran and Arafat. First, Iran has always distinguished between the broad Palestinian population on one side and Arafat and his top aides on the other side. Iran has established and maintained relations with other Palestinian organizations. Second, the cooling of relations with the PLO never implied a suspension of hostility toward Israel. The troubled relations Tehran has had with Arafat have not led to better relations with Israel. The two issues have been separated.

For several years, Israeli and American intelligence agencies have accused Iran of supporting Hamas (Islamic Resistance Movement) and Islamic Jihad, both of which carry out suicide attacks against Israeli targets within Israel itself and in Gaza and the West Bank. The Iranians categorically deny any military or financial links with these two militant organizations. Instead, Iranian officials confirm their strong ties with Hizbollah in Lebanon and claim moral support for these two Palestinian organizations. Any attempt to understand the Iranian connection with Palestinian terrorist organizations and Tehran's role in the Palestinian violence against the Israelis should take three factors into consideration. First, for a long time, particularly before the September 11 terrorist attacks in the United States, Hamas received substantial funding from sources in the Arab states in the Persian Gulf and from some Muslims in the West. Second, both Hamas and Islamic Jihad are Sunni Muslim, whereas Hizbollah is Shi'ia. There is a sectarian difference between the Palestinian organizations and Iran. Third, the violence against Israeli citizens and targets should be explained less by the foreign support that Hamas and Islamic Jihad receive (from Iran and/or other sources) and more by the continuing lack of a political solution to meet the minimum aspirations and the continuing deterioration of socioeconomic and political conditions for the majority of Palestinians. It is a reasonable assumption that if and when these conditions improve, the incentives for violence will decrease. Put differently, the violence between Palestinians and Israelis is better explained by the internal dynamics of the conflict than by foreign assistance from Iran or any other state.

Despite Tehran's uneasy relations with Palestinian organizations, the Islamic Republic has strongly rejected and denounced almost all initiatives to make peace between Israel and the Palestinians. This strong Iranian opposition is based on ideological and strategic considerations. On the ideological side, since the revolution Iranian officials have viewed the Palestinian issue as a struggle between Islam and the global oppressive powers (the United States and Israel). This perception has two implications: the legitimacy of the political regime in Tehran is reinforced by its opposition to Israel and any peace agreement with it; and neither Arafat nor any other leader has the right to give away "even an inch of the Islamic land of Palestine."[71] On the strategic side, Iran sees a hostile United States as the prime mover behind the peace process. Thus any peace agreement would establish U.S. hegemony and a new order in the Middle East. Iran would be isolated under such a scenario.

In closing, it is important to underscore two points. First, since Iran is not a direct party in the Arab-Israeli conflict, its means to influence this conflict and the peace process are limited. To be sure, Iran could strengthen its relations with Palestinian organizations that object to Israel's survival. Still, with the exception of south Lebanon, Iran's assistance and role in the conflict with Israel have not been significant. Second, Tehran has already paid a very high price for its opposition to the peace process. U.S. economic sanctions on Iran are largely in response to Tehran's opposition to a peaceful settlement of the Arab-Israeli conflict. Since the late 1990s, some Iranian intellectuals and officials have argued that Iran's stand on the Palestine issue should be guided less by ideology and more by the country's national interests. If the Palestinians recognized Israel and accepted a peaceful negotiation with it, the argument goes, why would Iran reject Israel? Indeed, Iranian president Muhammad Khatami has repeatedly stated that if the Palestinians reach an agreement with Israel, Iran will accept it and will not take any action to prevent its implication.

The Arab-Israeli conflict should be seen more as a symbolic issue and less as a security threat to Iran. The Islamic Republic does not need to be more Palestinian than the Palestinians themselves. For Tehran, "Israel remains a foreign policy rather than a security issue."[72] Unlike the Arab-Israeli conflict, Iranian support for Hizbollah in the fighting against Israel in southern Lebanon represented a national security challenge to the Jewish state and a proxy war between Tehran and Tel Aviv that lasted for almost a quarter century.

Iran, Israel, and Hizbollah

On May 24, 2000, a quarter century after Israel became entangled in Lebanon and fifteen years after it declared a "security zone" covering 10 percent of the territory, the Israeli occupation of southern Lebanon ended.[73] The Israeli occupation and Hizbollah's successful efforts to liberate southern Lebanon represented the closest that Tehran and Tel Aviv came to a military confrontation. This proxy war was the outcome of three developments: the socioeconomic and political mobilization of the Lebanese Shi'ias, which started in the second half of the twentieth century; the Israeli invasion and occupation of parts of Lebanon beginning with the 1978 Litani Operation and the more extensive 1982 Operation Peace for Galilee; and the expansion of traditional Iranian ties with the Lebanese Shi'ia community following the 1979 revolution. As a result, what began as a hesitant self-assertion movement of the economically deprived and politically marginalized Lebanese Shi'ias was transformed into a radical military and political force in the 1980s, which presented Israel and the West with one of the most determined opponents in the Middle East.

Lebanese policy was long dominated by two sects, the Maronite Christians and the Sunni Muslims. The large Shi'ia community was marginalized and poorly represented in the country's economic and political leadership. This neglect, however, has not always been the case. Indeed, in the eleventh century, when the Fatimid dynasty ruled a large part of the Middle East, the Shi'ias in Lebanon and elsewhere enjoyed tremendous privileges. This good time did not last. Beginning in the twelfth century, the plight of the Shi'ias was worsening while the conditions of the Christians and Sunni Muslims were improving. According to Barbara Harff, "The twentieth century witnessed the rapid descent of the Shi'ias into poverty and powerlessness. Reaching about 17 percent of the population by the time of the French Mandate (1920), they were badly represented and exploited by their clan leaders, some of whom enjoyed French support."[74] Although accurate socioeconomic data are not readily available, it is clear that by any reasonable measure the Shi'ias fared poorly either in comparison with other Lebanese sects or in absolute terms.

When Lebanon won its independence from France in 1943, the Shi'ias were recognized, on the basis of a 1932 census, as the third largest communal group, after the Maronite Christians and the Sunni Muslims. Representatives from these two dominant groups reached an unwritten agreement called the National Pact, which became the political basis for the country's independence. The pact divided the most important positions in the Lebanese administration based on religious affiliation. The presidency and the post of army commander were given to the Maronites, while the premiership was given to the Sunnis. Meanwhile, the Shi'ias were given the speakership of the Chamber of Deputies (parliament), a largely symbolic job.

The Shi'ias' lack of economic and political power was soon to be transformed. During the 1950s and early 1960s, Lebanon was engaged in a comprehensive process of rapid social and economic modernization. Despite their weakness, the Shi'ias participated in this process. Exposure to mass education and rapid urbanization raised the Shi'ias' political consciousness and awareness of their limited share of wealth and power and made them available for political mobilization. These young Shi'ias, however, lacked a political forum to voice their concerns. Many Shi'ias joined pro-change and antiestablishment political parties, mainly communist, socialist, and Arab-nationalist.

These secular parties failed to adequately address the growing Shi'ia political demands and economic aspirations. The prominent role that Musa al-Sadr assumed in the 1960s and 1970s provided the Shi'ia community with the leadership it was looking for. Al-Sadr, a charismatic leader, was born in Qom, Iran. He pursued an education in Islamic jurisprudence (fiqh). He moved to Lebanon, which he claimed as his ancestral home, in 1960 and launched a campaign for social justice. In the mid-1970s, al-Sadr "founded a movement called Afwaj al-Muqawamah al-Lubnaniyah (Battalions of the Lebanese Resistance), but quickly became known by its acronym, AMAL, which means hope."[75] Al-Sadr mysteriously disappeared in Libya in 1978.[76] Though initially allied with and trained by the PLO, by the end of the 1970s AMAL was at odds with the Palestinians and their Lebanese allies. The movement resented the PLO domination in south Lebanon and the high price the Shi'ias were paying in the Israeli retaliatory attacks. As a result, AMAL militiamen and elements of the PLO engaged in serious fights against each other. Thus, despite great differences between the Lebanese Shi'ias and the Israelis, some members of AMAL and the Shi'ia community saw the Israeli invasion of south Lebanon as a means to rid them of the PLO. Instead of liberating the area from PLO domination, the Israeli army established itself as an occupier force. Meanwhile, instead of trying to ally itself with the Shi'ias, the Israeli army humiliated and provoked them.

These incorrect expectations that the Israeli army would expel the PLO and leave in conjunction with humiliation and provocation alienated a large segment of the Shi'ia community and weakened AMAL. Within AMAL there were a number of defections. Some top leaders rejected the movement's relative moderation and demanded a strong stand against Israel. "One faction led by Hussein Musawi accused AMAL of collaboration with Israel and of deserting its Islamic principles and formed another movement called Islamic AMAL."[77] A more serious challenge was the defection of another group led by Hassan Nasr Allah, who created Hizbollah in 1982. The founding of Hizbollah was reinforced by the deployment of thousands of Iranian Revolutionary Guards, whose main purpose was to fight the invading Israeli army.

The creation of Hizbollah and the deployment of Iranian Revolutionary Guards were the main achievements of Iran's Lebanese policy. Ironically, the expansion of Iran's presence and influence in Lebanon were triggered by the Israeli invasions of south Lebanon. Thus, in the early 1980s the expansion of Iranian influence in south Lebanon had coincided with a growing frustration among Lebanese Shi'ias due to social mobilization and intense demands to renegotiate the distribution of political power between the country's main religious and sectarian groups. The Palestinian military operations against Israel, which led to retaliatory Israeli attacks and eventually Israeli occupation of southern Lebanon, had further complicated the political and security environment in Lebanon. Meanwhile, the success of the revolution in Iran created enormous excitement among the Shi'ias in Lebanon for many reasons. First, the majority of Shi'ias in both Iran and Lebanon are Ithna Ashariyah (Twelvers). According to John Esposito, "These are the followers of the twelve imams regarded as the rightful successors of the Prophet."[78] They constitute the major subdivision within Shi'ia Islam. Second, the two communities have always had close ties. Many of the Lebanese ulama (religious leaders) receive their theological education and training in Iran. Indeed, writes Helena Cobban, "When Iran's new Safavid ruler decided in the early sixteenth century that Shi'ism should be the official religion of his new state there, he imported scores of ulama from Lebanon to teach the new belief to his formerly Sunni subjects."[79] Third, the overthrow of the shah demonstrated dramatically what a well-organized and mobilized Shi'ia community could do.

Given these strong traditional links between the Shi'ias in Iran and those in Lebanon, Tehran poured substantial financial and military resources into Lebanon. These resources were used to arm Hizbollah and to run an array of social services, including hospitals, schools, and sanitation services. These massive resources were intended to achieve several goals. First, Tehran's efforts to export its Islamic revolution to the Gulf states did not succeed. Given its socioeconomic and political dynamics and the traditional close relations between Iran and the Lebanese Shi'ia community, Lebanon was seen as a country where another Islamic revolution might materialize. Second, the involvement in Lebanon provided a means for confronting the United States and Israel. Indeed, the successful Islamic resistance to the Israeli invasion is seen in Tehran as the second great Islamic victory after the Iranian revolution itself. Third, Iranian support for the Lebanese Shi'ias demonstrated the Islamic revolution's commitment to the cause of the disinherited and oppressed classes in the Muslim world.

The Lebanese Shi'ias largely welcomed the growing Iranian role and influence in their country. Tehran's commitment to the oppressed masses corresponded to the Lebanese Shi'ias' perception of their historical experience and their place in Lebanon's political and economic system. Iran provided financial assistance to the victims of the Israeli invasion and to those who were involved in resisting the Israeli occupation. According to Ehteshami and Hinnebusch, "Iran practiced what it preached, as the Revolutionary Guards provided credible leadership in resistance to the invasion."[80]

These mutual interests between Iran and the Lebanese Shi'ias were substantially reinforced by Israeli invasion and occupation of parts of Lebanon. In March 1978, responding to a Palestinian hijacking of a bus that resulted in the deaths of nine Palestinians and thirty-seven Israeli civilians, Israel launched its biggest punitive raid to date, known as the Litani Operation. An estimated 1,100 Lebanese and Palestinians, mostly civilians, perished in the ensuing Israeli assault.[81] Moreover, hundreds of thousands of southern villagers had to leave their homes and move north toward Beirut. This vast migration contributed to the radicalization of the Shi'ias.

Despite these heavy casualties, the 1978 invasion failed to achieve its goal of removing the PLO bases and fighters away from Israel's northern borders with Lebanon. The massive 1982 invasion, known as Operation Peace for Galilee, sought to finish the job by completely destroying the PLO political and military forces and driving it out of Lebanon.[82] An assassination attempt on the life of an Israeli ambassador to Britain served as the trigger for the 1982 invasion.[83] This massive Israeli attack substantially added to the radicalization of the Lebanese Shi'ias, weakened the moderate AMAL, and ironically facilitated the creation and rise to power of Hizbollah. Initially, the Shi'ias in the south assisted the Israeli efforts to drive out the PLO. Instead of taking advantage of this Shi'ia cooperation, Israel preferred to work with its client militia, the South Lebanese Army. Gradually this policy as well as the Israeli occupation of parts of Lebanon made a large part of the Shi'ia community Israel's most radical enemy. Hizbollah led the Shi'ias and Lebanese against Israel.

The U.S. State Department's authoritative *Patterns of Global Terrorism 2003* describes Hizbollah and its activities:

> Hizbollah was formed in 1982 in response to the Israeli invasion of Lebanon. This Lebanon-based radical Shi'ia group takes its ideological inspiration from the Iranian revolution and the teachings of the late Ayatollah Khomeini. Hizbollah is dedicated to liberating Jerusalem and eliminating Israel and has formally advocated ultimate establishment of Islamic rule in Lebanon. Nonetheless, Hizbollah has actively participated in Lebanon's political system since 1992. Hizbollah is closely allied with, and often directed by, Iran but has the capability and willingness to act alone. Although Hizbollah does not share the Syrian regime's secular orientation, the group has been a strong ally in helping Syria advance its objectives in the region.[84]

Two points need to be underscored in this description. First, dissatisfied with AMAL's moderation, Iran played a direct role in founding Hizbollah. Still, there is no doubt that the party is an indigenous organization with specific and limited goals within Lebanon. Its primary agenda was ridding Lebanon of the Israeli occupation, not liberating Palestine. Second, throughout the 1980s, Hizbollah focused on fighting the perceived enemies of the Lebanese Shi'ias with little, if any, indications of political role. The end of Lebanon's civil war in the late 1980s in conjunction with the rise of moderate elements within the Iranian leadership since the early 1990s have facilitated the increasing role Hizbollah has played as a political party in the Lebanese political system. Since 1992 the party has participated in Lebanon's parliamentary elections and expanded its network of social services, including schools and hospitals.

The party operates its own radio and TV stations and has its own Web site. Hizbollah's most important achievement is the successful resistance to the Israeli occupation of the so-called "security zone" in south Lebanon, which led to Israeli withdrawal in May 2000.

Following the Litani Operation in 1978, the United Nations Security Council issued resolution 425 demanding an immediate and unconditional withdrawal of Israeli troops from Lebanon, and the United Nations Interim Force in Lebanon (UNIFIL) was created to oversee the full implementation of the resolution. Israel rejected the resolution and, instead, maintained a presence in southern Lebanon. The 1982 Operation Peace for Galilee further reinforced Israeli military presence in Lebanon. Before it retreated to the international borders in 1985, the Israeli army created the security zone, a strip approximately 440 square miles (about 10 percent of Lebanon's territory), providing a buffer north of the Lebanese-Israeli borders. The zone was protected in collaboration with a mainly Christian militia called the South Lebanon Army, which was armed, trained, and financed by Israel.

This plan did not work. Instead, Hizbollah engaged Israel in a long-term war of attrition. In classic guerrilla fashion, Hizbollah exploited the vulnerability of fixed Israeli positions in the security zone by using long-distance attacks with mortars and antitank rockets, as well as devastating roadside bombs. Equally important, by videotaping and televising its military attacks, Hizbollah engaged in a psychological warfare with Israel and eventually succeeded in mobilizing the Israeli public against the war in Lebanon.

Gradually, the Israeli public grew weary of the stalemate in Lebanon and the slowly mounting casualty toll. Indeed, Alan Philps described the war in Lebanon as "Israel's Vietnam."[85] In the late 1990s, Israeli society was deeply divided on the wisdom of maintaining the security zone in southern Lebanon. Some Israelis viewed the zone as contributing to the protection of Israeli towns in the north, next to the borders with Lebanon. On the other hand, some Israeli strategists came to the conclusion that a war against a guerrilla army in a foreign country cannot be won. A grassroots movement called the Four Mothers (their sons were killed in Lebanon) helped to galvanize Israeli public opinion in favor of a withdrawal. At the end, increasing numbers of Israelis saw no advantage to staying in southern Lebanon.

Building on this public resentment, Israeli prime minister Ehud Barak decided to abandon the old strategy of a ground occupation that nullified all of Israel's technological advantages to a new one that relies on an aerial offense. Learning from the experience of the Gulf War and the war in Kosovo, the Israeli government decided that fighting from the air would allow Israel to use its superior capabilities. The cornerstone of this strategy, writes Tony Allen-Mills, was "a shift from fighting a guerrilla war against Hizbollah to relying on massive deterrence (i.e., a threat to strike at the Syrian army stationed in Lebanon if it helps the guerrilla)."[86] Accordingly, the Israeli army carried out the withdrawal from southern Lebanon (code name Operation Stamina) in May 2000. The operation was accomplished without the loss of a single life. Still, some Israelis voiced concern that Hizbollah portrayed their withdrawal as an outright defeat.

Given the significant role Iran has played in creating and supporting Hizbollah, the Israeli withdrawal was seen as a victory for the guerrillas as much as for the Islamic Republic. Little wonder, the Iranian foreign minister, Kamal Kharazi, was the first foreign dignitary to visit Lebanon shortly after the Israeli pullout, which he described as a "victory for all Muslims around the world." Iranian officials argued that the Israeli withdrawal validated their long-standing argument that military resistance and martyrdom, not negotiations, were the only way to liberate Arab and Muslim lands.

In closing, three conclusions can be drawn from the Israeli creation of and withdrawal from the security zone. First, there is no doubt that the Israeli withdrawal from south Lebanon is the greatest achievement for Hizbollah. The religiously motivated guerrillas succeeded in forcing the technologically superior and more powerful Israeli army to leave the security zone. The group's secretary general, Hassan Nasr Allah, proclaimed that his fighters had won the only Arab victory over Israel in more than fifty years. Second, the Israeli decision to pull out of Lebanon was, relatively speaking, easy to take because Israel makes no explicit territorial claims on Lebanon. In other words, withdrawing from south Lebanon was much simpler than pulling out from territory such as the West Bank, Gaza, or the Golan Heights, where there are territorial claims and Israeli settlers. Third, the Israeli pullout of south Lebanon left an important issue unresolved. A 100-square-mile area known as Shebaa Farms is located at the corner where the Syrian, Israeli, and Lebanese borders meet, and ownership of this farmland has been disputed. Israel insists that Shebaa Farms was part of the Golan Heights it seized from Syria in 1967, and therefore its ownership must be decided in negotiations with Damascus. Meanwhile, Israel has accepted that a small part of Shebaa Farms is Lebanese and left it as part of its overall withdrawal from south Lebanon. Lebanon has said that Shebaa Farms is all Lebanese territory and that Israel should leave it to comply with the 1978 United Nations resolution 425.[87]

An assessment of Iran's role in Lebanon since the early 1980s suggests that Tehran undoubtedly has tremendous influence over the Shi'ia community in Lebanon. Tehran, however, does not completely control or determine the policy that the Lebanese Shi'ias pursue. Hizbollah leaders pay a lot of respect and take into consideration Iran's wishes, but they make their own decisions. Since 1982 when Iran helped create Hizbollah, the Iranian leadership's perception of the group's role in Lebanese and regional policies has evolved. Top Iranian officials have endorsed Hizbollah's active participation in Lebanon's political system. The prospect for an Iranian-style revolution in Lebanon, if it ever existed, is long gone. This does not mean that the Iranian influence in Lebanon is waning. It is not. Developments in Iran will continue to be watched closely by the Lebanese Shi'ia community and have their own ramifications in Lebanon.

To sum up, the low-intensity proxy military confrontation between Iran and Israel in Lebanon started in the early 1980s, and since the Israeli withdrawal from south Lebanon in May 2000 it has substantially waned. Since the mid-1980s, strategists in the two countries have paid increasing attention to a possible direct military confrontation that might be triggered by nuclear proliferation.

Nuclear Proliferation

Nuclear bombs are the deadliest weapons ever invented. This why they are often described as the "great equalizer" in the sense that their possession diminishes the gap in conventional military power between strong and weak nations. However, they are also the most difficult weapons of mass destruction to manufacture or acquire. Western powers and Israel have suspected that Iran has been secretly developing nuclear capability since the mid-1980s. Iran, a signatory to the Treaty on the Non-Proliferation of Nuclear Weapons (NPT), categorically denies these accusations.

An examination of Iran's motivations to acquire nuclear capability reveals a deep concern about national security within a regional and international context that has grown more hostile and dangerous to the Islamic regime since the 1979 revolution. Stated differently, Iranian strategists feel threatened by the growing nonconventional capabilities of several of their neighbors and also by the deployment of American troops next to their borders in almost all directions. Conflicts with the United States, Israel, and Iraq are often cited as the main justification for Tehran's nuclear drive. Iran has had hostile relations with the United States since the Pahlavi regime was overthrown in 1979. Since then, the Islamic Republic has held what Ehteshami calls an "almost paranoid and conspiratorial view of the United States' role and action in the Middle

East" and has seen almost every U.S. initiative as a direct or indirect attack on Iran's national interest.[88] Iran's strategic standing in the international system has further worsened since the collapse of the Soviet Union in 1991 and the emergence of the United States as the sole superpower. This unchecked sole superpower has been very suspicious of Tehran's intentions and nuclear program.

Since the early 2000s, the mutual suspicion between Washington and Tehran has heightened. In October 2001, American troops were deployed to Afghanistan, where they overthrew the Taliban regime. In March 2003, American troops were deployed to Iraq, where they toppled Saddam Hussein's regime. Despite the fact that both the Taliban and Saddam Hussein were Iran's sworn enemies, the American military presence on Iran's eastern and western borders (as well as in the Arab states on the Persian Gulf on the southern borders and in Central Asia on the northern borders) is a matter of great concern to the regime in Tehran. This suspicion was further reinforced in 2002 when President George W. Bush called Iran a member of an "axis of evil," along with Iraq and North Korea, in his State of the Union Address. Speeches concerning a desire for a "regime change" in Tehran have further fueled Iranians' concern. Finally, the 2003 war in Iraq has sent a mixed signal to Iran. On one hand, the United States was not provoked to attack Iraq. Rather, it was a preemptive strike. This clearly suggests that Washington is ready to use its overwhelming might to prevent the proliferation of weapons of mass destruction. On the other hand, the United States' more benign and less confrontational response to North Korea's nuclear activities suggests that acquiring a nuclear device can serve as a deterrent. Some members of the Iranian political/security establishment believe that a nuclear capability is the only guarantor of the nation's independence and the regime's survival. The aim of acquiring such capability, as Shahram Chubin argues, would be to "deter the United States before it 'bullies' the Islamic Republic."[89]

Iranian leaders find Israel a much more straightforward cause of their interest in acquiring nuclear capability. Iran, even under the shah, opposed the Israeli nuclear asymmetry in the Middle East and Israel's refusal to sign the NPT. Accordingly, the Pahlavi regime sought to establish its own nuclear program and called for the creation of a Middle East nuclear-free zone. The leaders of the Islamic Republic perceive Israel as having the most extensive chemical, biological, and nuclear arsenal in the region and a formidable conventional force as well. Within this context, an Iranian nuclear capability can serve as a deterrent against potential Israeli attacks.

Finally, Iraq poses the most obvious and direct security threat to Iran, which might explain the Iranians' interest in developing nuclear capability. In recent memory, the war with Iraq (1980–88) was much more violent than any confrontation Tehran had with other adversaries. Indeed, Saddam Hussein's wide use of chemical weapons against Iranian targets in 1988 forced the Iranians to accept a cease-fire that favored the Iraqis. Within this context, "deterring Iraq became the principal rationale for the revival of Iran's nuclear program in the mid-1980s."[90]

Relations between Tehran and Baghdad are complicated. True, under Saddam Hussein, hostility between the two countries peaked, but his removal does not guarantee a peaceful coexistence. The two nations still have a territorial dispute over Shat al-Arab. Furthermore, Tehran has strong ties with several factions within the Iraqi Shi'ia population, which might help or hurt relations between the two countries. In short, any speculation on the political and strategic orientation of post-Saddam Iraq is risky and unproductive. The Iranians believe that they should be prepared for any outcome.

The roots of Iran's pursuit of nuclear capability lie in the closing years of the Iran-Iraq War, though the shah had laid the groundwork for an indigenous Iranian nuclear capability during the 1970s. Ironically, Iran's nuclear program began with the assistance of the United States. This included a research reactor and a number of hot cell laboratories for handling radioactive materials. In 1974 the shah established the Atomic Energy Organization of Iran and stated that Iran would "without a doubt have nuclear weapons very soon."[91] France and Germany also contributed to Iran's nuclear program, signing several agreements with the shah to provide Iran with enriched uranium, nuclear reactors, and research centers.

Shortly after the revolution, Ayatollah Khomeini froze the country's nuclear program on the ground that nuclear weapons were immoral. This stand, however, was reversed in 1985 because of Iraq's heavy military attacks. Tehran's efforts to revive its nuclear program have since been restrained by intense American pressure. U.S. pressure gained momentum in 2002 when an Iranian opposition group, the National Council of Resistance, publicly disclosed the locations of two secret nuclear facilities in Iran. These revelations prompted investigations by the International Atomic Energy Agency (IAEA). International inspectors found that Iran, in violation of its nonproliferation commitments, had pursued a clandestine fissile material production program for eighteen years and that it was "further advanced in its enrichment program than anyone had suspected."[92] In response to this development, the United States, the European Union (EU), and the IAEA have pursued different strategies to impose a tight international scrutiny on Iran's nuclear program.

American diplomats have sought to persuade their European and Asian counterparts as well as officials from the IAEA to refer Iran to the United Nations Security Council, where broad sanctions can be imposed. The EU agrees with the United States that a nuclear Iran would pose a threat to regional peace and a challenge to the nonproliferation regime. The Europeans, however, are less convinced than the Americans (and the Israelis) that Tehran is trying to acquire nuclear weapons. Furthermore, Brussels does not see sanctions and threats of military strikes as the best way to address Iran's nuclear ambition. On the contrary, they might push Tehran to withdraw from the NPT and end its cooperation with the IAEA. Instead, European powers prefer what may be described as a "conditional engagement" with Iran. Since the early 2000s, Brussels and Tehran have negotiated a Trade and Cooperation Agreement (TCA). Given that Iran's application to join the World Trade Organization has been blocked by the United States for several years and that the EU is Iran's major trade partner, the TCA would substantially help the Iranian economy. The EU is using economic and diplomatic incentives to persuade Iran to abide by the norms of the nonproliferation regime.

Finally, since late 2002 the IAEA has been vigorously investigating Iran's nuclear program. The IAEA Board of Governors has issued several statements underscoring two important points. First, Iran's nuclear activities have not been completely in line with its commitments to the NPT. In other words, Tehran violated some of its obligations under the NPT. Second, despite these violations and some serious irregularities, the IAEA has not found credible evidence that Iran seeks to develop nuclear weapons.

Tehran's efforts to build an indigenous nuclear infrastructure and its intense negotiations with the EU and the IAEA as well as the diplomatic and economic confrontations with the United States suggest several conclusions. First, Iranian officials assert that they are interested in nuclear power for peaceful purposes and that it will help free up oil and gas resources for export, thus generating additional hard-currency revenues. Furthermore, they argue, Iran does not want to fall behind in nuclear industry technology with its wide-ranging applications and that Iranian technicians need to familiarize themselves with this technology. Second, Iran's nuclear program has received substantial assistance from foreign sources, particularly Russia, China, and Pakistan. Iranian personnel have developed such extensive knowledge and technology that they might be approaching the point of self-sufficiency.

Third, Iranian officials confirm that Iran has the right to uranium enrichment under the NPT and that, given the country's experience, it cannot rely on the international community to guarantee supply fuel. Foreign suppliers, the

Iranians argue, are subject to political pressure. Fourth, Iran's motivations are not regime-specific. The support for a nuclear capability is shared across the Iranian political spectrum (moderates and hard-liners). It started under the Pahlavi dynasty and is likely to continue regardless of the political orientation of the regime in Tehran. Fifth, Iran has already invested substantial financial and technological resources, as well as national pride, in building its nuclear program. It is highly unlikely that the Iranians will agree to abandon it completely.

A complicating factor in the debate over Iran's nuclear ambition, and indeed the entire nonproliferation regime, is Israel's own status as an undeclared nuclear power. Israel is widely recognized as the world's sixth-ranking nuclear power, "much closer, in quality and quantity, to France and Britain than to India and Pakistan."[93] Even the IAEA considers Israel a nuclear power.[94] Israel, India, and Pakistan are the only countries with nuclear facilities that have not signed the NPT. Furthermore, Israel forbids outside inspections of its nuclear facilities. This tolerance of Israel's nuclear weapons program outside of the NPT has led Iran and other Middle Eastern countries to question the legitimacy and validity of the nonproliferation regime. Iranian officials argue that Israel's nuclear capability "poses the gravest danger to the security and stability of the Middle East."[95]

Shortly after its creation as the Jewish homeland in 1948 and following the horrors of the Holocaust in which 6 million European Jews were murdered, Israel began showing an interest in acquiring nuclear weapons as the ultimate deterrent. This nuclear capability was meant to help the new state overcome two disadvantages: small population and lack of territorial depth. During this early stage of building nuclear capability, the country lacked the necessary indigenous materials and expertise and had to depend on foreign sources. France, more than any other country, provided crucial assistance to Israel.[96] In the mid-1950s, France pledged to assist in developing nuclear arms and agreed to supply a "sizable plutonium-producing reactor, which was built at Dimona in the Negev desert."[97] In addition, in 1955 Israel and the United States signed a general agreement for peaceful nuclear cooperation including an agreement for the purchase of a small research nuclear reactor.[98]

Israel has been considered a special case in Washington's nuclear nonproliferation policy. The Kennedy and Johnson administrations demanded that U.S. officials be allowed to inspect the Dimona reactor. Israel reluctantly yielded, and a number of visits took place during the 1960s. These visits reinforced American suspicion of Israel's nuclear ambition and caused some friction between the two countries, which culminated in Israel's refusal to sign the NPT in 1968. From an American perspective, Tel Aviv's signature would have meant that it renounced its nuclear weapons program. Apparently the United States lacked either the political will or the power (or both) to persuade Israel to join the NPT. Accordingly, in 1969 President Nixon reached an agreement with the Israeli prime minister, Golda Meir, in which Nixon agreed to maintain a low profile on its nuclear program and Meir agreed not to talk about it. Since then, all American and Israeli administrations have adhered to this agreement.

At least two factors shaped this American tolerance of Israel's nuclear weapons program. First, since the establishment of Israel in 1948 and particularly before the 1970s, when it became a regional superpower, it has been seen as the victim in the Arab-Israeli conflict. A small country surrounded by numerous and more populous nations, who initially were not willing to accept its existence and sought to destroy it. Israel, the argument goes, has the right to defend itself and to deter its enemies from potential attacks. Second, Israel has a democratic political system similar to those in Western Europe and the United States. Washington sees a big distinction between nuclear weapons in pluralistic governments and under the control of dictators. In the words of Douglas Frantz, a senior U.S. official, "We tolerate nuclear weapons in Israel for the same reason we tolerate them in Britain and France."[99]

Accordingly, the United States imposed very few restrictions, if any, on Israel's efforts to develop its nuclear capability in the 1950s and 1960s. Since then, Washington apparently has accepted Israel's nuclear exceptionalism. The issue, as Cohen and Graham stated, has evolved into an "off-limits subject for American foreign policy."[100] Shai Feldman notes, "Israel pretended not to have nuclear weapons and the U.S. pretended to believe this."[101] This American stand and Israel's disengagement from the nonproliferation regime have increasingly been under criticism. Many analysts argue that Israel is a major beneficiary of the NPT and the nonproliferation norms, and it is in the country's best interest to be part of them. Similar criticism has been voiced regarding how the issue of Israel's nuclear capability is being handled domestically. The country's nuclear program has never been subjected to self-examination or public scrutiny.

Despite this sensitivity to transparency and restrictions on public debate, some analysts argue that the Israeli public strongly supports the government's nuclear policy.[102] Other analysts suggest that this public support has eroded over time and that the country's nuclear strategy should be opened for discussion and cease to be a fait accompli "made in secrecy with little or no governmental, parliamentary, or public oversight."[103] This disagreement over Israel's nuclear posture has further intensified since 2000. There is no consensus on how Israel should respond to the growing controversy over Iran's nuclear program.

Israeli officials do not believe the claim that Iran's nuclear program is solely for peaceful purposes. Rather, the Israelis charge that Iran is secretly developing a nuclear weapons program. They also accuse Tehran of deceiving the international community and having no plan to abandon its nuclear weapons ambition. Tehran, the Israelis argue, is negotiating with the IAEA and the EU only to buy time and that the countdown to a nuclear Iran has already begun. Still, the Israeli analysts differ in their assessment of when Iran would be seen as irrevocably on the road to developing nuclear weapons. Several characteristics of a potential Israeli attack against Iran's nuclear facilities can be identified.

First, Israel's concerns over Iran's nuclear capability are magnified by the fact that Iran already possesses a surface-to-surface missile known as Shehab-3. In addition to the fact that the Shehab-3 can reach every point in Israel, it has multiple warheads, so that one of them can act as a decoy, confounding the Israeli defense system. Second, Israeli officials have been deliberately ambiguous regarding the course of action they might take. Rather, they confirm that all options are being weighed to prevent Iran from achieving nuclear weapons capability and that Israel will not rely on others. Third, Israeli officials have argued that the cost of doing nothing regarding Iran's nuclear program may be the most expensive outcome. They suggest that if the international community fails to act against Iran in a timely fashion, Israel could strike preemptively as it did against Iraq's nuclear facilities in 1981.

Fourth, the possibility of an Israeli attack on Iran's nuclear installations similar to the one on Iraq in 1981 is complicated. Iran learned from the Iraqi experience and has taken precautions against such preemptive action. Iranian nuclear installations are reported to be scattered throughout the country, in urban areas and in underground locations, and are protected by sophisticated defense systems. Equally important, the Israeli attack on Iraq in 1981 did not terminate that country's nuclear ambition and probably encouraged Saddam Hussein to develop chemical and biological weapons. Fifth, despite these potential drawbacks of an Israeli military strike against Iran's nuclear facilities, the Israeli government has sought to buy military equipment to facilitate such an attack if the need arises. These include American-built F-16 warplanes, designed with extra fuel tanks to allow them to reach Iran, and precision-guided "smart bombs." These bombs were originally developed for penetrating hardened Iraqi command centers located deep underground. Sixth, in response to these sophisticated weaponry systems and the repeated Israeli threats, Iranian officials have warned Israel of the severe consequences of an attack on their country and threatened to target Israel's nuclear reactor at Dimona.

To sum up, the discussion of Israel's nuclear capability and policy suggest three conclusions. First, Israeli officials have never confirmed or denied their country's nuclear arsenal. Rather, they have deliberately maintained a policy of nuclear ambiguity, or "deterrence through uncertainty." By not confirming their possession of nuclear weapons, the Israelis avoid subjecting their country to international criticism and possible sanctions. On the other hand, by not denying the existence of these weapons, the Israelis keep their enemies (Arabs and Iranians) guessing. This deliberate ambiguity has enabled Israel to achieve strategic deterrence without paying a political price. In remarks to the Israeli Army Radio in July 2004, Prime Minister Ariel Sharon said, "Our policy of ambiguity on nuclear arms has proven its worth, and it will continue."[104] Second, a fundamental component of Israel's nuclear policy is the right to preemptively strike nuclear facilities established by its adversaries. The 1981 attack on Iraq's nuclear reactor was a case in point. A report presented to Sharon on existential security matters in January 2003 declared, "Today, more than ever, Israel must include appropriate preemption options in its overall defense strategy. Israel's main focus must be on preventing a coalition of Arab states and/or Iran from coming into possession of weapons of mass destruction."[105]

Third, Israeli officials have always been suspicious of universal global arms control agreements. They argue that the NPT and proposals to make the entire Middle East a nuclear-free zone are premature. Rather, they insist that a comprehensive peace that resolves all the region's political disputes should be reached first. All major players (Arabs and Iranians) should agree on such a framework, and Israel should be fully accepted and integrated into the Middle East's economic, diplomatic, and security systems. In other words, a genuine peace should precede an arms control treaty.

Iran and Israel: The Road Ahead

The fall of the shah and the rise of an Islamic regime shattered any formal ties between Iran and Israel, but it did not completely alter their shared geopolitical interests. Therefore, ideology aside, geopolitical interest kept the channels between Tehran and Tel Aviv open. These channels have never completely
· closed, although the level of activity has varied. This variation reflects the ri-

valry between pragmatism and dogmatism in Tehran. Put differently, an Iranian foreign policy driven by ideological considerations would be characterized by hostility toward Israel while a foreign policy guided by national interests would be receptive to some level of coexistence with and accommodation to the Jewish state

On the Israeli side, there are also two competing approaches in shaping the country's stand on Iran. One school emphasizes the geostrategic significance of Iran as a non-Arab, non-Sunni Middle Eastern state, which for a long time had good relations with Jews and Israel. The proponents of this theory argue that the extremist tone in the current Iranian leadership is temporary and that Tel Aviv should establish and maintain contacts with the Iranian people, who would outlast the Islamic Republic. Most important, Israel will always be concerned about the welfare of the Iranian Jewry. The other Israeli school believes that the Islamic regime in Tehran is here to stay and that Tel Aviv should wake up from the peripheral policy.

Given these conflicting theories in both Tehran and Tel Aviv, a major shift in the verbal confrontation or, more accurately, the cold war between Iran and Israel is highly unlikely. The long-term relations, either hostile or friendly, between the two countries will be shaped by developments in at least four areas. First, since the establishment of the Islamic Republic, a major characterization of Iranian policy has been factionalism. Moderate and extremist elements have pursued different and occasionally contradictory policies and objectives. The moderate camp is less hostile toward Israel than the conservative camp. Despite some current and expected setbacks, moderation and pragmatism are gaining ground at the expense of extremism. Second, since 1979 Iran has considered the United States its main enemy. Diplomatic relations between the two countries were severed in 1980, and more than two decades later, President Bush labeled Iran as a member of a global "axis of evil." The Israeli factor features in this extreme hostility between Washington and Tehran. The cold war between Tel Aviv and Tehran can be seen as both cause and effect of the tension between Tehran and Washington. In other words, the animosity between Iran and Israel aggravates the already tense American-Iranian relations. Meanwhile, a rapprochement between Washington and Tehran will not take place without some relaxation and pacification of Iranian-Israeli hostility.

Third, a major area of contention between Tehran and Tel Aviv is the continuing violence between the Israelis and the Palestinians. Iran's sympathy and support for the Palestinians have been persistent in Iranian policy since the late 1940s, long before the Islamic revolution. The escalation of violence and the deterioration of the Palestinian plight further deepen the animosity toward the Israelis. A fair and peaceful settlement of the Arab-Israeli conflict would tremendously contribute to regional stability and remove a major source of tension between Tel Aviv and Tehran. Fourth, the high level of uncertainty regarding Iraq will continue to influence relations between Iran and Israel. Until the fall of Saddam Hussein's regime in 2003, both Tehran and Tel Aviv perceived Baghdad as their most dangerous enemy. The Iraqi army participated in the Arab-Israeli wars and fought a long and bloody war with Iran from 1980 to 1988. Iran and Israel coordinated their efforts to undermine and weaken Iraq in the past. A repeat of these efforts cannot be ruled out. The future of Iraq and its role in the regional system following the 2003 war are highly uncertain.

3

Iraq and Israel

Unlike Egypt, Jordan, Lebanon, and Syria, Iraq does not share long borders with Israel. However, Baghdad has been one of the strongest Arab opponents of the Jewish state since its creation in 1948. Indeed, Israel has been technically at war with Iraq since 1948, when Baghdad participated in hostilities against Israel in the first Arab-Israeli war. According to Simon Henderson, "Iraq was the only participant in that war that refused to sign an armistice agreement with Israel in 1949 after the cessation of hostilities."[1] Iraq also fought Israel in the Six Days' War of 1967 and the Yom Kippur War of 1973. It took the lead against Egyptian president Anwar al-Sadat's peace overtures to Israel in 1977 and 1978 and opposed the Egyptian-Israeli peace treaty of 1979. More than any other Arab country, Iraq invested massive resources in building and stocking chemical and biological weapons as well as an active nuclear program in the 1980s.

In April 1990, Saddam Hussein warned that he would burn half of Israel if Israel attacked Iraq. During the Gulf War of 1991, Iraqi Scud missiles landed in Israeli cities. Furthermore, Saddam Hussein gave sanctuary to anti-Israel Palestinian groups and publicly endorsed suicide attacks as legitimate means to fight the Israelis and made payments to the families of Palestinians who carried them out.

Iraq's recent history and its political geography contributed to this hostile attitude toward Israel. First, in 1921 the provinces of Mosul in the north, Baghdad in the center, and Basra in the south were part of the Ottoman Empire. After the empire collapsed at the end of World War I, these three provinces were united to create the state of Iraq. Under British influence, a parliamentary system was installed; it failed, however, to prevent a direct military intervention in the political process. In 1936 and 1941, the first military coups in modern Arab politics occurred in Iraq.[2] In 1958, another military coup overthrew the monarchical regime and replaced the parliamentary system with a single party, effectively a one-man dictatorship that continued under Saddam Hussein. A major characteristic of the Iraqi political system, both monarchical and republican, is the lack of institutionalization. As a result, there have been frequent and violent changes of power. These include King Faisal I (1921–33), King Ghazi (1933–39), and Regent Abdullah in the 1940s and early 1950s while King Faisal II (1939–58) was an infant. Under the republican system Abd al-Karim Qasim ruled from 1958 to 1963 and was toppled by Abd al-Salam Aref, who was killed in 1966 in a helicopter crash and was succeeded by his brother Abd al-Rahman Aref until he was overthrown in 1968 by the Ba'ath Party under the dual leadership of Ahmad Hassan al-Bakr and Saddam Hussein. The latter declared himself president in 1979 and ruled Iraq brutally until his regime was toppled by an American-led international coalition in March 2003 and he was arrested in December 2003. Under all these regimes, writes Tim Niblock, "political power has been the prerogative of a relatively small group of individuals who maneuvered in cliques to attain power."[3]

Second, the political geography of Iraq presents both opportunities and constraints for the country's foreign policy. Iraq is blessed by massive oil reserves and substantial agricultural resources. These resources suggest that Iraq has the potential to play a leading role in the Gulf region and the broader Middle East. This leadership role has been challenged and enforced by the country's location on the fringe of the Arab world sharing borders with two non-Arab Middle Eastern states, Iran and Turkey. These natural resources in conjunction with the strategic location have formulated a national perception that Iraq should play a leading role in protecting the Arab world from non-Arab regional powers, particularly Iran and Israel. Ironically, throughout history, says Ahmad Yousef Ahmad, "not only has Iraq been unable to fulfill that role; it has also suffered from the invasion of great powers and their overbearing influence."[4] The American-led international coalition's invasion in March 2003 was the latest episode.

Iraq's domestic instability and the general perception of the country as a defender of the Arab cause have contributed to the adoption of a hostile attitude toward Israel. In the following sections the main forces that shaped Baghdad's attitude toward Israel will be examined. These include the tense relations with the United States (1958–2003), the Ba'ath Party's theoretical ideological orientation (radical Arab nationalism), and the composition of the Iraqi population (ethnic division between Arabs and Kurds). Then the few direct confrontations between Iraq and Israel will be analyzed. The list includes the plight of the Iraqi Jews, Israel's support to the Kurdish rebellion in northern Iraq in the early 1970s, Baghdad's participation in the Arab-Israeli wars, Israel's reaction to the Iran-Iraq War and the Persian Gulf War, and Israel's raid on Iraq's Osiraq nuclear reactor in 1981. The concluding section provides some preliminary discussion of the Israeli reaction to the 2003 war. The study demonstrates that the Iraqi-Israeli confrontation has lacked any hint of compromise or rapprochement and has been characterized by mutual suspicion and hostility.

Determinants of Iraq's Attitude toward Israel

Probably more than any other Arab country, Iraq is blessed with abundant resources. The country holds the world's second largest oil reserves after Saudi Arabia, it is rich in water supplies, and it is neither overpopulated nor underpopulated. Furthermore, until the 1991 Gulf War it had one of the best-educated populations in the Arab world. Given these economic potentials, the Iraqi leaders have always aspired to lead the entire region. In pursuing such ambition, they occasionally had to compete with their Syrian and Egyptian rivals. In addition, given the centrality of the Arab-Israeli conflict and the plight of the Palestinians in Middle Eastern policy, Baghdad has been intensely involved in the dispute with Tel Aviv. Despite the fact that Iraq does not share borders with Israel, Baghdad, until the collapse of Saddam Hussein's regime in 2003, adopted the most militant stand against Israel in the Arab world.

Relations with the United States

From the late 1950s until the collapse of Saddam Hussein's regime in 2003, a major theme of Iraqi foreign policy had been a strong mistrust of Western powers, particularly Great Britain and the United States. This characterization was in response to the conditions under which Iraq was created. After World War I, Iraq, which was previously part of the Ottoman Empire, was put under British mandate until its independence in 1932. This independence, however, did not reduce the British influence over Baghdad's domestic and foreign policies. During World War II, Great Britain reoccupied Iraq and replaced an independent, anti-British government with one more trustworthy to the Allies. The British continued to play a significant role in Iraqi policy until the monarchy was overthrown and a republican system was established in 1958.

The peak of the monarchical Iraq's alliance with Western powers was reached in the mid-1950s. In 1954 Iraq signed a military aid agreement with the United States, and a year later, Baghdad broke diplomatic relations with

Moscow, which were first established in 1944. The apex of this Western orientation was reached when the Baghdad Pact was concluded in 1955 between Iraq, Turkey, Iran, Pakistan, and Great Britain. The major purpose of this alliance was to prevent the spread of communism and to create a territorial buffer against Soviet expansion in Southwest Asia and the Middle East. It confirmed Baghdad's dependency on Western allies to ensure its national security and economic development. This open alliance with Western powers and the absence of other Arab participants contributed to the collapse of the monarchical regime in July 1958. Iraq withdrew from the Baghdad Pact in March 1959 and terminated the bilateral military assistance agreement with the United States two months later.

Iraq's foreign policy orientation has changed dramatically since the 1958 coup, yet every regime in Baghdad has adopted a strong anti-Western, particularly anti-American, stand. Four factors shaped Baghdad's policy toward Washington. U.S. support for Israel has always been featured negatively in its relations with Iraq. Strong pan-Arabism sentiments have always dominated Iraqi history and policy. Little wonder, then, that even under the monarchy Iraqi regimes have strongly identified with Arab nationalism and presented themselves as the vanguard in the Arab struggle against Israel. The close cooperation between Washington and Tehran that was followed by hostility after the Pahlavi regime's collapse has had its own effect on U.S.—Iraqi relations. Since 1958 there have been numerous successful and unsuccessful coups in Iraq. A common denominator has been a fascist and nationalist ideological drive. The rhetoric generated by this attitude and support for it among intellectuals and other constituencies have made cooperative policies with the West extremely difficult. To a great extent, post-1958 Iraqi regimes have established a close political, economic, and military alliance with the Soviet Union and its successor, Russia. These overall warm relations between Moscow and Baghdad, which had few but significant setbacks, have further deepened the rift between Baghdad and Washington.

Although interests often coincided between Moscow and Baghdad, differing stands and goals have occasionally caused strain. Iraqi withdrawal from the Baghdad Pact was followed by a resumption of relations with the Soviet Union and clear pro-Soviet foreign policy orientation. According to Mark Katz, "When the Ba'ath Party seized power for the first time in February 1963, Soviet-Iraqi relations declined sharply as the Ba'ath and the Iraqi Communist Party fought each other. Soviet military aid to Baghdad ceased and was only restored to its former level after the November 1963 coup, which ousted the Ba'athists and brought General Aref to power."[5] When the Ba'ath Party regained power in 1968, the new regime adopted a pro-Soviet foreign policy orientation, similar to the one adopted by its predecessors. It also supported leftist and nationalist movements against conservative governments in the Middle East.

A dramatic improvement in Iraqi-Soviet relations was formalized in 1972 when the two countries signed a twenty-year treaty of friendship and cooperation. Baghdad and Moscow were engaged in hostility against the United States and its allies in the Middle East. Tehran and Tel Aviv, in cooperation with Washington, were providing military and financial assistance to the Kurds in their fighting against Iraq. Meanwhile, Baghdad was supporting a Marxist insurgency against the conservative pro-West government in Oman. This formal alliance between Moscow and Baghdad further deepened the rift between Baghdad and Washington. As a result, the United States consolidated its relations with Iran, Iraq's sworn enemy. Indeed, the mid-1970s witnessed the closest cooperation ever between Washington and Tehran.

Relations between Moscow and Baghdad, however, considerably cooled down in the second half of the 1970s. Several developments restrained their cooperation. First, the skyrocketing of oil prices following the 1973 Arab-Israeli war provided Iraq, and other oil producers, with substantial revenues. These massive revenues fueled Iraq's aspirations to plan and implement ambitious social and economic development. Some Iraqi officials were not satisfied with the poor quality of Eastern bloc goods and felt the need for modern Western products and technology. In mid-1970s Iraq started buying sophisticated weapons from France. Overall, Baghdad's increasing economic power made it more confident and less dependent on Moscow. Second, in March 1975 Iraq signed agreements with Iran, which temporarily ended their territorial dispute and stopped Tehran's support to the Kurdish rebellion in Iraq. This agreement significantly improved Iraq's national security and enabled the regime in Baghdad to assert its control and sovereignty over the Kurdish provinces in northern Iraq.

Third, Egypt started negotiating a peace treaty with Israel, which the two sides signed in 1979. These Egyptian steps to make peace with Israel were largely seen in the Arab world as a separate movement and resulted in temporary Egyptian isolation in the region. This provided Iraq with a historic opportunity to expand and assert its claims for Arab leadership. Accordingly, Baghdad improved relations with Riyadh and other Arab conservative states, ended its support for the separatist movement in the Sultanate of Oman, and championed Arab opposition to the Egyptian-Israeli peace treaty. This rising Iraqi role was further enhanced by the political turmoil in Iran, which eventually led to the toppling of the Pahlavi regime and the establishment of the Islamic Republic. Fourth, in the late 1970s the Soviet leaders sought to consolidate relations with Marxist regimes over which they could exercise greater leverage.[6] Writes Barry Rubin, "Such was the model followed with greater or lesser success in Afghanistan, Ethiopia, and the People's Democratic Republic of Yemen (South Yemen)."[7] This Soviet policy further weakened ties with Baghdad.

The Iran-Iraq War (1980–88) provided a rare opportunity to improve relations between Washington and Baghdad. Ayatollah Khomeini's rise to power in Iran had drastically altered the dynamics of Middle Eastern policy and security. The Ba'ath Party returned to power in a 1968 coup, and Saddam Hussein was considered the strongman behind the scenes until 1979, when he officially became president. Despite Hussein's brutality, Washington and other regional and Western powers perceived him and Iraq as the only barrier standing between Khomeini and the Middle East. As a result, the 1980s witnessed the warmest phase in the overall troubled U.S.-Iraqi relations. At the outbreak of the war, the United States declared its neutrality. But when the Iranians liberated the territories they had lost to the Iraqis and went on the offensive, Washington tilted toward Baghdad.

Thus in September 1984 diplomatic relations, which Baghdad broke in response to American support to Israel in the 1967 Arab-Israeli war, were restored. This resumption of diplomatic relations was facilitated by the removal of Iraq from the U.S. State Department's list of states sponsoring terrorism. "More quietly," writes Rubin, "the United States gave Iraq satellite photographs of Iran's military positions and operations."[8] Meanwhile, members of Congress were upset by Iraq's use of chemical weapons against Iran and its own Kurdish population. Legislation was proposed for trade and financial sanctions, but the Reagan administration successfully amended the bill so that the question of sanctions was left to the president's discretion. In the end, no sanctions were imposed on Iraq.

The most serious test of U.S. accommodation occurred in May 1987, when a French-built Iraqi Mirage fighter accidentally fired two missiles at the USS *Stark*, a frigate steaming in international waters in the center of the Persian Gulf. In the resulting explosion, thirty-seven sailors were killed and many more were injured. Following this incident, the United States moved quickly to commit naval forces to the region in order to escort oil tankers, but, according to Simon Henderson, "it blamed Iran—not Iraq—for the dangerous environment that allowed the accident to occur in the first place."[9]

It is important to reemphasize that rapprochement between Washington and Baghdad was not based on any trust between the two governments. Rather, they found a mutual enemy in Khomeini's revolution. While these short-range interests had created a temporary harmony, they could not overcome the deep gulf of mistrust that separated the two countries. The end of the Iran-Iraq War brought back the suspicion that had characterized U.S.-Iraqi relations since 1958. By the spring of 1989 and after a long debate in Washington on how to "handle" Saddam Hussein, the Bush administration decided on a policy of constructive engagement with Iraq, hoping that such a policy would lead to Saddam Hussein's moderation. Iraq was the ninth-largest customer for U.S. agricultural goods.[10] Indeed, what was remarkable about U.S. policy toward Iraq in this transitional period between the end of the Iran-Iraq War in 1988 and the beginning of the Gulf crisis in 1990 were Washington's consistent efforts to improve relations with Saddam Hussein's regime. According to Paul Gigot, "There were more carrots than sticks. Washington never drew a line in the sand."[11] The Iraqi president, however, became more aggressive. Still, the Bush administration pursued this constructive engagement until Iraq invaded Kuwait in August 1990.

The end of the Persian Gulf War in February 1991 was supposed to have ended the conflict between Iraq and the United States. Instead, Operation Desert Storm turned out to be only the first of a series of hostilities between the two countries, which included military operations and economic sanctions. The American objectives in this long confrontation have evolved from containing Saddam Hussein to destroying Iraq's weapons of mass destruction and finally bombing Baghdad. A new chapter in U.S.-Iraqi relations has yet to be written following the 2003 war.

Two conclusions can be drawn from this brief examination of U.S.-Iraqi relations. First, the United States and Iraq have never had warm relations. For a short time in the 1980s their national interests overlapped and for pragmatic reasons they worked together to face the Iranian challenge. Remarkably, in just two years Iraq was transformed from a virtual U.S. ally to the first Arab country to fight a war against the United States. This underscores the deep mistrust, which characterizes the relations between Washington and Baghdad. When Iraq was created in 1921, the British enjoyed the greatest leverage as a foreign patron. The Soviet (Russian) influence has replaced that of Great Britain since the 1958 coup, and Baghdad has adopted a radical leftist and nationalist stand in both domestic and foreign policy. Diplomatic relations with the United States were severed in 1967 in response to American support to Israel during the Six Days' War. Relations were restored in 1984 but broken following the Iraqi invasion of Kuwait in 1990. The toppling of Saddam Hussein's regime and American and British occupation of Iraq represented a turning point in the country's domestic and foreign policies. Washington has a fresh opportunity to reshape Baghdad's foreign relations.

Second, this extensive mistrust between the United States and Iraq has manifested itself over two principal issues: Persian Gulf security and the Arab-Israeli conflict. The animosity between Washington and Baghdad, until the 2003 war, can be seen as both a cause and an effect for the hostility between Baghdad and Tel Aviv. Iraq's opposition to the United States was driven partly by American support for Israel. At the same time, a rapprochement with Washington would not have happened as long as Baghdad maintained its fiery rejection of Israel's existence and policy. Until the 2003 war, this militant Iraqi stand was reinforced by the ideological framework of the Ba'ath Party.

The Ba'ath Party

The Ba'ath Party, which dominated Iraqi policy from the 1960s until 2003, perceived itself as the embodiment of Arab nationalism and the one movement that would finally drive home the Arabs' secular dream of political unification and economic prosperity. In order to understand the role the Ba'ath Party played in articulating and guiding the Iraqi policy, a brief discussion of the party's history, structure, and ideology is in order.

In the early 1940s two Syrian intellectuals, Michel Aflaq, a Greek Orthodox Christian, and Salah al-Din Bitar, a Sunni Muslim, founded the Ba'ath Party. According to Edmund Ghareeb, "Both men had studied at the Sorbonne in the 1930s, where they came in contact with Marxist, Hegelian, and nationalist ideologies and philosophies."[12] The party was founded at a time when Syria was still under French mandate. This led the Ba'athists in two directions. First, the party developed into a national liberation movement against the French occupation and against imperialism in general. Second, the young leaders of the Ba'ath called for a more assertive approach to pan-Arabism than the one adopted by the "old generation" of Arab politicians. This new vision of Arab unity was based more on socialist ideals and less on liberal-democratic principles. The defeat of Arab armies in the 1948 war with Israel reinforced the failure of traditional politicians and the need for new leadership and vision. The party spread to Iraq through the recruitment of Iraqi students studying in Damascus and Beirut and the arrival in Iraq of a number of Syrian teachers who carried with them the seeds of Ba'athist ideas.

During the 1950s, the Ba'ath was a clandestine party, and its members were subject to arrest if their identities were discovered. The Ba'ath joined with other parties in opposing the monarchy and participated in the activities that led to the 1958 coup. The Ba'ath's role, however, was limited. Still, given its ideological orientation, the Ba'athists hoped that the new republican government would favor pan-Arabism, particularly a union with Egypt. It is worth pointing out that Nasser of Egypt was then perceived as the champion of Arab unity. These expectations did not materialize, and instead the Iraqi leadership was split between General Abd al-Karim Qasim, who led the 1958 coup and the communists, on the one hand and the nationalists and Ba'athists on the other hand. This confrontation was further escalated in November 1959 when a group of Ba'athists attempted to assassinate Qasim.[13] Their failure led to a temporary breakdown in the party's organization and the arrest of many of its members. As a result, the Ba'ath was forced underground again, and experienced a period of internal division as members debated over which tactics were most appropriate to achieve their political objectives. The party's second attempt to overthrow Qasim, in February 1963, was successful, and it resulted in the formation of the country's first Ba'ath government. The party, however, was more divided than ever between idealist and pragmatic members. Because of this lack of unity, writes Helen Metz, "the Ba'ath's coup partners were able to outmaneuver it and, within nine months, to expel all Ba'athists from the government."[14] The party then reorganized under the direction of General Bakr as secretary general with Saddam Hussein as his deputy. Both men were determined to bring the Ba'ath back to power. In July 1968, the Ba'ath finally staged a successful coup and stayed in power until the 2003 war. The history of the Ba'ath Party demonstrates that it succeeded in gaining and maintaining political power less by the appeal of its programs to a large segment of the Iraqi population and more through conspiracies between a few individuals.

At least three characters of the Ba'ath Party's structure can be identified. First, "most accounts of the party suggest that it had a highly structured organization, comparable in many ways to a communist party, with a central committee, a carefully elaborated ideology, and an agreed line endorsed by the party congresses."[15] Furthermore, throughout its history the size of the Ba'ath Party had been a matter of speculation. No precise account has been made public. Second, the hierarchy within the party was based less on ideological purity and more on personal and family ties. Third, from its early years, the Ba'ath Party recruited converts from a small number of college and high school students, intellectuals, and professionals—virtually all of whom were urban Sunni Arabs. The Shi'ias and Kurds were proportionally underrepresented.

These urban Sunni Arabs played a leading role in formulating the party's ideology. The main theme of this ideology is pan-Arabism. As the sixth clause of the Ba'ath Party's "permanent principles" reads: "The Ba'ath is a revolutionary party. It believes that its principal aims in realizing an Arab national renaissance and of building socialism will not be attained except by revolution and struggle."[16] The party's central slogans are "Unity, freedom and socialism" and "A single Arab nation with an eternal mission." The Ba'athists believe that the individual Arab states were all part of a single Arab nation and that their party constituted the vanguard of the new Arab nation. Indeed, this special role of the Ba'ath in leading the Arab nation came to be the party's dominant theme fairly early. Says John Devlin, "Its members were the new Arab generation, who would carry out its mission of raising society from the sleep into which it had fallen."[17]

Two important characteristics of this pan-Arabism and socialist ideological framework need to be underscored. First, the Ba'athists promoted their Arab nationalism call as a secular idea. Islam was seen as an important part of Arab heritage, but Arabism, not Islam, was seen as the glue that ties Arab citizens (Muslims and Christians) together. Second, the Ba'athists believe that economic wealth of the country belongs to the people, represented by the government. Still, property and inheritance are two natural rights that are protected within the limits of the national interest. In other words, the Ba'athist vision of socialism tolerated some form of individual ownership.

In closing, three conclusions need to be highlighted. First, within the context of radical pan-Arabism, the Ba'athists had employed various derogatory terms to describe Israel and to express contempt for Zionism. The rhetoric of many Ba'athist leaders indicated that the very existence and survival of Israel were denied. Despite the extreme animosity the Ba'athists expressed toward Israel, it is noticeable that, rhetoric aside, Iraq's real contribution to the Arab-Israeli conflict had been limited. Iraq's rhetoric was much louder than its deeds. Second, writes Ofra Bengio, "The founding fathers of the Ba'ath Party were neither the first nor the last to take up the issue of Arab unity. Indeed, the Ba'ath's record on pan-Arabism is less than impressive."[18] Iraq's actual attempts at unity with Egypt and Syria came to nothing. Ironically, despite the Ba'ath's attempt to champion pan-Arabism, it is the only Arab regime that sought to completely swallow another Arab country (Kuwait in 1990). Furthermore, major Arab states such as Egypt, Syria, and Saudi Arabia fought against the Ba'ath regime in the 1991 war and did not oppose its toppling from power in 2003. Third, the Ba'ath's strong emphasis on pan-Arabism alienated Iraq's large ethnic non-Arab minorities, particularly the Kurds.

Human Geography

For centuries Iraq was part of the Ottoman Empire. Following the empire's defeat in World War I, the British authority combined three Iraqi provinces into a single nation-state. From the very beginning Iraq has comprised several ethnic and religious communities: Arabs, Kurds, Turkomans, Assyrian, Sunni Muslims, Shi'ia Muslims, Christians, and Jews. Since 1921, a major challenge to the Iraqi governments has been how to transform these multiethnic and multisectarian communities into an Iraqi national identity.

This ethno-religious fragmentation of Iraq has been further complicated and reinforced by considerations of geography. The three major groups are concentrated in specific regions. The majority of the Kurds (20 percent of the population) reside in the north, the Arab Sunnis (20 percent) are mostly in the center of Iraq, and the Arab Shi'ias (60 percent) dominate the south. Each of these communities has had its own political aspiration. The Arab Sunnis, who have dominated the political system in Baghdad since the state was created, have always emphasized pan-Arabism sentiments and have attempted, unsuccessfully, to unite Iraq with other Arab states at different times. As far as the Shi'ia majority is concerned, writes Charles Tripp, the response to Iraq's projection primarily as an Arab state has been mixed: "On one hand, a section of lay Shi'ias embraced pan-Arabism, believing that it would put them on an equal footing with their Arab Sunni compatriots; on the other hand, those Shi'ias who remained closer to the spiritual leadership of the community mistrusted the Arab Sunnis' scheme and maintained some connection and loyalty to their co-sectarians in Iran."[19]

Having a culture distinctive from both the Sunnis and Shi'ias, the Kurds have been consistent in resisting any attempt to assimilate them in a broad Arab society. Instead, they have sought to achieve a certain level of autonomy. The Kurds are the largest ethnic group in the Middle East without a nation-state. According to Charles MacDonald, "They are an Indo-European people who claim to be descendants of the Medes."[20] Their declared goal has been the recognition of their right to genuine autonomy within an independent Iraq. Every Iraqi regime since 1921 has dealt with the "Kurdish question" in one fashion or another. The history of Iraqi Kurds to achieve autonomy, at least until the 2003 war, can be described as repeated cycles of rebellion and repression and then accord with governments in Baghdad. Whenever the dominated Arab-Sunni regimes in Baghdad seemed weak, the Kurds sought to extract concessions and came close to achieving their goals. These concessions, however, were usually taken back once the authorities in Baghdad overcame domestic and foreign restraints.

To sum up, the Kurdish question has been the most serious challenge to the nation-state project in Iraq. As Monte Palmer argues, "It has reduced the prospect of national unity to a vague dream."[21] Furthermore, the inability of the Iraqi regimes and the Kurds to reach a satisfactory compromise to both sides has been a continuous source of strife, political instability, and a serious drain on the country's economic, military, and human resources. Furthermore, this continuous lack of satisfactory compromise has been used by foreign powers to further destabilize Iraq.

Before World War I, the Kurdish population lived under two Middle East governments: the Ottoman Empire and the Qajar Dynasty of Iran. The fall of the Ottoman Empire brought into independent existence a number of Arab states, two of which—Iraq and Syria—inherited a significant portion of the Kurdish population. "Of the two, Iraq acquired by far the largest number of the Kurds, who by this time had been stirred by the Western concepts of nationalism and self-determination."[22] These concepts of nationalism and self-determination were underscored in the Treaty of Sevres signed in 1920 between the Ottoman sultan and the Allied powers. In overseeing the breakup of the Ottoman Empire, the treaty granted Kurdistan local autonomy with the prospects of independence within one year if a majority of the Kurdish population desired independence and if the League Council considered Kurds capable of independence. Thus, shortly after the end of World War I, the Kurds seemed to have won the international community's endorsement to establish their own nation-state. The treaty, however, was never ratified by the Turkish Grand National Assembly. With the overthrow of the sultan and the establishment of a new Turkish republic under Mustafa Kemal Ataturk, the issue of an independent Kurdish state was dealt a heavy blow, and it never arose on the international level.

The Iraqi Kurds presented a different story. According to Graham Fuller, "The Kurdish-dominated province of Mosul might never have been included in Iraq at all were it not for the fact that it contained an oil-rich area of great interest to the British Empire."[23] The British sought to have Mosul province included within their mandate of Iraq rather than allowing it to go to Turkey.[24] The Kurds in Iraq demanded autonomy, the British were in no mood to accept the principle of self-determination in an area strategically and economically important to them. Since the early 1920s the Kurds have been involved in continuous fighting and negotiations with the Iraqi governments to secure some level of autonomy.

This Kurdish struggle to achieve autonomy and resist being assimilated into the broader Arab community of Iraq was generally weak until the late 1950s. Two factors contributed. First, Kurdish efforts to resist the British and Iraqi authorities were led by tribal chiefs who were more interested in regaining and maintaining the sort of autonomy that they enjoyed during the disintegrating period of the Ottoman Empire than in creating an independent Kurdish state. These tribal uprisings lacked a broad and well-defined Kurdish nationalism. Second, the other three Middle Eastern countries with large Kurdish minorities—Iran, Syria, and Turkey—were united in their domestic and foreign policy orientations. The three countries generally resisted the temptation to use their "Kurdish card" against one another's interests. Under these similar domestic and foreign policy structures and orientations, there was hardly any possibility for any of them to provide large-scale military aid to the Kurds without creating a serious international dispute that would involve not only the three Middle Eastern powers but possibly Britain and the United States.

Since the late 1950s the dynamics of internal Iraqi policy in conjunction with regional developments have substantially altered the Kurdish fight for autonomy. In July 1958 a group of officers led by Abd al-Karim Qasim overthrew the Iraqi monarchy and established a republican regime. The Kurds supported the military coup, believing that the new regime would be more sympathetic to their aspirations. These expectations were realized but only briefly. The early years of the Qasim regime witnessed close cooperation between the Iraqi government and the Kurds. The Kurdish leader Mullah Mustafa Barzani was allowed to return from his exile in the Soviet Union. General Qasim legalized the Kurdish Democratic Party (KDP) and allowed the publication of several Kurdish journals. Moreover, the new republican regime promulgated a provisional constitution stating that the Arabs and Kurds are considered partners in Iraq, and it recognized their national rights.

There were two reasons for these warm relations between Qasim regime and the Kurds in the late 1950s. Internally, General Qasim needed to consolidate his power base and neutralize his opponents from both the right and the left. These included the big landlords and the monarchists on one side and the

Nasserists and Ba'athists on the other side. Thus General Qasim generously armed the Kurds and often used them against rebellious tribes or military officers who did not agree with the regime's policies. Externally, the Qasim regime and the Kurds were united in their foreign policy orientation. Both sides were against the Baghdad Pact and close alliance with the West and conservative regional powers such as Turkey and Iran, and they advocated cooperation and friendship with the Soviet Union and communist countries.

However, Qasim started seeing the increased Kurdish influence as a threat to his authority. Moreover, having dealt with his opponents, General Qasim had little use for the Kurds. Accordingly, relations with the Kurds deteriorated in the early 1960s, and fighting resumed.

In 1963 the Qasim regime was overthrown in a coup led by Arab nationalists and Ba'athists. Later in the year, Arab nationalists led by Abd al-Salam Aref consolidated their grip on power and ruled Iraq until the Ba'athists launched a successful coup in 1968. During this very unstable period in Iraqi policy (1963–68), several factors further complicated the already troubled relations between the authority in Baghdad and the Kurds. Aref's regime accused the Kurds of supporting General Qasim. The Iraqi government also viewed the Kurds' close cooperation with the Iraqi communist party and the Soviet Union as a threat to domestic stability and national unity. On the other hand, the Kurds were suspicious of the Iraqi government's drive to merge with Egypt and Syria in a united pan-Arab state. This desire was evident from Iraq's participation in the tripartite unity talks in Cairo in 1963. According to J. M. Abdulghani, "The Kurds feared that Iraq's attempts to unite with Egypt and Syria might adversely affect and compromise the interests of the Kurdish minority in Iraq."[25]

Under these circumstances, mutual suspicion between the Iraqi regimes and the Kurds dominated their negotiations. Throughout the 1960s, the two sides engaged in temporary cease-fires, armistices, and extended negotiations lacking any substance. Not surprisingly, the two sides failed to reach a compromise, and fighting continued. This ebb and flow, which characterized relations between the Kurds and the various Iraqi governments, continued until the Ba'ath Party returned to power in 1968. The Ba'ath's rise to power represented a new violent episode in the confrontation between the Kurds and the Iraqi authority.

Several conclusions can be drawn from this brief discussion of the Kurdish question in Iraq. First, the Kurds have never been completely integrated in the Iraqi state. Culturally and politically the Kurds have succeeded in maintaining and even developing their own identity despite tremendous efforts by various Iraqi regimes to assimilate them. Second, since the early 1920s the Kurds have shown a great determination to achieve a high level of autonomy from the government in Baghdad. A major weakness of the Kurdish struggle, however, has been continuous divisions between Kurdish factions. These divisions are based on cultural and tribal differences within the Kurdish population. Third, in their long struggle for autonomy the Kurds have sought aid from any source willing to help them. All foreign powers interested in weakening the Iraqi government have been eager to assist the Kurds. The list includes the Soviets, Iranians, Turks, Americans, and Israelis. Fourth, this foreign involvement has further deepened the gap between the Iraqi government and the Kurds. Basically, the Iraqis have accused some Kurdish leaders of being agents of foreign powers and questioned their loyalty to the Iraqi state. Finally, whenever the Iraqi government has been weak, the Kurds have tried to take advantage and extract concessions from Baghdad, often with the support of Iraq's external enemies. On the other hand, whenever the Iraqi government has been strong, it has punished the Kurds for their cooperation with foreign powers.

To sum up, foreign intervention has always been a factor in the Kurdish question in Iraq. Foreign powers have sought to use the Kurds to destabilize the government in Baghdad. Meanwhile, the Iraqi regimes since 1921 have failed to articulate a successful strategy to deal with the Kurds and their foreign allies. This failure was fueled by domestic and foreign policy driven by radical Arab nationalism, and continuous tension with the United States shaped the Iraqi attitude toward Israel from 1948 until the 2003 war. The following episodes between Baghdad and Tel Aviv demonstrate how these determinants of Iraq's foreign policy have been played out.

The Jews of Iraq

When Israel was born in 1948, many Jewish leaders viewed the Jewish communities around the world as inherently part of the Jewish national identity in Israel. Bringing the aliyah (Jewish immigrants) home to Israel was a top priority.[26] Within this context, the large Iraqi Jewish community was considered a major target. Like the other Jews from Islamic countries, the Jews of Iraq were considered a key population reservoir that could tilt the demographic balance in Palestine in the Jews' favor. Indeed, as Simon Henderson argues, "Jewish history and Iraqi history have been interwoven since biblical times. The Old Testament patriarch Abraham came from Ur, in what is now the southern part of Iraq."[27] For most of this long history, the Iraqi Jews maintained their communal identity and were among the wealthiest and most fully integrated of all Jewish communities in Arab countries. They played a major cultural, social, and economic role in ancient and modern Iraq alike.

The Jewish presence in Iraq goes back more than two millennia. In fact, according to Abbas Shiblak, there was a time when Jewish scholarship in Iraq was the ultimate spiritual authority for world Jewry. "The renowned Babylonian Talmud was produced there, as were some of the most outstanding Jewish literary works."[28] For centuries the Jews of Iraq lived under Muslim Ottoman rule as dhimmis (tolerated protected subjects). Like the Christians, they were allowed freedom of worship, measures of communal autonomy, security of their lives and property. Despite some limitations imposed on them, Jews as well as Christians learned to make the best of it and even prospered at times.

The late nineteenth century witnessed the beginning of development and progress, bringing prosperity to the Iraqi Jewish community. The introduction of modern education paved the way for this economic prosperity. Shiblak writes, "Jewish educational prospects were substantially improved by the introduction of Alliance Israelite Schools by the Alliance Israelite Universelle of Paris in 1864."[29] Later more schools were opened, bringing modern methods of learning and foreign languages to the curriculum. This modern education contributed to a steady improvement of Iraqi Jews' economic and social positions. Generally, Jews were engaged in crafts, hawking, and small business. More significantly, the Jewish community played a prominent role in finance and foreign trade. Accordingly, many Iraqi Jews were of the upper and middle classes and generally were better off than the rest of the population.

This modern education not only led to economic prosperity but also had a significant positive impact on social mobilization. Until the beginning of the twentieth century, the Jews of Iraq were largely restricted to their own quarters in the main cities. Educational and economic opportunities, however, gradually eroded this system, and Jews became increasingly integrated into the Muslim society in Iraq. Members of the Jewish elite and educated middle class started to leave the old Jewish quarters and build houses in luxurious new Muslim neighborhoods. Most of the Jews lived in Mosul, Baghdad, and Basra. According to Moshe Gat, "Throughout the history of the Iraqi Jewish community, the largest number of Jews was always concentrated in Baghdad."[30]

Following World War I, the British mandate provided great opportunities for Iraqi Jews to prosper. According to Daphne Tsimhoni, "The Iraqi Jews became the main source for British recruitment of professional local manpower into the newly established administration owing to their westernized education and their knowledge of both Arabic and English."[31] In other words, given their early exposure to Western education, the Jews served as a link between the local Muslim population and the West. This prosperity of the Iraqi Jews was protected and endorsed by the monarchy. Under the monarchical regime, the Iraqi Jews, like other minorities, were guaranteed basic rights: freedom to practice their religion, freedom to establish their own schools, equal civil rights, and equal opportunities in government jobs.

This relative prosperity did not last long. By the mid-1930s several developments threatened the delicate relations between the Jews and the larger Iraqi society. First, tension increased between Jews and Muslims. A growing number of Muslims graduated from schools and sought employment opportunities in the Iraqi administration, which was already filled with Jews. In other words, the competition between increasingly better-educated Muslims and Jews for government jobs was intensified. Second, the political system in Baghdad suffered from growing instability. In 1933 King Faisal died and was succeeded by his son Ghazi, who lacked his father's experience. Within this context, the Iraqi army initiated two coups d'etat, the first ever in the Arab world. As in many other countries, political instability became fertile ground for extreme ideologies and ethnic and religious conflicts. Third, the rise of pan-Arabism during the 1936–39 Arab revolt in Palestine fueled anti-Zionist propaganda. As a result Jews were increasingly seen as collaborators with British imperialism. Fourth, the international system had a significant impact on the dynamics of religious strife within Iraq. Nazi propaganda was appealing to some segments of the Iraqi population. The victory of Nazi Germany in Europe in the early stages of World War II reinforced the pro-German feeling among some Iraqi politicians and senior army officers.

The establishment of the state of Israel in 1948 and the outbreak of the first Arab-Israeli war, in which the Iraqi army participated, dealt a heavy blow to the Jewish community in Iraq. These developments underscored the large gap between Jewish identity and Arab nationalism. Persecution and discrimination against the Iraqi Jews intensified, and eventually most left for Israel. Indeed, the Iraqi Jewish community faced the gravest threat to its survival during this period. The Iraqi authority took several initiatives to contain and undermine a massive Iraqi Jewish immigration to Israel. These included restricting the freedom of movement of the Iraqi Jews and prohibiting them from leaving the country except in extraordinary circumstances. Another significant step was taken in August 1948 when, writes Moshe Gat, "the Iraqi government announced that all Jews who had left the country for Palestine since 1939 and had not returned would henceforth be considered criminals who had defected to the enemy and would be tried in absentia by a military tribunal."[32] These policies generated mutual suspicion and resentment between the Iraqi Jews and the rest of the population.

Despite these grave threats to the mere existence and survival of the Iraqi Jewish community, Israel was reluctant to become involved openly. The reason for this reluctance was concern that such involvement could be seized on by the Iraqi government as proof that the Jews were collaborating with Israel. Still, Israel did not abandon the Iraqi Jews. Instead, Israel sought to intensify international pressure on the Iraqi government to authorize the legal departure of its Jewish citizens. At the same time, Israeli agents tried to smuggle Iraqi Jews out of the country.

Given the intense international pressure, the regional tension following the creation of Israel and the end of the first Arab-Israeli war, and growing alienation of Iraqi Jews, which led to domestic turmoil, the authority in Baghdad enacted a denaturalization law in March 1950. According to Yehouda Shenhav, "The law—valid for one year—enabled the Jews to leave the country after renouncing their citizenship." By enacting this law the Iraqi government had a twofold goal. It wanted to rid the country of disruptive elements, and it wanted to assure those who had no desire to leave that the government would guarantee their full rights. This goal was based on Baghdad's view that most, if not all, of the potential emigrants would be the poorer Jews, while most of the upper classes, who were engaged in commerce and finance, would stay. As a result, normal economic activity could be restored and the social tension would be contained. Another significant step in this direction was taken in March 1951 by issuing a complementary law that ensured the supervision and management of the property of Jews who had been deprived of their Iraqi nationality. "All told," Shenhav adds, "more than 100,000 Jews were brought to Israel from Iraq in the period between May 1950 and June 1951."[33] Thus by 1952 the Jewish community in Iraq had virtually ceased to exist, much of its property had been confiscated by the Iraqi government, and only a few thousand Jews remained in Iraq.

The few Iraqi Jews who chose not to leave were mainly affluent members of the Jewish community who hoped that life would return to its previous state. Until the end of the monarchy in Iraq it seemed that this would be the major trend. It was with the establishment of the Ba'ath regime in Iraq during the 1960s that persecution resumed, leaving no choice for the remaining Jewish elite but to emigrate.

Four conclusions can be drawn from the plight of the Iraqi Jews. First, the mass immigration of the Iraqi Jews in the late 1940s and the early 1950s illustrates the complexity of the prevailing domestic, regional, and international environment. These include the impact of the British legacy, the creation of Israel, the growing sentiments of pan-Arab nationalism, and the policies of the Iraqi government. Second, considering the circumstances under which the state of Israel was created, many Israeli leaders viewed immigration as a central component of the state's national security and survival. Jews from all over the world were strongly encouraged to go to Israel. Third, as far as Iraq was concerned, the departure of the Jews meant the loss of a useful element of the economy and the administration. The decision to allow Iraqi Jews to leave the country was driven more by Arab nationalism and less by economic considerations. Fourth, the Jewish mass immigration out of Iraq was not grounded on individual initiative, although such initiative did exist. It was a large-scale escape operation. According to Eli Barnavi, "In 1947 the number of Iraqi Jews was thought to be 150,000; by 1952 only some 6,000 remained."[34] Most of these left at the beginning of republican rule in 1958. Under the Ba'athist regime, from 1968 to 2003, conditions deteriorated severely for the few hundred Jews still in Iraq. This mass immigration of Iraqi Jews marked the end of one of the most ancient and well-established Jewish diasporas.

Iraq and the Arab-Israeli Conflict

Israeli analyses of threats normally divide the Arab world into two geographic circles: "the inner circle of confrontation states and the outer ring of other adversaries."[35] The inner ring includes Jordan, which signed a peace treaty with Israel in 1994; Lebanon, which generally is not hostile toward Israel; Syria, which has always been seen as a relentless and sworn enemy; and Egypt, which was seen as Israel's principal opponent until the two countries signed a peace treaty in 1979. The outer ring contains hostile states such as Libya under Gaddafi, the Gulf monarchies, Sudan, and North African Arab states. For a long time most of these states denied Israel's right to exist and supported Palestinian organizations against the Jewish state.[36] Still, most Arab states that do not share borders with Israel have not taken an active combating role in the series of Arab-Israeli wars starting in 1948. Since late 2003 Gaddafi has agreed to cooperate with the international community to dismantle his country's nonconventional weapons program. This move signals a potential major change in Libya's foreign policy not only toward the West but also potentially toward Israel as well. Similarly, Tunisia, Algeria, Morocco, and Mauritania have been more accommodative to Israel. Somehow Iraq does not fit in this categorization. Despite lacking a common border with Israel, Iraq participated in the 1948, 1967, and 1973 wars. In none of these wars did the Iraqi army play a central role. Nevertheless, Baghdad's participation illustrates its commitment to the Arab-Israeli conflict and the impact of this conflict on Iraq's domestic policy.

The thrust of the Iraqi approach toward Israel is that Arabs can deal with the Jewish state only through strength, a formula that essentially rejects negotiation. Indeed, Baghdad's militant and uncompromising stand on the Arab-Israeli conflict has been both firm and consistent since the late 1940s throughout the Arab-Israeli wars and the peace negotiations that followed them. The approach post-Saddam Iraq will take toward the Jewish state is yet to be decided.

As soon as the British left Palestine in May 1948, a war broke out between Israel and Egypt, Syria, Iraq, Trans-Jordan (soon to be called Jordan), and Lebanon. Saudi Arabia sent a military contingent that operated under Egyptian command, and Yemen declared war on Israel but did not take any military action. This first Arab-Israeli war (called the War of Independence by the Israelis) lasted from May 1948 until January 1949. Iraq had a substantial military presence in this conflict. Like the other Arab armies, at the end of the war the Iraqi forces lost and went home. As a result of the 1948 war Iraq had lost the use of its oil pipeline to Haifa. Writes Avner Yaniv, "Israel was willing to consider Iraq's resuming use of the pipeline on condition that this be part of a larger understanding between Baghdad and Tel Aviv."[37] Iraq not only refused such an offer but also refused to negotiate and sign a cease-fire agreement with Israel as the other Arab countries had done.

Shortly after hostilities stopped, Israel negotiated and signed armistice agreements with Egypt, Lebanon, Jordan, and Syria. Some territorial adjustments were made and endorsed in these agreements. The signing of these armistice agreements marked the formal end of the first Arab-Israeli war. According to Benny Morris, "The state of the war had been replaced by a de jure state of non-belligerency. Subsequently the international community and, to a somewhat lesser degree, the former combatants themselves, were to recognize the armistice lines as de facto international frontiers."[38] These agreements, however, were not considered peace treaties and did not provide for many of the features that normally govern the relations between neighboring states at peace with each other, such as diplomatic and trade ties. Small wonder, other wars broke out.

As a member of the Eastern Front, Iraq participated in the 1967 Arab-Israeli war. After the war, Iraq maintained a sizeable force in Jordan as an indication of Iraqi commitment to the conflict. Equally important, following the stunning Arab defeat in this war Baghdad adopted an extremist stand on any peaceful settlement to the conflict. With the Ba'ath Party in power after July 1968, Iraq aligned itself with those Arab states and other factions of the Palestine Liberation Organization (PLO) that rejected UN Security Council resolution 242 and all other attempts to find a peaceful solution. Most prominent was the Rogers Plan, put forward by the United States in December 1969 and accepted by Israel, Egypt, Jordan, and the Soviet Union by July 1970. Instead, Iraq committed itself to "the goal of liberating the whole of Palestine by means of armed struggle."[39]

Iraq's commitment to the Palestinians was tested in 1970. Earlier that year there had been a number of serious clashes between members of the various Palestinian guerilla organizations and the Jordanian army. The root cause of the clashes was King Hussein's unwillingness to allow the Palestinian military organizations to attack Israel from Jordan. More specifically, the king was concerned about the challenge the Palestinians appeared to pose to his own authority. At the beginning of September, the Jordanian army began an all-out attack on the Palestinian guerillas. By the time the fighting ended, according to media reports, hundreds were killed and thousands more were injured, mostly Palestinians. In response to this elimination of the Palestinian resistance, Iraq declared that it would not remain idle. Rhetoric aside, the Iraqi troops, which were stationed in Jordan, did nothing to stop the Jordanian army's attack on the Palestinians.

Three years later, the Yom Kippur War broke out. The Iraqi government claimed that it had been excluded from the planning for this war by Syria and Egypt. As soon as the news reached Baghdad, Iraq started preparing a special force to support the Syrian army liberating the Golan Heights. The Iraqi armored division, however, arrived late after the tide of battle had turned, and it seemed as if the Israeli forces were heading for Damascus. Within days of the Iraqi forces' arrival, the Syrian government accepted a cease-fire with Israel without consulting Iraq. According to Charles Tripp, "This gave the Iraqi government the pretext it needed to withdraw its troops from Syria, expressing disapproval of the cease-fire—a disapproval that turned into vituperative denunciation in 1974 with the Syrian signing of the disengagement agreements with Israel."[40]

In the aftermath of the Yom Kippur War, several developments strengthened and consolidated the Iraqi government's stand domestically and region-ally. Saddam Hussein signed the Algiers agreement with the shah in March 1975. The Kurdish rebellion in northern Iraq collapsed a few weeks later, and the government was able to expand its authority over the entire country. At the same time, the Iraqi government was enjoying the massive increase in oil revenues following the first oil price shock in 1973–74. Thus the new oil money and the settlement of the Kurdish question combined to give an un-precedented boost to the Ba'ath Party's confidence.

Baghdad used this financial and political power to enhance its claim over Arab leadership and championed opposition to the peace process led by Egyp-tian president Anwar al-Sadat. In a turning point in the Arab-Israeli conflict, Sadat went to Jerusalem and spoke before the Israeli Knesset (parliament) in 1977. This marked a major departure from the previous norms of seeking a comprehensive peace—not a unilateral one. Sadat's move provoked wide-spread Arab anger, and many Arab leaders felt the need to publicly condemn Sadat's unilateral approach and show solidarity with the Palestinians and the other "frontline" Arab states (Jordan, Lebanon, and Syria). "Saddam Hussein was increasingly tempted to assert his own and Iraq's pretensions to fill the leadership vacuum."[41] The Iraqi leader sought to create a viable anti-Sadat front. Representatives of Algeria, Libya, South Yemen, Syria, and the PLO met in Tripoli in December 1977 and in Algiers in February 1978. Iraq refused to endorse these efforts on the ground that they implied an indirect acceptance of UN Security Council resolution 242, which calls for Arab recognition of Israel in return for Israeli withdrawal from occupied Arab lands. In other words, Iraq accused the participants in the Tripoli and Algiers conferences of not being radical enough.

In an attempt to ensure a major role for himself and to assert Iraq's regional leadership, Saddam Hussein invited Arab leaders to meet in Baghdad in No-vember 1978 to coordinate their response to the Camp David accords between Egypt, Israel, and the United States. The Baghdad summit, however, did not go beyond threatening to take various economic sanctions against Egypt if and when it signed a peace treaty with Israel. When this did happen in early 1979, there was no further mention of sanctions, and a second lower-level Baghdad summit opted merely for the diplomatic isolation of Egypt. This amounted to Egypt's expulsion from the Arab League and the transfer of the League's head-quarters from Cairo to Tunis. This Iraqi-led opposition to the peace process did not stop Egypt from making peace with Israel, but it deepened Tel Aviv's concern about the direction of Iraqi policy.

This Iraqi radical stand against Israel does not necessarily mean that Baghdad has had close relations with the Palestinians and their main representative, the PLO. Indeed, such ties have not always been friendly. Both the internal conflicts in Iraq and Baghdad's isolation in the Arab world contributed to the creation of tension between the PLO and the Iraqi government. "In order to have its own surrogate within the Palestinian movement," writes R. D. McLaurin, "Baghdad founded the Arab Liberation Front (ALF) in 1969. The motive behind the creation of the ALF was to have an Iraqi counterpart to the Syrian-sponsored Sa'iqa."[42] The ALF believed that only through general Arab participation and mobilization would the Palestinians be able to achieve their political goals. In contrast, other Palestinian organizations rejected the principle of general Arab participation in their activities, on the ground that it would expose the Palestinian movement to the divisions within the Arab world.

In addition, Baghdad provided safe haven to radical Palestinian leaders such as Abu Nidal and Abu Abbas and endorsed some of their operations. Abu Abbas found refuge in Baghdad after being expelled from the PLO for masterminding the 1985 hijacking of the Italian cruise ship *Achille Lauro* and killing an elderly American tourist. In 1990 Abu Abbas planned and carried out a raid on the beach at Tel Aviv. This terrorist operation placed the PLO in an intolerable position vis-à-vis the United States and led to suspension of relations between the two sides. Shortly after the collapse of Saddam Hussein's regime in 2003, American troops captured Abu Abbas, who then died in custody.

Despite these terrorist attacks, which occasionally spoiled the PLO's efforts to negotiate peace agreements with Israel and the United States, Yasser Arafat maintained good relations with Saddam Hussein for most of the 1980s and 1990s. He supported Saddam Hussein in the Iran-Iraq War and backed the Iraqi invasion of Kuwait in 1990. Saddam Hussein, on the other hand, publicly supported suicide attacks against Israeli targets and launched missile attacks against Israel in the Gulf War in 1991. Thus the Iraqi role within the Palestinian movement has been seen more as a spoiler of the policies that were not in line with Baghdad's strategy and interest. Iraq pursued this policy primarily through its influence over a few radical Palestinian organizations.

Two conclusions can be drawn from this discussion of Iraq's involvement in the Arab-Israeli conflict. First, Iraq was a participant, though not a central actor. Iraq fought in the 1948, 1967, and 1973 wars, led the Arab opposition to Sadat's peace initiative to make peace with Israel, and tried to manipulate the Palestinian movement to serve its own regional interests. Second, Israel's relations with Iraq have ranged from direct to indirect confrontation. As far as the

Israelis were concerned, Iraq was distant, and a confrontation with it was quite unnecessary. "The trouble, however, was that it was precisely this distance that made Iraqi policy so aggressive."[43] Baghdad was in the position to fuel rhetoric without paying a price. In other words, Iraq had used the Arab-Israeli card to advance its ambition of regional leadership. The next two sections analyze Israel's reaction to Iraq's attempts to expand its influence in the Middle East, which resulted in two bloody wars.

Israel and the Iran-Iraq War (1980–88)

In September 1980 the Iraqi army invaded Iran, hoping for a quick victory. In explaining this attack, the Iraqis cite Iran's provocations, particularly calling upon the Shi'ias and Kurds in Iraq to overthrow the Ba'ath regime. Accordingly, from Iraq's perspective, the military attack on Iran was mainly defensive to protect the country's national unity. On the other hand, many analysts believe that the political turmoil during and after the Islamic revolution of 1979 presented an opportunity for Saddam Hussein and the Iraqi leadership to take advantage of temporary instability in Iran, their powerful, larger, and more populated neighbor. Despite signing an agreement in March 1975 to settle the territorial dispute between the two countries over Shat al-Arab and other bilateral issues, Baghdad was not satisfied and sought to extract concessions from the new regime in Tehran.

Regardless of the real motives behind the Iraqi attack on Iran, the outcome was disastrous for both sides. With an estimated 1 million dead and injured, there is no doubt that it was a gross strategic miscalculation. After initial Iraqi success, the Iranians were able to put their act together and stop the Iraqi advances. Furthermore, after liberating the territories they lost in the first few months of the war, the Iranians went on the offensive and insisted that they would not stop the war as long as Saddam Hussein remained in power. Concerned about the stability of the whole Gulf region, the Gulf monarchies and Western countries provided substantial financial and military assistance to Iraq. As a result, neither Tehran nor Baghdad was able to bring the war to a decisive end. The increasing isolation of Iran and Iraq's widespread use of chemical weapons were major reasons for the Iranian army's collapse and Saddam Hussein's declaration of victory. "But the victory was to prove increasingly hollow," according to Phebe Marr.[44] Iraq emerged from the war economically dependent on the West and its regional allies.

This eight-year war between the two giant Persian Gulf powers had a significant impact on Israel. Tel Aviv's two archenemies were destroying each other's military capabilities. The Arab world was polarized by this long war, with Syria allying with Iran and almost all other Arab countries supporting Iraq. Regional and international attention shifted from the Arab-Israeli conflict to the war in the Persian Gulf. All these developments served Israel's strategic interests. For eight years Tel Aviv enjoyed a high level of relative security on its eastern front. However, this did not last.

Israel's initial reaction to the Iran-Iraq war was driven by its perception of the two belligerent states. Baghdad has a legacy of enmity toward Tel Aviv. This enmity was demonstrated repeatedly after the Jewish state was born in 1948. More than 100,000 Jews left Iraq in the late 1940s and early 1950s; Iraqis participated in the 1948, 1967, and 1973 Arab-Israeli wars and strongly opposed the Egyptian peace initiative; and Baghdad's nuclear ambition underscores the deep hostility toward Israel. On the other hand, since its inauguration, the revolutionary regime in Tehran has adopted an uncompromising stand against Israel, denying it the right to exist. Despite the record of Iranian hostility, Israelis seemed eager to identify potential positive developments. Recognizing the value of the pre-revolution relationship with Iran, its geostrategic nature, and the presence of a large Jewish community, Israelis have thought of potential improvements in relations between the two non-Arab Middle Eastern states. This view was further reinforced by Israeli leaders' belief that the Khomeini regime was but a short-lived episode in Iran's long history.[45] Thus Israel's overall attitude was to support Iran and try to build and maintain good relations with the Iranian people in anticipation of a post-Khomeini era. Israel continued its own supply of limited amounts of arms to Iran and played a key role in facilitating U.S. deliveries during the Iran-Contra affair (1985–86).

Israeli support began to wane in the mid-1980s. in response to increasing signs that Iraq was softening its stand on the Arab-Israeli conflict. Iraqi fatigue from the war and Baghdad's desire to win Washington's support appeared to have generated a more pragmatic Iraqi approach to the entire Arab-Israeli issue. As a result, Baghdad stopped its opposition to the Egyptian-Israeli peace treaty and the attempts by other Arab states to negotiate with Israel. Equally important, the Iraqi government repeatedly announced that the PLO was free to negotiate a peaceful agreement with Israel and that any agreement acceptable to the Palestinians would be endorsed by Baghdad.

Three characteristics of the Iraqi stand on the Arab-Israeli conflict in the mid-1980s can be identified. First, the Iraqi leaders' statements showed growing signs of softening their opposition to the peace process. No longer did the Iraqi leaders present their country as the leading Arab state in the confrontation against Israel. It is important to point out that this new moderation was intended mainly for American ears. Inside Iraq there was not much change in the rhetoric against Israel. Second, despite this relative moderation, the Iraqi stand was ambiguous. Iraq never offered explicit recognition to Israel. Iraqi leaders never talked about specific steps to make peace with Israel. Third, many Iraqi officials indicated that their country considered Iran to be a greater danger than Israel to the Arab world. This notion was further reinforced by increasing Iranian hostility toward Israel. Iranian propaganda repeatedly stated that the road to Jerusalem goes through Baghdad. In other words, in order to "liberate Palestine," Muslims must defeat the Iraqi regime in Baghdad. Furthermore, Iran created and supported Hizbollah in Lebanon, which was engaged in intense fighting against Israeli and Western interests in the region.

The hardening of the Iranian position and the apparent moderation of the Iraqi regime prompted Israeli leaders to take a fresh look at their stand on the Iran-Iraq War and reevaluate their policy with Iraq. They explored avenues of limited rapprochement with Iraq, aimed at encouraging Iraqi moderation. In line with this thinking, Israel announced that it would not oppose the construction of a pipeline from Iraq to the Jordanian port of Aqaba near the Jordanian-Israeli border. Furthermore, writes Joseph Alpher, "Tel Aviv suggested that Baghdad should reopen the long-defunct pipeline linking Kirkuk in northern Iraq to the Israeli coastal city of Haifa as a means of solving Iraq's oil-export difficulties."[46]

In the final stage of the war, several developments pushed Israel further from Iran and closer to Iraq. First, the strongest denial of Israel's right to exist was coming from Iran and Hizbollah, while most Arab states had, explicitly or implicitly, accepted that Israel was there to stay and they would have to negotiate a peaceful settlement. In other words, Israeli leaders were increasingly seeing threats to their country's national security from the peripheral Shi'ia Iran and less from the Sunni-Arab heartland, including Iraq. Second, the advent of the American reflagging operation was an unmistakable sign of a clear American "tilt" toward Iraq. Israeli leaders understood the need to coordinate their policy on the war with that of their strategic ally, the United States. Any Israeli support for Iran would have been considered contradictory to America's growing backing to Iraq. Third, the outbreak of the Intifada (Palestinian uprising) in 1987 emphasized for many Israelis the primary importance that should be attached to the Arab-Israeli peace process, for which Israel would require the goodwill of the United States, Egypt, and Jordan—all of whom were friendly, if not actually allied, with Iraq. In response to these developments, Israel distanced itself from any association with a pro-Iranian stand.

In mid-1988 Iran and Iraq agreed to end hostilities. The cease-fire initially was welcomed in Israel. Israeli leaders came to realize that the war had outlived its usefulness and had generated a regional arms race in both conventional and nonconventional weapon systems. Israel's initial reaction was soon replaced by a more complex assessment of the implications of the end of hostilities. The real concern in Israel was whether Iran and Iraq would focus their resources on internal construction or pursue foreign adventures, including renewing threats to Israel. Domestic rehabilitation seemed to be the likely option for Iraq. The Ba'ath regime had been reassuring the Iraqi people that with the end of the war "it would turn to domestic reconstruction to help alleviate the suffering of the population, to reward it for its support and sacrifices during the war, and to provide a 'safety valve' as a way of preventing future anti-regime reactions."[47]

This scenario, however, never materialized. Instead, the Iraqi leadership opted for a radical stand on both regional affairs (i.e., Baghdad's relations with its neighbors in the Persian Gulf region) and the Arab-Israeli conflict. Shortly after the end of the war with Iran, Iraq intensified its rhetoric against the Jewish state. Israeli leaders were particularly concerned about two potential threats from Iraq. First, overjoyed by its victory over Iran, Baghdad claimed that it had won a war against a non-Arab power for the first time in modern Arab history. These claims reinforced the Iraqi leaders' aspirations for a leadership role in the Arab world. The eight-year war between Tehran and Baghdad served Israeli strategic interests. The "eastern front" concept, a focus of much discussion and expectation during the 1970s, "became a complete mirage with Syria preoccupied with the civil war in Lebanon and the peace with Egypt holding firm."[48] After the cease-fire was declared between the Iranian and Iraqi armies, fears persisted in Israel that the eastern front concept might reemerge and become a reality.

The other Israeli concern was that new and deadly weapons systems, including ballistic missiles and chemical warfare capabilities, would become available to the large and battle-hardened Iraqi army. During the hostilities Baghdad acquired and effectively used chemical weapons against its Iraqi Kurdish population and against Iranian troops. In addition, Iraq acquired and employed ballistic missiles against civilian population centers in the so-called "war of the cities" with Iran. These missiles could reach targets in Israel, as happened during the Gulf War in 1991. From an Israeli point of view, "this was the first time ever that an Arab country that is not a frontline state had the capability of attacking Israel with a surface-to-surface missile without dispatching expeditionary units to one of the confrontation states."[49] Finally, Tel Aviv was concerned about Baghdad's efforts to develop nuclear capability. Israel's continued public reports on Iraq's nuclear activities led to the Iraqi threats to retaliate against Israel if the Israelis were to attack Iraqi facilities.

Three conclusions can be drawn from the Israeli reaction to the eight-year Iran-Iraq War. First, the intense hostilities between two of Israel's archenemies substantially served Tel Aviv's security interests. The underlying Israeli reaction was a great satisfaction at seeing Iran and Iraq destroying and exhausting each other's military and economic capabilities instead of employing them against the Jewish state. Second, Tel Aviv's stand on the war was adjusted to respond to regional and international developments. In the early phase of fighting, Israel maintained some contacts with elements in the Iranian military, as had been demonstrated in the Iran-Contra affair. Later in the war, Israeli leaders considered easing tension and even cooperating with Iraq. This "Iraqi option," however, was never implemented.

Third, the end of the cold war and the final collapse of the Soviet Union had a significant impact on the confrontation between Baghdad and Tel Aviv. Iraq suffered from the loss of the Soviet Union as a supporter and a balancer against the West. The blow was also severe ideologically. The obvious failure of the Soviet model of state-controlled development, similar to the one adopted by the Ba'ath Party, raised questions regarding the overall policy the Iraqi government had pursued. Finally, the incremental weakening and final collapse of the Soviet Union meant that hundreds of thousands of Soviet Jews were allowed to immigrate to Israel. Many of them were well educated, and they substantially contributed to Israel's demographic, economic, cultural, and military capabilities.

The Israeli leaders realized that the period of the Iran-Iraq War was unique and that with the end of hostility a new regional system was emerging with a great deal of uncertainty. Iraq emerged with massive conventional and nonconventional military capabilities, but with a collapsing economy. Saddam Hussein's invasion of Kuwait in August 1990 was largely driven by these two outcomes of the war with Iran (strong army and weak economy). The invasion of Kuwait opened a new chapter in regional and international policy, and Israel had to respond.

Israel and the Gulf War (1990–91)

On August 2, the Iraqi army invaded Kuwait and within a few hours was able to occupy the entire country. The invasion and the subsequent Gulf War represented a major turning point in Iraqi foreign policy, regional alliance, and the international system. Previously Iraqi leaders had denied Kuwait the right to exist as an independent and sovereign state and claimed that Kuwait was part of Iraq. But only Saddam Hussein carried out a large-scale military action to substantiate and pursue these claims. Furthermore, inter-Arab conflicts are not unusual. On a few occasions Arab armies have fought each other. However, the Iraqi takeover of Kuwait was the first time in modern Arab history that one Arab country had completely absorbed another one. In response, traditional adversaries were persuaded to put their differences aside, at least temporarily, to face the Iraqi aggression. Syria, Egypt, Saudi Arabia, and Israel were together in the international coalition against Iraq. Finally, the Gulf War demonstrated the emergence of a post–cold war international system. Instead of supporting the opposing sides in the conflict, the United States and the Soviet Union worked together to end the crisis.

In addition to the Iraqi claims over the whole of Kuwait, Baghdad accused Kuwait of ruining its economy by overproducing oil and driving prices down. Most important, the roots of the Iraqi invasion can be found in the collapse of the Iraqi economy as a result of the eight-year war with Iran. At the start of the war Baghdad had substantial foreign exchange reserves. These reserves were completely depleted by the third year and, instead, turned into massive foreign debts. Kamran Mofid estimated the total cost of the war to Iraq at $452.6 billion. This sum represents only the monetary cost of the war. It does not include inflationary costs, the loss of services and earnings by the many hundreds of thousands of people killed, the depletion of national resources, the postponement of crucial development projects, or the cost of the delayed training and education of the young people. These represent precious lost opportunities. Finally, Mofid's figure "does not include the cost of welfare payments to the hundreds of thousands injured in the war, who were not able to contribute fully to the creation of wealth for the national economy."[50] In short, it can be argued that the Iraqi leaders thought invading and absorbing Kuwait would solve their country's deteriorating economic conditions.

The evolution of the crisis showed that Saddam Hussein had seriously miscalculated the international response to the invasion . The international community was not willing to allow Iraq to be the dominant influence over the supply and pricing of the world's oil. The crisis demonstrated the fundamental changes in the international system since the days of the cold war. The Soviet Union, previously Iraq's principal supporter, joined the United States in condemning the invasion and offered diplomatic support in the United Nations for resolutions condemning Iraq, imposing economic sanctions on it, and legitimizing the use of force in the event of an Iraqi refusal to withdraw from Kuwait. Similarly, the occupation of Kuwait demonstrated a gross underestimation of Washington's resolve. Apparently Saddam Hussein was convinced that the United States lacked the political will to go to war and would therefore refrain from reacting militarily to Kuwait's conquest.

The Iraqi occupation of Kuwait and the subsequent war was not related to Arab-Israeli conflict. Tel Aviv played no role in the events that led to this conflict. Nevertheless, Israel found itself involved in the war in at least three ways. First, Saddam Hussein sought to link his occupation of Kuwait to the Israeli occupation of Palestinian territories. Second, in an attempt to get Israel involved in the fighting and break the international coalition, Iraq launched missile attacks on Israeli targets. Third, the war changed the dynamics of the Arab-Israeli conflict and provided new incentives to pursue a comprehensive peace.

Just a few weeks after Iraq's attack on Kuwait, Saddam Hussein claimed that Iraq was not the only Middle Eastern country to have seized territory by force. Baghdad, he argued, would agree to review the Kuwaiti question if Israel declared itself ready to abandon the territories it had occupied in 1967.[51] Iraq's assessment (or hope) was that this argument would make it hard for any Arab country to reject or ignore this linkage. Israel naturally would refuse. The outrage over the crisis would thus be deflected from Iraq to Israel. Pressure on Baghdad to evacuate Kuwait would be turned aside, and Kuwait would remain under Iraq's control. This attempt to link the Gulf crisis to the Arab-Israeli conflict did not work and, indeed, turned out to be another major strategic miscalculation.

During the Gulf War, thirty-nine Iraqi Scud missiles armed with conventional warheads were launched against Israel. These were the first strikes of consequence at Israeli targets since the 1948 war. Iraq's intention was to undermine the international coalition; therefore, it sought to provoke Israel into military retaliation, hoping that this would make it politically impossible for the Arabs to remain in the coalition. Without their political backing, the war against Iraq would stop and attention would shift to the Arab-Israeli conflict. In addition, successful missile attacks on Israel would bolster Saddam Hussein's prestige in the Arab world and inflame popular sentiment. Israel, however, was determined not to be used as a tool to break the coalition.[52]

Faced with Iraq's Scud missile attacks, Israel responded with extraordinary self-restraint. This course of action was very different from that implied by the deterrent image Israel had been projecting toward the Arab world in general and toward Iraq in particular. Traditionally, Israeli deterrence was designed to compel neighboring Arab states not to attack its territory with large conventional forces. This was to be achieved by promising that, if attacked, Israel would take the battle to the enemy's territory and destroy the attacking forces there. Israel's decision not to respond to Iraq's surface-to-surface missile attacks was driven by four considerations:

First, Israeli leaders understood that their military retaliation would complicate the task of maintaining the Arab states' participation in the anti-Iraq coalition. Given the severe hostility that had characterized the relations between Baghdad and Tel Aviv, Israel had clear interest in seeing Iraq's military capabilities destroyed. Therefore, by not responding to the Iraqi missile attacks, the coalition remained intact and continued to pursue its objectives. Second, the United States exerted tremendous pressure on Israel, demanding that Tel Aviv not play any role in inter-Arab conflict. Israeli leaders knew that showing sensitivity to Washington's strategy and paying attention to its demands would further strengthen relations between the two countries. This policy paid off. According to Joseph Alpher, "During the Gulf crisis the United States shipped two batteries of modified Patriot antiaircraft missiles, together with their American crews, so as to provide Israel with some antimissile protection."[53] This was the first time in Israel's history that American combat units were sent to take an active part in its defense. The fact that some of the Iraqi missiles reached Israel demonstrates that the Patriots were not very effective.

. Third, Israel's ability to retaliate against Iraq's missile attacks was restrained by the international coalition's refusal to coordinate its military operations with Israel. Without such coordination Israeli forces could not have been involved in an area that formed part of the coalition's theater of operations. In the end, there was nothing that Israeli forces could have done more than the Americans' massive bombing of Iraq. Fourth, writes Shai Feldman, Israel's restraint was also made easier by the fact that "the damage caused by Iraq's missile attacks during the war remained limited. Although considerable structural damage was incurred, the number of casualties caused by these attacks was minuscule."[54]

These Iraqi Scud missiles attacks on Israel have had significant military and strategic ramifications. First, these attacks demonstrated that hostile states that do not share borders with Israel still can inflict harm on the Jewish state. These missiles, potentially coupled with chemical, biological, and nuclear warfare capabilities, have substantially altered the security environment in the whole Middle East. Nonconventional capabilities and the methods to deliver them became an option in the warfare in the region. Second, despite these attacks, it is important to point out that Saddam Hussein refrained from using chemical warheads, which he had used in the war against Iran (1980–88). This demonstrates that Israel's deterrence policy was not a complete failure. Certainly Tel Aviv's unspecified threat of massive retaliation deterred Saddam from using his chemical weapons. In other words, the Iraqi leader's decision to refrain from attacking Israel with chemical weapons was driven by his fear of possible Israeli nuclear reprisal.

Finally, the war provided significant momentum for a comprehensive peace between Israel and its Arab neighbors. The main reason behind this momentum was American determination to reassure the Arab partners in the anti-Iraq coalition that the United States had formulated a plan for peace. Several months after the end of hostilities, Washington succeeded in convening an international conference in Madrid to negotiate a peaceful settlement to the Arab-Israeli conflict. The major regional and international powers were represented, and several joint committees were created to address various aspects of the conflict (e.g., water and arms control). This opportunity, like many others, however, was missed. The military and political outcomes of the Gulf War did not create the "right" environment to negotiate peace. First, the Arab world was severely divided and polarized by the war. Major Arab states such as Egypt, Syria, and Saudi Arabia supported the United States and sent military units to fight side by side with the American, British, and French troops against the Iraqi army. But a few Arab states such as Jordan and Yemen supported Iraq. Second, Palestinians in the West Bank and Gaza Strip generally were in favor of the Iraqi takeover of Kuwait. Moreover, despite some ambiguity and conflicting statements, the PLO voted against the Arab League resolution opposing Iraq's action, and Yasser Arafat supported Saddam Hussein.

Third, at the end of the war the United States turned down Tel Aviv's request for U.S. guarantees of housing loans to facilitate the integration of Jewish immigrants from the Soviet Union. One reason for this uncommon public American pressure on Israel was Washington's attempt to present itself as an honest broker in the Arab-Israeli conflict. The 1992 Israeli elections resulted in an improvement of U.S.-Israeli relations on this matter, as the policy of the newly elected Labor government on settlements in the West Bank met the preferences of the Bush administration in connection with the loan guarantees. In short, despite a little tension between the Bush administration and the Likud-led Israeli government, the war confirmed American strategic and security commitments to Israel. All these developments combined left the major parties in the Arab-Israeli conflict with few incentives to reach a breakthrough in the peace process. The outcome of the Madrid conference was a slow and modest progress toward a comprehensive peace. The breakthrough came a few months later when the Palestinians and Israelis directly negotiated and signed the Oslo agreement.

Two conclusions can be drawn from the experience of the Gulf War and its aftermath. First, the Gulf War, like the 1980–88 Iran-Iraq War, shattered the concept of Arab unity and neutralized the Arabs' capacity to form an effective eastern front against Israel. As a result, the likelihood of a war between Israel and its Arab neighbors was substantially reduced. Second, for Israel the Gulf War was an almost unqualified blessing. "It ensured that Israel would not have to handle Saddam alone and that the United States would maintain a hegemonic presence in the Middle East as long as the Iraqi threat persisted."[55] In short, the Gulf War drastically altered the regional military balance to Israel's advantage. This was important in order to make up for the Israeli loss to Iraq on the Kurdish question in the mid-1970s.

The Kurdish Card

Since its creation in the early 1920s, writes R. D. McLaurin, "Iraq has been a mosaic of religious, ethnic, linguistic, regional, and ideological groups."[56] The continuous efforts by various Iraqi regimes (monarchical, Ba'athist, and nationalist) have achieved a modest success, at best, in creating a national Iraqi identity and integrating all these diverse groups. By far the most critical challenge that has faced Baghdad is the Kurdish question and the failure to solve it peacefully. This problem has comprised both internal and external aspects. In the domestic political context, the Kurds, on the basis of their ethnic and linguistic differences from the Arab majority, have pressed for a certain level of autonomy within the Iraqi state. In their struggle for autonomy, the Kurds have sought aid from foreign sources. Naturally, foreign powers who came to the Kurds' aid have their own objectives. The intense fighting between the Kurds and the Iraqi government in the first half of the 1970s reflected this overlap of Iraqi Kurds' aspirations and foreign powers' strategic interests. During this episode a triangular coalition of three powers—Iran, the United States, and Israel—began to lend financial, political, and military support to the Kurdish insurgents. Their aim was to embroil Iraq in domestic turmoil and immobilize her military capabilities.

After returning to power in 1968, the Ba'ath Party leaders confirmed their desire to reach a comprehensive solution to the Kurdish problem. This strategy was driven by domestic and foreign developments. Domestically, the Ba'athists wanted to consolidate their hold on power, neutralize their opponents, and achieve a high level of political stability. Externally, the Ba'athists planned for an active role in the confrontation with Israel and the pursuit of Arab unity as well as solving territorial disputes with Iran. The Ba'ath leaders understood that an active Kurdish insurgency would weaken them internally and undermine their foreign policy agenda. In other words, the Ba'ath leaders sought a settlement of the Kurdish problem as a means of strengthening national unity, which was considered a prerequisite for an effective Iraqi role in the Arab-Israeli confrontation and the struggle for Arab unity.

Given these incentives, representatives of the Iraqi government and the Kurds negotiated a fifteen-point agreement known as the March Manifesto of 1970. This agreement met many of the Kurds' demands, including "recognition of their language as an official language, a promise that one of the vice presidents of the Republic would be a Kurd, and proportional representation in the revolutionary command council, cabinet, civil service, and the armed forces."[57] This agreement was considered a significant watershed in Ba'ath-Kurdish relations. However, the March Manifesto was never implemented. Differences over the definition of autonomy proved hard to resolve. More specifically, three obstacles undermined this opportunity to reach a peaceful solution to the Kurdish question.

First, the March Manifesto did not make any specific commitment about sharing oil revenues from Kirkuk. Kirkuk is a province in the north of Iraq with a mixed population of Kurds, Turkomans, and Arabs. Most significant is the presence of oil in this area. The Kurds contended that the province should fall within their autonomous region, on grounds of having a Kurdish majority. The government claimed that only some parts of Kirkuk had a Kurdish majority, and therefore only those parts should be included in the autonomous region. It was obvious that the government was unwilling to give up its direct control over a region important to the economy of the entire country. It is hard to imagine that any political regime in Baghdad would surrender control over Kirkuk to the Kurds. Second, implementation of the agreement was postponed for four years, yet within two years serious tensions and clashes had begun again, leading to a complete breakdown and war by 1974. As Graham Fuller argues, "It would appear that Baghdad had never seriously intended to implement the agreement and was only playing for time to gain strength against the Kurds."[58] Third, the United States, Iran, and Israel encouraged the

Kurdish leadership to reject the agreement.[59] Each of these foreign powers had its own reasons to support the Kurds.

U.S. support was driven by at least three motives. Washington viewed Baghdad as a radical, ultra-nationalistic, and pro-Soviet client. Iraq severed diplomatic relations with the United States in response to U.S. support for Israel in the 1967 Arab-Israeli war. Meanwhile, Baghdad signed a Friendship Treaty with Moscow in 1972 and subsequently bought substantial Soviet arms. Furthermore, in 1972 Baghdad nationalized the Iraqi Petroleum Company (IPC), which was seen as another blow to Western interest in the country. Second, American help to the Kurds would weaken Iraq and, as a result, would strengthen Iran, then a close U.S. ally. In the early 1970s, cooperation between Tehran and Washington reached its peak. The shah refused to participate in the Arab oil embargo imposed against the United States following the outbreak of the 1973 Arab-Israeli war. The shah also continued his policy of selling oil to Israel and maintained good relations with the Jewish state. Third, American assistance to the Kurds would keep the Iraqi military away from any confrontation, directly or indirectly, with Israel. By keeping the Iraqi army busy fighting the Kurds in northern Iraq, Baghdad was restrained from sending large units to fight Israel along with the Syrians in the 1973 war. As Henry Kissinger acknowledged, "Only one Iraqi division was available to participate in the October 1973 war."[60]

Given these incentives, the United States provided the Kurdish rebels with arms and ammunition. The Kurds were eager to cooperate with the United States. Some Kurdish leaders were suspicious of the ultimate intentions of Iran and viewed Washington as a more reliable partner in their fight against Baghdad. Despite this trust, U.S. aid to the Kurds suddenly came to an end once the Iranians reached an agreement with the Iraqis and suspended their aid to the Kurds. This holding of U.S. assistance underscores Washington's limited goal: weakening the Iraqi government and not helping the Kurds to achieve autonomy or independence. This goal was shared by Iran and Israel.

The Kurdish question in Iraq has always reflected the degree of tension between Baghdad and Tehran. The issue assumed greater or lesser significance according to the temperature of overall relations between the two countries. Given the long Kurdish struggle against different Iraqi regimes, Tehran has sought to manipulate this struggle for its own national interests. By playing the "Kurdish card" (supplying arms, money, and advisors to the Kurds), Iran was able to achieve several goals. First, Iran's support for the Kurds forced Iraq to keep a big part of its army and air force in the north to fight the Kurdish rebels, and so Tehran did not need to mobilize its military forces along the Iraqi borders in the south to settle the territorial dispute with Baghdad over Shat al-Arab. Second, both the Kurds and the Iranians wanted to hinder Baghdad's drive to unite with other Arab countries. The Iraqi leaders' attempt to champion Arab unity represented a serious challenge to the non-Arab Kurds and Iranians. Third, concerned about the close relations between Baghdad and Moscow following the signing of the 1972 Friendship Treaty, Iran had interest in weakening the Iraqi government and preventing Soviet penetration of the region. Fourth, providing military and financial assistance to the Iraqi Kurds had another significant advantage to the shah. In return for this assistance, the Iraqi Kurds were inclined to return the favor by handing over to the shah's government many Iranian Kurdish dissidents who had sought refuge in the Iraqi Kurdish region.

Accordingly, Iran played a leading role not only in directly supplying arms, training, and advisors to the Kurds but also in facilitating a growing Israeli cooperation with the Kurds. It is important to point out that Iranian assistance to the Kurds was restrained by concern about spillover effects on the sizeable Kurdish minority in Iran.

Israeli support for the Kurdish rebellion in Iraq was shrouded in secrecy until 1980, when the Israeli prime minister, Menachem Begin, officially disclosed that "Israel had provided the Kurdish guerrillas with money, arms, and instructors from 1965 to 1975."[61] Israel had strong reasons to back the Kurdish rebels. First, Iraq was the most aggressive Arab state in her verbal attacks on Israel. Iraq was the only Arab state that had fought against the creation of Israel in 1948 and had refused to sign an armistice. The Kurdish insurrection engaged the Iraqi army in intense fighting far from Israel's eastern front. For Israel there were obvious advantages in having an ally such as the Kurds who knew the terrain and knew how to fight. Second, supporting the Kurds incited them to facilitate the smuggling of Iraqi Jews out of Iraq. Tens of thousands of Iraqi Jews moved to Israel. Still, thousands were left behind. Many of them took advantage of the coordinated efforts by Israel and the Kurds to leave Iraq. Third, forging an alliance with the Kurds was part of the broader periphery doctrine that Israel pursued from the mid-1950s to the late 1970s. According to this policy, Israel sought to establish ties and build alliances with non-Arab and non-Sunni communities and states in the Middle East. The non-Arab Iraqi Kurds were an important target of this periphery policy.

The Kurds were interested in receiving assistance from any source in their intense fighting with the Iraqi government. The Kurds and the Israelis shared similar geopolitical circumstances—being a small ethnic (the Kurds) or religious (the Jews) community surrounded by a hostile Sunni Arab majority. Furthermore, some Kurdish leaders believed in the Israelis' ability to influence U.S. policy in favor of the Kurds.

Eager to weaken the Iraqi government, Iran helped to put together this alliance between the Iraqi Kurds and Israel. Weapons deliveries were a central component of this relationship. Following the 1967 and 1973 Arab-Israeli wars, weapons deliveries increased sharply, especially of sophisticated Soviet arms, which the Israelis had captured from Arab armies. Another significant Israeli contribution was in 1966, "when the Mossad (Israeli intelligence agency) helped set up Parastin (meaning 'protection' in Kurdish), the Kurds' intelligence organization."[62]

In return for Israeli support, the Kurds mounted a large-scale offensive against Iraqi troops in 1967, which made it difficult for Iraq to dispatch large military units to help Syria during the 1967 war. Similarly during the 1973 Arab-Israeli war, there was "desultory talk of the Kurds' opening a second front to keep Iraq from transferring troops to help the Syrians on the Golan Heights."[63] This option, however, was rejected by the United States on the grounds that the Kurds would be defeated in such an offensive.

The powerful American, Iranian, and Israeli support convinced the Kurds that they could resist Baghdad's attempt to impose its own version of autonomy on them. On the other hand, the Iraqis increasingly viewed the Kurds as agents of foreign powers. Within this context, a full-scale military confrontation erupted between the Kurds and the Iraqi government in 1974. Due to the sophistication of the weapons used, the new fighting was tough and intensive. Despite arms supplies from the United States, Iran, and Israel, the Kurdish rebels were not able to withstand the Iraqi army. In response, the shah sent units of the Iranian army to fight alongside the Kurds. This was a significant escalation of the fighting between the Kurds and the Iraqi government and threatened to switch the conflict into an open war between Baghdad and Tehran. It was a war that neither side wanted.

The shah was trying to cultivate the Arab states on the Persian Gulf. He wanted to ensure a dominant role for Iran in a regional security system. In addition, both Iran and its Arab neighbors needed to coordinate their oil policies to maximize their profits and stabilize global oil markets. The rising hostility with Iraq would damage these strategic and economic Iranian interests. At the same time, escalated fighting began to take a heavy toll on the Iraqi army, and the Iraqi leadership became convinced that an understanding with Iran was necessary to bring the war to an end.

Saddam Hussein, then Iraq's vice president and de facto ruler, concluded that in order to defeat the Kurdish uprising, he needed to reach an agreement with Iran. Several Arab leaders played the role of mediators between the two countries, including King Hussein of Jordan and President Houari Boumedienne of Algeria. Their efforts bore fruit when a meeting between the shah and Saddam Hussein took place during the Organization of Petroleum Exporting Countries summit. This meeting resulted in the signing of the Algiers agreement in March 1975, in which the shah agreed to end his support for the Kurdish uprising in Iraq "in return for Baghdad's concessions on a number of border adjustments between the two countries."[64] These included Iraq's acceptance of the Thalweg Line, or mid-channel of the Shat al-Arab (Arvand Rud, as it is called by the Iranians) as the boundary between Iran and Iraq.[65] Saddam Hussein's concession on this point was a bitter blow to the prestige of his regime, eventually forcing him to renounce the terms of the Algiers agreement and invade Iran in September 1980. Within hours of the announcement of the Algiers agreement, Baghdad launched a major offensive against the demoralized Kurdish rebels, and the Kurdish resistance collapsed a few weeks later. Thousands of Iraqi Kurds sought refuge in Iran, and Kurdish leader Mullah Mustafa Barazani settled in Tehran before moving to the United States, where he died of cancer in 1979.[66]

An assessment of the Algiers agreement suggests that Iran emerged with territorial and prestige gains. Iranian support for the Kurds never aimed at an autonomous or independent Kurdish entity. Rather, the shah wanted to maximize pressure on Saddam Hussein in order to extract concessions. The Iraqi government, on the other hand, made painful territorial concessions but was able to crash the Kurdish rebellion and restore its control and sovereignty over the entire country. The agreement laid the groundwork for the most stable period (1975–80) in Saddam Hussein's reign. The United States scored some points by pressuring Iraq to accept a subordinate place in the regional balance of power. For Israel, the outcome of this agreement was mixed. As long as fighting between the Kurds and the Iraqis continued, Baghdad was distracted from the Arab-Israeli conflict. On the other hand, like Iran, it is unlikely that Israeli aid to the Kurds aimed at establishing an autonomous or independent Kurdish identity.

Undoubtedly, the Kurds were the losers. They paid the price of being used as an instrument in a game dominated by foreign powers with different agendas than their own. This defeat led to a major split within the Iraqi Kurdish community. The KDP, led by Barazani and his sons, dominated the Kurdish struggle for autonomy for a long time. "Following the March 1975 agreement a faction led by Jalal Talabani broke with the KDP and formed the Popular

Union of Kurdistan, attracting many who had found Barazani's tribal leadership hard to reconcile with their own nationalist and socialist principles."[67] The March 1975 agreement, however, did little to reconcile the Kurds to the status quo. Instead, they bided their time, awaiting the next opportunity when the particular configuration of regional forces would allow them to challenge their subordination to the central government in Baghdad.

The heavy American, Iranian, and Israeli involvement in aiding and fueling the Kurdish rebellion in the early 1970s suggests several conclusions. First, viewed from Baghdad, the Kurds have always constituted a potentially disaffected population that has presented many opportunities for outside powers to play mischievous roles in Iraq's affairs. Second, the Kurds have never, in the course of Iraqi history, been integrated into the political life of Iraq in any meaningful manner. Their political and military successes have come primarily through the intervention of foreign powers with their anti-Iraqi agendas. The disagreement over the role of the Kurds in the post-Saddam government is the latest manifestation of the failure to assimilate them into an Iraqi national identity. Third, this foreign support for the Kurds increased as the Kurdish leadership saw in it the only effective method for forcing Iraq to give more concessions. The Kurdish leaders, however, failed to realize that by allying with foreign powers they surrendered the fate and destiny of their national movement to forces that have objectives distinctive from Kurdish nationalism. Fourth, the early 1970s episode showed the convergence of the Iranian, American, and Israeli interests in weakening the Iraqi government. Destabilizing Iraq was a constant goal shared by these three states. Once the Kurds had outlived their usefulness, they were abandoned and sacrificed by their patrons. The collapse of the Kurdish rebellion in 1975, however, did not bring the Iraqi-Israeli low-level war to an end. Rather, a direct confrontation between the two sides took place in 1981.

The Israeli Raid on Osiraq

On June 7, 1981, two formations of U.S.-built aircraft left Etzion Airbase near Eilat, Israel, for a preemptive strike on the Osiraq nuclear reactor, which was built to manufacture a nuclear device. According to Jed Snyder, "Eight F-16 Falcon aircraft escorted by six F-15 Eagles dropped a total of sixteen 2,000–pound iron bombs on the reactor facility."[68] The Israeli action represented the first preventive strike against nuclear facilities, which established an international precedent.

The Iraqi attempt to develop nuclear capability was part of a broader Arab effort to counter Israel's nuclear program, which started in the early 1950s in Dimona. Originally, the Egyptian president, Gamal Abd al-Nasser, took the lead by inviting German scientists to help Egypt establish a counteroffensive strategy. Under heavy Israeli diplomatic pressure, the German government stopped its cooperation with Egypt. Nasser's appeals for assistance from the Soviet Union and China were unsuccessful. After the 1967 war, politically weakened and lacking financial resources, Nasser abandoned the idea of establishing a nuclear option in Egypt. Arab aspirations for a nuclear capability, however, did not end with Nasser. Saddam Hussein had seriously sought to acquire and develop nuclear capability. His efforts were driven by personal and national ambition to lead the Arab world as well as strong anti-Israel and anti-Iran sentiments. Baghdad's enormous oil revenues in the 1970s were used to fund the country's nuclear program.

Saddam Hussein approached several foreign powers to assist him in acquiring nuclear capability. Both the Soviet Union and Italy provided some help, but France showed more enthusiasm. Realizing that the French nuclear industry was advanced and seeking clients, Saddam Hussein approached the French government initially soliciting a general nuclear cooperation accord. This accord was signed during Premier Jacques Chirac's trip to Baghdad in 1974. A more detailed agreement was signed in 1976, which provided Iraq with a complete nuclear research center including Osiraq. The reactor was scheduled to be operational by the end of 1981. The fact that Saddam Hussein came very close to fulfilling his nuclear ambition incited Israel to launch a preemptive raid on Iraq's nuclear facilities and destroy them.

Several dynamics shaped and drove the Israeli leadership's decision to initiate a military strike against Osiraq: first, Iraq's declared radical stand on the Arab-Israeli conflict and its persistent denial of the Jewish state's right to exist; second, the failure of Israel's diplomatic efforts to prevent foreign powers, particularly France, from providing technical assistance to Iraq's nuclear program; and, third, the assessment that international safeguards, documented in international treaties, would not be an effective barrier to Iraq's efforts. In 1959 Baghdad joined the International Atomic Energy Agency (IAEA), and ten years later it signed the Non-Proliferation Treaty (NPT) and ratified it in 1974. The safeguards system did not provide for aggressive sanctions. Instead, it offered an effective warning mechanism that, in Israeli opinion, was not sufficient to contain Iraq's ambition to make a nuclear device. Fourth, Israeli prime minister Menachem Begin wanted to maintain Israel's nuclear monopoly in the Middle East. The creation of the Iraqi reactor would have threatened such a monopoly. Following the raid, Israeli leaders repeatedly confirmed their commitment to prevent Arab countries from acquiring or developing weapons of mass destruction and to maintain their country's nuclear monopoly. Later, this became known as "Begin's doctrine." Thus Israeli leaders' perception of a growing Iraqi threat underscored by Iraq's declared animosity toward the Jewish state and the inadequacies of international safeguards had contributed to the decision to attack and destroy Osiraq.

The decision to destroy the Iraqi nuclear reactor was finally made in late 1980, and the Israeli air force and intelligence started planning several contingencies and training for the operation. At least two factors were considered in choosing the date for executing this operation. First and most important was the question of when the Iraqi reactor would become operational. Israeli military experts could not agree on a specific date. According to Amos Perlmutter, "Estimates in that respect ranged between September 1981 as the earliest timeframe and 1985 as the latest."[69] Israeli experts and politicians, however, agreed that Iraq was trying to manufacture a nuclear device and that these nuclear capabilities, if they materialized, would be used against Israel. Second, there was some speculation that Begin had chosen early June for the attack in order to maximize the domestic political benefit. "Pre-election polls in Israel were forecasting a defeat for the Likud Party, which would have resulted in Begin's downfall."[70] By launching this military action against Iraq's nuclear reactor, the argument goes, Begin was able to remove a significant threat to Israel and, at the same time, increase his personal appeal and his party's chances for reelection.

Condemnation of the Israeli military action was virtually universal. A few days after the attack, the UN Security Council convened to consider the appropriate response. In addition to condemning the attack, Baghdad demanded that the United Nations should impose economic and political sanctions against Israel. To avoid an American veto, Iraq softened its position. Accordingly, on June 19, 1981, the Security Council passed resolution 487 condemning the military attack by Israel as a "clear violation of the Charter of the United Nations and the norms of international conduct."[71] The resolution also called on Israel to refrain from any such action in the future and recognized the rights of Iraq and other states to establish programs of technological and nuclear development for peaceful purposes. Finally, the resolution called on Israel to open its facilities for IAEA inspections and to compensate Iraq for the loss of the facility.

In response, Israel told the UN Security Council that it had no confidence in the Non-Proliferation Treaty safeguards and that its action should be seen as a legitimate right to self-defense. Not surprisingly, Tel Aviv "refused either to pay compensation to Baghdad or to open its nuclear facilities to international inspections."[72]

Equally important was the IAEA's reaction. Undoubtedly, the Israeli raid on Osiraq was seen as a vote of no confidence in the international safeguards as established by the IAEA. Hence the raid opened up the possibility that other countries would follow suit and replace the nonproliferation regime with pre-emptive strikes. Considering this challenge to established international rules, the IAEA expressed its opposition to the Israeli military action. Initially, Arab delegations demanded that Israel should be expelled from the IAEA. However, due to American pressure, Arab states softened their position and accepted a mild resolution that urged the IAEA to suspend Israel's membership but stopped short of calling for its expulsion. The resolution also condemned Israel and called upon members to stop all financial and technical aid to it.

Even though the American intelligence community was aware of Israel's concerns about the nature and purpose of the Iraqi nuclear reactor, the timing of the bombing was a total surprise. There is no evidence that the United States was aware of this operation. The Israeli attack, indeed, pushed Washington to an uneasy position. On one hand, in the early 1980s fundamental strategic developments were reshaping the Persian Gulf region. Shortly after the Iranian revolution, diplomatic relations between Washington and Tehran were severed. Meanwhile, Baghdad was moving away from close alliance with the Soviet Union and was, instead, courting good relations with moderate Arab states and the United States. In short, Washington and Baghdad were examining prospects for improved relations. On the other hand, the United States has always voiced its opposition to nuclear proliferation and its unquestionable commitment to its alliance with Israel and to the security of the Jewish state.

Given these restraints, the Reagan administration issued a very measured response that balanced a recognition of Israel's concern about a potential nuclear threat with considerations of U.S. strategic interests in the Middle East (maintaining good relations with Arab states) as well as U.S. arms transfer policies. Besides condemning the Israeli raid, Reagan ordered the suspension of the delivery of four F-16s "pending completion of a review to determine if a violation of the U.S.-Israeli agreement on arms sales had occurred."[73] Officials in the Reagan administration assured their Israeli counterparts that the suspension was temporary. The suspension was officially lifted in August, only two months after the Israeli raid. Despite this very mild American reaction, it is important to point out that the suspension was a rare event in the history of U.S.-Israeli relations.

Naturally, the Arab world strongly condemned the Israeli raid. The attack hurt Arab pride and deepened the perception of Israel as an aggressor. Despite this uniform and straightforward Arab condemnation, some Arab leaders felt a sense of relief with the destruction of Iraq's potential nuclear capability. Traditionally, Iraq has many rivals within the Arab world and in the broad Middle East. These include Saudi Arabia, Syria, and Egypt, as well as Iran and Turkey. It is reasonable to assume that these countries shared Israel's concerns regarding Iraq's nuclear program. Finally, for the Egyptian president, Anwar al-Sadat, the raid amounted to a personal insult. Only three days after Sadat met with Menachem Begin, Israel bombed Osiraq, leaving the impression that the Egyptian president was told in advance about the Israeli raid.

The raid on Osiraq has had long-term strategic ramifications for the Arab-Israeli peace process and for the proliferation of weapons of mass destruction (WMD) in the Middle East. The brilliant execution of the military operation undoubtedly enhanced the credibility of Israeli deterrence. Paradoxically, this same success has further deepened the Arabs' sense of alienation and victimization. This sense of weakness in confronting Israeli might was not transformed into a rush to sign peace agreements with Israel. Rather, it created a general feeling of despair, which, among other factors, has led to more violence against the Israelis and renewed efforts to acquire different types of unconventional weapons.

The destruction of the Iraqi nuclear reactor has had mixed impact on the long-term prospects for the proliferation of weapons of mass destruction in Iraq and the Middle East. The attack dealt a heavy blow to Saddam Hussein's ambition to acquire nuclear capability and sent a clear signal to other Arab leaders with similar ambitions. Bombing Osiraq removed a potential threat to Israel and certainly enhanced its national security. The successful raid, however, underscored the Iraqis' and Arabs' sense of inferiority and the necessity to take some action to balance and counter the Israeli nuclear monopoly. Ironically, the proliferation of chemical and biological weapons in the Middle East can be seen, at least partly, as the Arabs' response to the Israeli nuclear monopoly. Furthermore, the Israeli raid was a major reason for the Ba'athist regime's determination to acquire a nuclear device in the late 1980s and early 1990s.

What Lies Ahead for Iraq and Israel?

In comparison with other Middle Eastern states, Iraq has adopted the most militant stand against Israel for more than five decades. The violent exodus of Iraqi Jews, Iraqi participation in the 1948, 1967, and 1973 Arab-Israeli wars,

Baghdad's leading role in opposing the peace process and sponsoring radical Palestinian organizations, and the missile attacks on Israel during the 1991 Gulf War all demonstrate the Iraqis' hostile attitude toward the Jewish state. This animosity can be explained, at least partly, by the nature and characteristics of the Iraqi state.

Domestically, since Iraq was created as a nation-state following World War I, the country has been ruled by a narrowly based minority, the Sunni Arabs. Despite tremendous efforts by different Iraqi regimes, the state has not succeeded in assimilating all the ethnic and sectarian groups into a coherent national identity. In order to divert attention from this failure and to strengthen the appeal for Iraqi and Arab nationalism, Baghdad has embarked on several foreign policy adventures. In addition to participating in the Arab-Israeli wars, Iraq invaded Iran in 1980 and Kuwait in 1990. Since 1980, Iraq has experienced three devastating wars as well as twelve years of comprehensive economic sanctions.

The impacts of the Iran-Iraq War and the Gulf War have been discussed above. The strategic ramifications of the 2003 war on Israel are uncertain. Still, some tentative conclusions can be drawn. First, the ability of the Arab states to form an eastern front (Iraq, Syria, and Jordan as well as the Palestinians) against Israel has considerably diminished. This front has always been considered by the Israeli strategic planners as more dangerous than the northern and southern fronts because it is closer to the center (the Jerusalem/Tel Aviv/Haifa triangle). Second, Iraq's armed forces suffered heavy losses in the 2003 war. Shortly after the collapse of Saddam Hussein's regime, the United States disbanded the remains of the army and began building a new one, trained and equipped under American supervision. Iraq's intelligence and security organizations went through a similar process. The war also removed the threat of Baghdad's employment of WMD. All these developments have enhanced Israel's strategic posture in the Middle East. Third, the drying up of the funds Saddam Hussein sent to the families of suicide bombers is not only a financial blow; it is also a significant setback to morale among Palestinians who oppose peace negotiations with Israel. No Arab regime is likely to choose to replace Saddam in this role. Fourth, the 2003 war in Iraq has what can be called "demonstrable effects." By toppling the Hussein regime, which was said to have refused to cooperate in destroying its WMD, other regional powers with interest in developing these weapons are likely to adjust their policies. One case in point is Libya's decision to closely adhere to international nonproliferation norms and regimes shortly after the ouster of Saddam Hussein.[74] Similarly,

Iran negotiated agreements with the IAEA and the European Union to ensure its nuclear program was not aimed at making nuclear weapons. The European economic and diplomatic incentives (the good cop) and the American military and political threats (the bad cop) are believed to have persuaded the Iranians to accept a more rigid international inspection of its nuclear facilities.

Fifth, what happened in Iraq sends a clear message to Israel's adversaries on what the United States, Tel Aviv's closest ally, is willing to do. The American military and political presence in Iraq is likely to enhance the Israeli standing in the region. Sixth, in the aftermath of the 2003 war, the Israeli government turned its attention to other regional adversaries, particularly Iran and Syria, demanding swift action by the United States and the international community to strip them of WMD and to encourage regime change. However, the active involvement of Israeli intelligence in exaggerating the threat of Hussein's WMD "has been a blow to Israel's credibility."[75] Finally, a revival of the Haifa-Mosul pipeline to pump Iraqi oil to Israel's major port city cannot be ruled out. The resumption of Iraqi oil shipments (halted when Israel was established in 1948) would provide Israel with badly needed oil supplies. This potential cooperation with Israel is not likely to happen soon. It will take some time to establish security and stability in Iraq. Meanwhile, as long as tension exists between Israel and Syria, Lebanon, and the Palestinians, it is highly unlikely that Iraq will engage in any close cooperation with Israel.[76]

Since the 2003 war, the Iraqi political system has been subjected to a comprehensive process of reconstruction. The analysis in this chapter suggests that a more stable political regime in Baghdad, when it happens, is likely to pursue peaceful relations with its neighbors, including Arabs, Iranians, and Israelis.

4

The Gulf Monarchies and Israel

The kingdom of Saudi Arabia was established in the early eighteenth century through an alliance between two dynasties, the Saudi and the Wahhabi. The heads of these two dynasties, Muhammad ibn Saud and Muhammad ibn Abd al-Wahhab, agreed that the former would be in charge of political issues while the latter would control the religious domain. Despite some ups and downs, the alliance has persisted until today. In formulating their stand on the Arab-Israeli conflict, Saudi policy makers have tried to accommodate pressures from opposite directions. First, the kingdom holds approximately one-fourth of the world's proven oil reserves and is the world's largest oil producer and exporter. Little wonder, the Arabs have long debated the use of this strategic commodity in their struggle against Israel and its major ally, the United States. Except during the 1973 Arab oil embargo, Saudi leaders have adamantly resisted mixing oil and policy.

Second, since its creation as a nation-state in 1932, Saudi Arabia has confronted serious threats from leaders of more populous and powerful regional states such as Nasser of Egypt, Ayatollah Khomeini of Iran, and Saddam Hussein of Iraq. Given the kingdom's limited military capability, in comparison with these three regional powers, Riyadh was unable to defend itself. Instead, a major component of the country's security strategy has been a reliance on the United States. Considering Saudi Arabia's massive oil resources and its prominent role in global energy markets, Washington has always demonstrated firm commitment to the security of Saudi Arabia. This close strategic cooperation between Washington and Riyadh has always been a major source of tension and embarrassment for the Saudi royal family in both the Arab and Islamic worlds as well as domestically. The dilemma facing the Saudi policy makers has been how to explain their close cooperation with the United States, Israel's closest ally, to their conservative constituency at home and to the Arab and Muslim peoples and governments.

The massive hydrocarbon wealth, the important religious legitimacy of the Saudi regime, and the close cooperation with the United States have all shaped the kingdom's approach to the Middle East conflict. Four basic characteristics of the Saudi stand on the Arab-Israeli dispute can be identified. First, during the cold war, Saudi officials sought "to underscore the early association between Zionism as a political movement and the socialist ideology and the communist political backing it received in the initial stages of Israel's creation."[1] Furthermore, the Saudis claimed that Israel was largely responsible for the Soviet penetration of the Middle East in the second half of the twentieth century. They argued that Israel's military victory in the 1948 war substantially contributed to the collapse of conservative governments and the rise of a radical form of pan-Arabism in several key Arab states such as Egypt, Syria, and Iraq. The plight of millions of Palestinians has further radicalized Arab policy. This political environment, the argument goes, facilitated Soviet penetration of the Middle East and put pro-Western regimes, such as Saudi Arabia, on the defensive. Second, the Saudi attitude toward Israel is also shaped by religious and cultural factors. Most Arab and Muslim countries hosted large Jewish communities before the establishment of Israel in 1948. Relations between the predominantly Muslim populations and these Jewish minorities were not always easy, but the idea of Jews and Muslims living side by side was more or less accepted. For the Saudis and the other Gulf monarchies, however, this notion of a peaceful coexistence between Muslims and Jews and a Muslim majority accommodating a Jewish minority was absent. William Quandt writes, "No significant Jewish community existed in the Arabian Peninsula outside of Yemen in modern times."[2] Many Saudis and other Arabs have failed to see any distinction between Judaism as a religion and Zionism as a political movement.

Third, Israeli control over Muslim holy sites in Jerusalem since the 1967 war has further intensified Saudi hostility toward the Jewish state. As the guardians of the two holiest places in Islam—Mecca and Medina—the Saudis could not be indifferent to the third holiest site in Islam, al-Aqsa Mosque in Jerusalem. Finally, the centrality of the Palestinian issue in Arab and Muslim policies as well as the presence of large Palestinian expatriate communities in Saudi Arabia and the other Gulf monarchies have shaped the kingdom's relations with the Palestinians. Generally, Riyadh enjoyed good relations with the Palestine Liberation Organization (PLO) and its leader, Yasser Arafat. Occasionally relations between the two sides deteriorated due to leftist and secular orientations within the PLO, which contradict conservative Saudi policy. Accordingly, the

Saudis have established and maintained relations with other Palestinian organizations such as Hamas, which is occasionally seen as a rival to the PLO. Arafat's support for Saddam Hussein in the 1991 Gulf War dealt a heavy blow to PLO relations with the Saudis and other Gulf monarchies. Despite these periodical but significant setbacks, the Saudis have demonstrated strong commitment to the Palestinian cause. Like other Arabs, the Saudis believe that the creation of a Palestinian state with real authority and sovereignty is the right way to end the Arab-Israeli conflict and contain nationalist, leftist, and Islamist radicalism in the region.

In the following sections the main forces that shaped the Saudi attitude toward Israel will be examined, namely, Islam, oil, and relations with the United States. The Saudi policy toward the Arab-Israeli conflict will be analyzed. Particular attention is given to the Saudi leading role in the Arab oil embargo in 1973, Saudi peace plans of 1981 and 2002, and the kingdom's diplomatic and financial role in supporting the Palestinians and other Arab states in both launching wars and making peace with Israel. Finally, the chapter discusses the limited diplomatic relations between Israel and the other five Gulf monarchies (Bahrain, Kuwait, Oman, Qatar, and the United Arab Emirates). In September 1994, the six Gulf monarchies agreed to lift the secondary and tertiary boycott on direct dealings with Israeli companies until peaceful negotiations were successfully concluded between Israel, Syria, and Lebanon. The Gulf monarchies have not adopted an identical approach toward the Jewish state. Diplomatic contacts and trade relations have been established between Tel Aviv and both Muscat and Doha.

Strained opposition to Israel and the generally moderating role that the Gulf monarchies play in the Arab-Israeli conflict can be explained by their close strategic relations with the United States. In addition to Washington's pressure on the Gulf monarchies to adopt a moderate stand on the Arab-Israeli conflict, domestic opposition pulls them in the opposite direction, particularly in Saudi Arabia. Given the characteristics of the Saudi domestic constituency as well as the kingdom's prominent role in the Arab and Islamic worlds, Riyadh is likely to be slow and cautious in normalizing relations with Israel if a comprehensive peace agreement is reached.

Saudi Arabia's Attitude toward Israel

Saudi Arabia, like so many of its neighbors, "is a nation of paradoxes."[3] The country is the birthplace of Islam, but increasingly the main challenge to Saudi national security is Islamic fundamentalism. Saudi Arabia holds the world's largest oil reserves, but a growing number of Saudis are unemployed and living in poverty. For more than half a century the kingdom has been an ally to the United States. However, despite these close official ties, some Saudi citizens have been involved in terrorist attacks against the United States, most notably on September 11, 2001. One of the major problems facing the Saudi leaders has been how to explain to their domestic constituency their close cooperation with the United States, Israel's closest ally. Members of the Saudi royal family have always sought to hide or play down their close and extensive ties with Washington. Meanwhile, Riyadh has tried, unsuccessfully, to use its energy and financial leverage to pressure the United States to adopt an evenhanded approach to the Arab-Israeli conflict. Washington, on the other hand, has endeavored to persuade the Saudis to play a moderate role in the Middle East conflict and to tone down their rhetoric against the Jewish state. The Saudi attitude toward Israel has been largely formulated by three factors: Islam, relations with the United States, and oil.

Islam

Islam, as it is interpreted by the religious establishment, has the most powerful influence on the Saudi policy. Islamic norms and values are seen as the foundation and the guide for social and economic life in the kingdom. Furthermore, adherence to the main tenets of Islam is used to legitimize domestic and foreign policy decisions. Accordingly, the Qur'an is the kingdom's constitution, and the Shari'ia (Muslim code of law) is the source of laws and regulations. This dominant role which Islam plays in almost all aspects of life in Saudi Arabia is drawn from two sources: the kingdom's control of the two holiest cities in Islam and the historic alliance between the Saud royal family and the Wahhabiya Islamic movement.

Both Mecca and Medina are located in Saudi Arabia. Mecca is the birthplace of Islam and where the Great Mosque is located. Practicing Muslims all over the world face the Great Mosque in their prayers five times a day. All Muslims are required to make a pilgrimage (hajj) at least once if they are physically fit and able to afford it. In this holy journey, according to Islamic teachings, believers visit certain sites in Mecca and perform certain rituals. More than 2 million Muslims from all over the world make this journey every year. Medina is where Muhammad resided after he left Mecca. This move was a turning point in the history of Islam. From Medina, the Prophet was able to convert a growing number of people to Islam, and the religion has spread throughout the world. Millions of Muslims visit the Prophet's grave in Medina every year. Little wonder, Saudi Arabia is of unparalleled importance to the more than 1 billion Muslims, and Saudi leaders assume special responsibility toward Muslim nations and peoples. Accordingly, since the early 1980s the king of Saudi Arabia has designated himself "Custodian of the Two Holy Shrines."

The second source of Islamic dominance in Saudi Arabia is the alliance between the Saud royal family and the Wahhabiya Islamic movement. In the early eighteenth century Muhammad ibn Saud, the founder of the Saudi dynasty, needed a political/religious movement to support his aspiration to unite and rule the tribes and provinces that constitute the modern-day Saudi Arabia. Thus he forged an alliance with Muhammad ibn Abd al-Wahhab, a charismatic religious leader with numerous followers and an appealing Islamic doctrine. Abd al-Wahhab is the founder of a religious movement known in the West as Wahhabiya. The followers, however, call themselves Muwahhidun (Unitarians). They regard themselves as Sunnis, following the school of Ibn Hanbal, the founder of one of the four jurisdictional schools in Sunni Islam, as interpreted by Ibn Taimiya, a prominent theology scholar. The movement opposes any innovation and calls for the purification of Islam by returning to the basic teachings of the Qur'an and the Prophet's traditions. The two leaders, Muhammad ibn Saud and Muhammad ibn Abd al-Wahhab, agreed that should they succeed in imposing their partnership on their neighbors, the former would be in charge of socioeconomic and political issues and the latter would control religious affairs.

Their alliance succeeded in defeating rival tribal chiefs and taking over most of modern Saudi Arabia, including the holy cities of Mecca and Medina. This first Saudi kingdom, however, was crushed by Egyptian forces acting in the name of the Turkish sultan in the early nineteenth century. At the turn of the twentieth century, Muhammad ibn Saud's grandson, Abd al-Aziz ibn Abd al-Rahman al-Saud, known in the West as Ibn Saud, sought to consolidate his family's power. He was able to follow and repeat his grandfather's victories, and he quickly expanded his rule over the entire modern-day Saudi Arabia and made it a nation-state in 1932. The alliance with the Wahhabiya was a main reason for Ibn Saud's success. The movement provided the ideological justification for the expansion of Saudi rule. In addition, "the Wahhabiya provided Ibn Saud with an army known as the Ikhwan (brethren), which was formed in 1912."[4] The Ikhwan began as "a group of religious zealots dedicated to reasserting the austere Wahhabi doctrine among the tribes of Najd."[5] The Ikhwan were able to win for Ibn Saud every battle they fought. However, political and ideological disagreements weakened the close alliance between Ibn Saud and the Ikhwan. Fearing for his throne, Ibn Saud recruited a new army drawn from loyal tribes to counter the Ikhwan, whom he eventually crushed in 1929. Despite this confrontation, the alliance between the Saudi royal family and the Wahhabiya movement has endured. Followers of the movement control large parts of the religious, judicial, and educational bureaucracies in the kingdom.

It is important to point out that the prominent role of Islam in Saudi Arabia has served both the royal family and its opponents. Islamic symbols and principles have been utilized to legitimize the political regime in Riyadh. On the other hand, opponents of the political establishment, particularly since the Gulf War in 1990–91 and increasingly following the 2003 war in Iraq, have used the same Islamic teachings to question the legitimacy of the royal family and to rally support against certain Saudi policies, both at home and abroad. Indeed, the main opposition to the Saudi government comes from religious groups and individuals who use Islamic terminology.

In addition to using religion in Saudi domestic policy, Islam plays a significant role in formulating the kingdom's foreign policy. In general terms, the Saudi perception of the world is drawn from the Qur'an. Instead of seeing the world divided between developed and underdeveloped countries (have and have-nots) or capitalist and communist, the Saudi view of the world conforms far more closely to the classical Islamic view. Writes David Long, "This is basically a bipolar world composed of Dar al-Islam, or the territory under divine Islamic law, and Dar al-Harb, the territory of war, that is, outside the rule of God's law."[6] Within this context Saudi Arabia plays a significant role in promoting cooperation with other Muslim countries and organizations and providing economic aid to poor Muslims. Riyadh, for example, took the initiative to establish the largest Muslim governmental organization, the Islamic Conference Organization (ICO), in 1969. Besides the ICO, the kingdom provides political and financial support to nongovernmental organizations such as the Muslim World League and the World League of Muslim Youth. Moreover, the kingdom has consistently established and maintained ties with Muslim organizations all over the world in order to build mosques and promote the Saudi version of Islam. Finally, the Saudis supported Muslim groups in their wars against non-Muslims such as the Afghanis against the Soviet Union and the Bosnians in their war against the Serbs.

With regard to non-Muslims, the Saudi cooperation with the Christian West is in line with Islamic principles. Christians and Jews are known in Islam as Ahl al-Kitab, People of the Book. In other words, they are monotheists who subscribe to a divinely inspired revelation. Islamic tenets permit cooperation and peaceful relations with followers of other monotheist religions (Christians and Jews).

Israel occupies a different position in the Saudi perception of the international system. Saudi officials have always emphasized a distinction between Judaism, which is recognized by Islam as a monotheist religion, and Zionism, which Riyadh considers an anti-Arab and anti-Islam political movement. The Saudis see Israel less as a Jewish state, where Muslims, Christians, and Jews can live in peace, and more as a Zionist entity, whose goal, according to the Saudis, is to occupy Arab and Muslim land. The Saudi opposition to Israel has further intensified since the 1967 war and the loss of the eastern part of Jerusalem, which houses the Dome of the Rock. According to Islamic traditions, the Prophet ascended to heaven from the Dome of the Rock. Israel's decision to make the unified Jerusalem its eternal capital following the 1967 war has further fueled Saudi hostility toward the Jewish state. The Saudi people and their government strongly oppose Israeli control and sovereignty over the Muslim holy sites in Jerusalem.

Two conclusions can be drawn from this discussion of the role of Islam in Saudi foreign policy. First, the Saudi regime looks to the religious leaders to approve important decisions and initiatives in the area of foreign policy. Their endorsement legitimizes the political action. However, according to Gregory Gause, "There is no case in recorded Saudi history where a foreign policy decision or initiative was rescinded or dropped because of publicly expressed disapproval by the religious establishment."[7] In other words, the ulama, religious leaders, have strong leverage, but they do not have veto power in foreign policy.

Second, in formulating its policy on the Arab-Israeli conflict, Saudi Arabia faces a dilemma similar to the one the Soviet Union faced when it was "forced to choose between serving as the vanguard of an international revolutionary movement and accepting the responsibilities of a nation-state in an international community."[8] Given the prominence of Islam in almost all aspects of life in Saudi Arabia as well as the country's leading role in the Arab and Islamic worlds, Riyadh cannot afford to show any public reconciliation with the Jewish state without real progress toward a comprehensive peace. Meanwhile, the Saudi state's national interests are not mutually exclusive with those of Israel. Above all, the United States is the main ally for both states. Furthermore, Riyadh and Tel Aviv found themselves on the same side against mutual enemies, such as Nasser of Egypt in the 1960s, Ayatollah Khomeini of Iran in the 1980s, and Saddam Hussein of Iraq in the 1990s.

Relations with the United States

For more than seven decades Saudi Arabia has been one of the closest allies the United States has in the Middle East and the Islamic world. Several economic and strategic interests are at stake, including oil supplies, Persian Gulf security, and militant Islam. Saudi Arabia's experience with the United States is different in many ways from that of other Arab and Muslim countries. The kingdom has never experienced the European colonization of the eighteenth and nineteenth centuries. Still suspicious of European intentions, Saudi leaders have long sought to forge close ties with the United States. This unofficial alliance has been founded on two basic pillars—Riyadh provides oil supplies and uses its leverage to maintain global oil prices at a reasonable level and, in return, Washington guarantees the kingdom's security from any external threats. For the most part, the two sides have kept their share of the bargain.

Determined to loosen what he saw as British hegemonic ambitions in the Arabian Peninsula, King Ibn Saud awarded a petroleum concession in al-Ahsa province to the Standard Oil Company of California. In other words, Saudi Arabia's vast oil reserves drew U.S. oil companies to the kingdom; they in turn helped to develop the capacities of the then newly established Saudi state. Several years later, diplomatic relations between the two nations were further consolidated when "a resident U.S. legation was established in Jidda, where the Saudi government preferred to keep foreign diplomatic missions."[9] Additionally, U.S. military engineers built an airport at Dhahran. The airport was supposed to be a staging base for the Far East theater of operations against Japan during World War II. The U.S. air forces controlled the facility until the early 1960s.

The most dramatic development in establishing relations between the United States and Saudi Arabia was the first meeting between the two heads of states. In 1945 Franklin D. Roosevelt hosted Ibn Saud aboard an American cruiser, the USS *Quincy*, in the Great Bitter Lake. The president, according to Saudi sources, assured the king that he would never do anything that might prove hostile to the Arabs and that his government would not change its basic policy in Palestine without consulting with both Jews and Arabs.[10]

This unofficial alliance should not be seen as dependency by Saudi Arabia on the United States. Rather, given the kingdom's massive oil reserves and its role in the Arab and Islamic worlds, the Saudi leaders have repeatedly distanced themselves from American policy and confirmed their independence from Washington. For example, following the outbreak of the 1973 Arab-Israeli war, Saudi Arabia led Arab oil-producing countries in imposing an oil embargo on the United States and other countries for their support to Israel. In the mid-1980s, when Washington refused to sell Riyadh sophisticated weapon systems, the Saudis signed a huge arms deal with Britain. On the other hand, a number of U.S. government agencies and members of Congress have repeatedly questioned specific features of Saudi policy. These include the Saudi record on human rights, particularly religious freedom and the status of women. Washington opposes Riyadh's boycott of Israeli products. Finally, since the early 2000s the issue of militant Islam has created the most serious crisis ever in American-Saudi relations.

Despite these few but serious differences between Washington and Riyadh, the kingdom has generally followed the U.S. line on strategic global issues. For most of the cold war years Saudi leaders perceived atheistic communism and the Soviet attempt to penetrate the Middle East as the main threats to regional and global stability. Accordingly, Saudi Arabia provided generous financial support to anticommunist movements in the Middle East and the rest of the world (e.g., Afghanistan and Nicaragua).

This general agreement between the United States and Saudi Arabia on global issues has not expanded to cover regional policy, particularly the Arab-Israeli conflict. The Saudis have long asserted that the continuing failure of the conflict and the Israeli occupation of Arab land and Muslim holy sites as well as the plight of the Palestinians are the main reasons for political instability in the Middle East. The United States, however, does not share the Saudi perception. Instead, Washington has claimed that instability was a response to Soviet policy during the cold war and the lack of genuine economic and political reform in most Middle Eastern states.

These differences between Saudi Arabia and its closest foreign ally, the United States, on the Arab-Israeli conflict have largely shaped the kingdom's role, both in the Arab-Israeli wars and in the several unsuccessful attempts to make peace. Riyadh resented Washington's support to Israel in the 1948, 1967, and 1973 wars. It provided financial support to frontline states (Egypt, Syria, and Jordan) as well as the PLO. The kingdom participated in the Arab economic boycott of Israel (which was partly lifted in the mid-1990s). Saudi Arabia also supported all resolutions in the General Assembly of the United Nations that condemned Israel. Riyadh opposed the Egyptian peace efforts in the late 1970s, which culminated in the signing of the first peace treaty between Israel and an Arab country in 1979. Two years later, then, Crown Prince Fahd proposed his own plan for an Arab-Israeli comprehensive peace. Similarly, in 2002 Crown Prince Abdullah presented his own plan to end the conflict. In short, the Saudi stand on the Arab-Israeli conflict can be described as restrained opposition to the Jewish state. Saudi Arabia has not gone as far as Egypt and Jordan in officially signing peace treaties with Israel, nor has the kingdom engaged in trade negotiations or given diplomatic recognition to Tel Aviv, as Qatar and Oman have done. On the other hand, Riyadh has adopted a more peaceful stand on the conflict than the one advocated by the Islamist Iran or Iraq under Saddam Hussein. In other words, the Saudi statements and policies suggest that the kingdom is willing to make peace with Israel under certain conditions and in the context of an Arab consensus.

In closing, three conclusions regarding the American-Saudi relations need to be highlighted. First, despite some serious crises and conflicting perceptions, the unofficial alliance between Washington and Riyadh is likely to endure. The two countries need each other. Massive Saudi oil supplies are essential to maintaining stability in global energy markets and prosperity in the international economy. Meanwhile, the United States has repeatedly proven itself a reliable security partner to the kingdom against its enemies

Second, allying with the United States has served the Saudi security concerns tremendously, but has also exposed the Saudi regime to domestic criticism and regional condemnation for the American military presence in the kingdom and the close relations between the royal family and the United States. Since the mid-1990s there have been several attacks on military and civilian American personnel in Saudi Arabia. Most noticeable was the 1995 attack in Riyadh, where five Americans were killed, and the 1996 attack in Dhahran, where nineteen Americans died. These attacks continued and were responsible, at least in part, for causing the bulk of American troops to be withdrawn from the kingdom and repositioned in neighboring Qatar in 2003.[11] Regionally, radical Arab leaders such as Nasser of Egypt, Saddam Hussein of Iraq, and Muammar Gaddafi of Libya have repeatedly accused Saudi leaders of contributing to the continued existence and increasing strength of Israel by allying themselves with the United States, which is Israel's main economic lifeline and military supporter.

Finally, despite the extensive military and economic ties between Washington and Riyadh, "there is no strong or vocal pro-Saudi constituency in the United States."[12] The close cooperation between the two countries seems to be only between the elites on both sides. The Saudi image in the United States has been tremendously tarnished since the terrorist attacks in September 2001. Indeed, Crown Prince Abdullah's peace plan of early 2002 can be seen partly as an attempt to improve his country's image in the United States.

Oil

With approximately 25 percent of the world's proven crude reserves, oil plays a prominent role in shaping Saudi Arabia's domestic and foreign policies. Oil revenues represent a large proportion of the country's gross national product and the bulk of its total export earnings. These financial earnings have been a major means of pursuing Riyadh's regional and international objectives.

Promising oil reservoirs were discovered in Iran, Iraq, and Bahrain early in the twentieth century. This hydrocarbon wealth was dominated by European companies, particularly from Great Britain. Meanwhile, indigenous leaders were interested in granting concessions to foreign companies in order to strengthen their rising economic and political power. Under these circumstances, in 1933 King Ibn Saud, who was suspicious of European intentions, "gave Standard Oil Company of California (Socal, later Chevron) a sixty-year exclusive right to explore for oil in an area in eastern Saudi Arabia covering 360,000 square miles."[13] The Californian-Arabian Standard Oil Company (CASOC) was formed to exploit the concession. According to George Lenczowski, "Three other companies acquired shares: Texas Oil Company (Texaco), Standard Oil Company of New Jersey (later Exxon), and Standard Oil Company of New York (originally Socony, later Mobil)."[14] A supplementary agreement was signed in May 1938, adding six years to the original agreement and enlarging the concession area by almost 80,000 square miles. It also included rights in the Saudi government's half-interest in the two neutral zones shared with Iraq and Kuwait.

Early exploration drilling in Saudi Arabia was not successful, and although the first well was completed in 1935, it was not until March 1938 that oil was struck in commercial quantities in the Dammam structure. First exports of oil took place in 1938 and continued at very modest levels until after World War II. But the event that transformed prospects for the oil industry in Saudi Arabia was undoubtedly the discovery of the Ghawar field in 1948, which proved to be the world's largest single oil-bearing structure. In 1944, CASOC was renamed the Arabian American Oil Company (Aramco). Aramco became the largest American investment in any foreign country and provided the Saudi state with massive revenues. The company also participated in social and economic services such as paving roads, building schools, and offering job training.

Unlike other foreign oil companies, Aramco had good relations with the host government and with the local Saudi population. The bitter dispute in the early 1950s between the Iranian authority and British Petroleum was very different from the smooth cooperation between Aramco and the Saudi government. In 1950 the Saudi government and Aramco reached an agreement on a modified system of profit sharing, which introduced the notion of the 50/50 division between the host country and the concessionaire. In 1973, the Saudi government took a 25 percent stake in Aramco. A year later, this share was increased to 60 percent, and in 1980 it was amicably agreed that Aramco should become 100 percent Saudi-owned, with the date of ownership backdated to 1976. This friendly and nonconfrontational change of ownership helped the two sides to maintain their cordial cooperation. The nationalization of Aramco made the Saudi government the determinant of its oil policies.

This expanding Saudi role in determining the kingdom's oil policy was most apparent in the creation of the Organization of Petroleum Exporting Countries (OPEC) and in setting the level of production and prices. In 1960 Saudi Arabia joined Iran, Iraq, Kuwait, and Venezuela in creating OPEC. Since then it has been the kingdom's preference, where possible, to work within the OPEC decision-making structure. As a founder and a leader of OPEC, Riyadh has always sought to reconcile its national interests with those of fellow members and has been engaged in consensus-building not only among OPEC members but also between OPEC and other major oil producers such as Russia, Mexico, and Norway. In spite of these efforts by Saudi Arabia and other oil producers to reach a consensus and present a coherent and unified front, OPEC does not always speak with one voice.

Traditionally, the organization's market power has been viewed as a trade-off between maximizing price and maximizing market share. Within OPEC, countries like Algeria, Nigeria, and Indonesia, for instance, contain relatively large populations and relatively small oil reserves. These countries, therefore, have tended (with numerous exceptions) to favor a strategy of short-term revenue maximization and to have relatively low political/social tolerance for the pain caused by low oil revenues. Countries with small populations and large oil reserves like Kuwait, the United Arab Emirates, and Saudi Arabia, on the other hand, have tended (also with exceptions) to favor a strategy of long-term revenue maximization and generally have been in a stronger position to weather price declines.

For the most part Saudi Arabia has succeeded in keeping oil prices at reasonable levels. This Saudi success is due to the kingdom's massive hydrocarbon resources and its willingness to play the role of "swing" producer, adjusting its production to accommodate other producers' production. This Saudi policy is based on the contention that excessively high prices are not in the kingdom's best interest. One of the most salient reactions could be the development of alternative or competing energy sources, which could undermine the importance of petroleum. In this respect, it is known that when petroleum loses its competitive edge, it will be difficult to recover it even if prices subsequently decline. Another response to high prices could be the exploration and development of oil in high-cost areas in non-OPEC countries, which in turn could lead to an increase in supply and exert downward pressures on prices, causing them to collapse.

With the development of steady oil income in the 1950s and the huge jump in that income in the 1970s, the Saudi government had the necessary financial resources to provide its citizens with an array of benefits including education, health care, and public employment. In foreign policy, the massive oil revenues enabled the kingdom to play an assertive and central role in both regional and international policy, particularly the Arab-Israeli conflict. With oil money, Riyadh was able to punish its adversaries and reward its allies. Saudi Arabia led an Arab oil embargo against the United States for its support to Israel in the 1973 Yom Kippur War. On the other hand, Saudi Arabia used its financial resources to contain radical Arab nationalism stemming from Egypt and Syria. Indeed, Riyadh was a major force promoting moderation of Arab policy in most of the 1970s.

This use of oil revenues to assert a central Saudi role in regional and international policies, however, has substantially faded in recent years. Since 1980, the Saudi population has more than doubled, while oil revenues, in real terms, have fallen sharply. According to the Energy Information Administration, "In constant $2000, the Saudi oil revenues in 1972 were $19.3 billion. By 1980 they skyrocketed to $223.2 billion, only to fall to $50.4 billion in 2003."[15] Put differently, "Saudi Arabia's per capita oil revenues, in inflation-adjusted dollars, in 1980 averaged $23,820. By 2003 they dropped to $2,112."[16]

These diminishing financial capabilities have had two direct impacts on the Saudi role in the Arab-Israeli conflict. First, the Saudi ability to punish adversaries and cultivate allies has been reduced. The benign approach that Qatar and Oman have adopted toward Israel since the early 1990s demonstrates the weakening of Saudi leadership in its own backyard. Saudi Arabia is not able to get the other five members of the Gulf Cooperation Council to speak with one voice with regard to relations with Israel. Second, despite the massive arms sales that followed the Gulf War in 1991, reduced oil revenues have forced the Saudi government to defer payments to some foreign suppliers and contractors, including those in the defense sector. Stable oil prices at relatively higher levels since 2000 have given a substantial boost to the Saudi economy and the kingdom's ability to pursue its foreign policy objectives.

For more than half a century, the Saudi leaders have sought to balance and reconcile pressure from opposite directions. With its close relations with the United States, the kingdom has supported moderation and opposed radical Arab nationalism. On the other hand, considering its domestic and foreign constituencies as the birthplace of Islam, there are limits to how far the Saudis can advocate moderation and pro-American foreign policy. These contradictory forces have shaped the choices the Saudi leaders have made in their policy in the Arab-Israeli conflict and their attitude toward the Jewish state. Naturally, oil revenues have been employed to promote the Saudi strategy and policy.

Saudi Arabia and the Arab-Israeli Conflict

In 1932 Ibn Saud declared the creation of modern-day Saudi Arabia and pronounced himself a king. For several years thereafter he was busy fighting other tribal chiefs and expanding the frontiers of the new state. Indeed, it took Riyadh several decades to finalize border agreements with its neighbors. Thus the emergence of a distinctive Saudi foreign policy was slow and reflected the kingdom's rising needs to play a role on the international scene. A significant development in this direction was the meeting held between Ibn Saud and Franklin D. Roosevelt in 1945. In addition to discussing bilateral relations, according to Saudi sources, Roosevelt made two promises to Ibn Saud: he would never do anything that might prove hostile to the Arabs, and the U.S. government would make no changes in its basic policy on Palestine without consulting with both Jews and Arabs. These two promises underscore the Saudis' perception of their country's leading role in Arab affairs; their mistrust of a growing Jewish immigration to what was then Palestine, which eventually led to the creation of Israel; the centrality of the Palestinian question in Arab policy; and their favorite method of containing the perceived Jewish threat in the region—dependency on the United States.

The Saudis, like the majority of Arabs, resented the creation of a Jewish state at the heart of the Arab world. The kingdom, however, adopted a different approach from that chosen by secular leftist-nationalist Arab regimes such as Egypt, Syria, and later Iraq. Instead of relying on the Soviet Union in the struggle against Israel, Saudi Arabia sought to lobby Western countries, particularly the United States, to exert pressure on the Jewish state. This was in line with a Saudi perception that atheistic communism was a greater threat to the Muslims and Arabs than Zionism. The repeated Arab defeats, the miserable plight of the Palestinian people, and Israel's control of Jerusalem and Muslim holy sites have further deepened Saudi resentment toward Israel.

To sum up, the Saudi stand on the Arab-Israeli conflict is that the Israeli occupation of Arab land is the major reason for instability in the Middle East. A just and comprehensive solution to the conflict cannot be achieved unless Israel withdraws from the Arab territories occupied in the 1967 war, including the eastern part of Jerusalem, where holy Muslim sites are located. In addition, an independent and sovereign Palestinian state should be established, and a fair settlement to the Palestinian refugees should be reached. In pursuing these goals, Riyadh has employed economic, financial, and diplomatic methods. These include participating in the Arab economic boycott against Israel, voting in the United Nations and other international organizations against the Jewish state, giving substantial financial aid to the Palestinians and other Arabs in their struggle against Israel, and proposing their own initiative to solve the Arab-Israeli conflict.

Unlike other Arab states, such as Egypt, Syria, Iraq, and Jordan, Saudi Arabia's involvement in the Arab-Israeli conflict was slow, employing more diplomatic and financial methods and fewer military ones. Despite the kingdom's animosity toward Israel, the Saudi leaders were more concerned about the Soviet penetration of the Middle East and the alliance Moscow forged with Cairo, Damascus, and Baghdad than with the threat posed by Zionism. For most of the 1950s and 1960s, the Soviet presence was seen as a national security issue, where the survival of the regime was at stake, while Zionism was viewed as a foreign policy concern, albeit a significant one. Indeed, during this period Riyadh was accused of helping Israel indirectly by allying itself with the United States, the major supporter of the Jewish state. The kingdom sent token military units to Jordan in the 1948 war, but these units were not involved in hostilities. According to Hermann Eilts, "In the 1956 war Saudi Arabia lost two small unpopulated islands to Israel. These two islands, Tiran and Sanafir at the entrance of the Straits of Tiran, had been lent to Egypt in the context of the Arab Collective Security Pact."[17] Saudi Arabia quietly recovered these islands following the signing of the Egyptian-Israeli peace treaty in 1979.

The 1967 war was a turning point in Saudi Arabia's involvement in the Arab-Israeli conflict. The kingdom has since resumed a leading role in drawing Arab strategy toward Israel. Two major developments explain this drastic change. First, as part of the stunning Arab defeat, Israel captured the eastern part of Jerusalem and united the entire city under Israeli sovereignty and pronounced it its eternal capital. In other words, al-Aqsa Mosque was no longer under Muslim/Arab control. The kingdom, being the birthplace of Islam, could not afford to be indifferent to this new situation. King Faisal, then in power, had prayed in al-Aqsa Mosque several years earlier and expressed his strong desire to revisit the holy site when Muslim sovereignty was restored. His wish was never fulfilled.

The second important outcome of the 1967 war was the defeat of radical Arab nationalism led by President Gamal Abd al-Nasser of Egypt. Before the war, the Arab world was sharply divided into two camps: the pro-Western conservative regimes and the radical socialist-nationalist states. This Arab cold war reached its peak in the proxy war between the Egyptian and Saudi armies in Yemen, where the two states supported opposite sides. Egypt's defeat in the 1967 war ended its involvement in the Yemeni conflict. Cairo became more concerned about liberating the territories it lost to Israel than supporting Arab revolutionary movements. Equally important, the heavy military defeat and the loss of Suez Canal revenues dealt a heavy blow to the Egyptian economy. Egypt became increasingly dependent on foreign aid and labor remittance from Arab oil-producing countries.

The Khartoum conference, convened in September 1967, was the first Arab summit to be held after the June 1967 war. The meeting demonstrated the growing role Saudi Arabia came to play in the Arab-Israeli conflict. It officially ended the undeclared cold war between the radical and conservative Arab states. The more confident Saudi leadership reached out to the badly weakened Egypt. Two resolutions adopted by the participant heads of states deserve special attention. First, the Arab leaders agreed to unite their political efforts on the international and diplomatic levels to eliminate the effects of the war and to ensure the withdrawal of Israeli forces from the occupied Arab lands. "The main principles that shaped the Arab stand were no peace, no recognition, and no negotiations with Israel as well as adherence to the rights of the Palestinian people in their country."[18] Second, King Faisal took the initiative to offer substantial financial assistance to the "frontline" states (Egypt, Syria, Lebanon, Jordan, and the Palestinians). The king persuaded Kuwait and Libya, two conservative oil-producing countries, to join in that effort. The goal was to compensate the "frontline" states for the losses of land and revenue resulting from the war.

These resolutions underscored some of the main constant characteristics of Saudi Arabia's stand on the Arab-Israeli conflict. First, the kingdom would not recognize the state of Israel as long as the Muslim holy sites in Jerusalem were under Israeli control. Second, despite the strong rejection of any negotiation with Israel, diplomatic and political efforts were not ruled out. Meanwhile, military force was not seen as the exclusive method for liberating the occupied Arab territories. Third, the Saudi role was mainly, if not exclusively, to provide financial support to the "frontline" states and the Palestinians. These financial resources have been utilized to strengthen moderation and pro-Western Arab regimes and to weaken extremism and radical Palestinian groups and Arab states. Fourth, a direct Saudi role in the military confrontation with Israel was not considered. The kingdom has never been an Arab frontline state. There has never been direct military confrontation with Israel.

The rapprochement between Riyadh and Cairo was further enhanced in 1970, when Anwar al-Sadat assumed the presidency after Nasser's death. During the almost two decades that he dominated Arab policy, Nasser opened the door for Soviet penetration of the Middle East and attacked Saudi strategy and interest. In contrast, Sadat always showed signs of being open to working with the United States, distancing Egypt from the Soviet Union, and allying with Saudi Arabia and other conservative Arab states. Little wonder, King Faisal sought to de-radicalize Egypt by pressing Sadat to get rid of the thousands of Soviet advisors who were invited in by his predecessor, Nasser. By eliminating the Soviet civilian and military presence in Egypt, King Faisal was hoping to convince the United States to adopt a balanced stand on the Arab-Israeli conflict. Faisal argued that if Egypt were to loosen its connection with the Soviet Union, the United States would be more willing to press Israel for a favorable settlement. Sadat agreed, and shortly after he became president, Soviet advisors were ordered to leave Egypt.

King Faisal tried to press the United States to reciprocate by adopting a more evenhanded attitude toward the Arab-Israeli conflict. Adeed Dawisha notes, "The king argued that justifying American support to Israel by reference to the Soviet presence in Egypt was no longer a valid stance; on the contrary, continued American support for post-1967 war Israel would be interpreted by Arab states as aggression by proxy."[19] The Arabs, the argument goes, would be further alienated from the United States, and the Saudi government's pro-West stand and close cooperation with Washington would be sharply criticized.

Despite heavy Saudi lobbying, the United States did not alter its basic approach to the Middle East. King Faisal felt personally deceived and embarrassed before Sadat. Consequently, Saudi Arabia's earlier moderation and insistence on the utilization of diplomatic means was gradually replaced by a belief that only through the use of military force and economic coercion could

Arabs liberate the territories they lost to Israel in 1967. This belief set the stage for the 1973 war and the employment of oil as a political weapon by Saudi Arabia and other Arab oil-producing countries.

In the early 1970s, Saudi Arabia increasingly placed its weight behind improving the Egyptian and Syrian military capabilities. An Egyptian-Syrian-Saudi triangle was forged where the three countries consulted periodically on strategic and military issues. This coordination between the Saudi financial muscle and the Egyptian and Syrian military forces produced one of the most successful military campaigns that the Arabs have ever launched against Israel. In addition to the initial military success, the kingdom led other Arab oil producers in imposing an oil embargo on the United States and a few other countries for their support to Israel.

Oil as a Political Weapon

With a relatively small population that long lacked adequate military traditions, Saudi Arabia has never presented itself as a military adversary to Israel, and its contribution to Arab armies in the series of Arab-Israeli wars has been understandably symbolic. The main assets the kingdom has are its massive hydrocarbon resources. With approximately 25 percent of total world oil reserves, Saudi Arabia is the global oil superpower. Given these substantial resources as well as the fact that the global economy runs on oil, many Arabs have called for the employment of this strategic commodity in their struggle against Israel and the main Western powers that support it. Already in 1946, at a conference in Bludan (Syria), the Arab League debated the use of oil as a weapon in its conflict with the Zionist program.[20]

The subsequent Arab-Israeli wars have further intensified the debate over using oil as a political weapon. Thus, in the 1956 war and the 1967 war, limited embargoes were implemented with little effect. In 1956, the United States was able to compensate for the embargo against Britain and France from its own domestic production. In 1967, Saudi government ordered Aramco to stop oil supplies to the United States and the United Kingdom, even though the kingdom had been fighting Egypt by proxy in Yemen for years. This embargo lasted for only four weeks and was intended primarily as a show of solidarity with fellow Arab states and to appease outraged Saudi and Arab public opinion, which ascribed the stunning Israeli military success to U.S. complicity. Meanwhile, Riyadh continued to ship jet fuel to U.S. forces in Vietnam. A major reason for this halfhearted and hesitant implementation of the 1967 oil embargo was the Saudi leaders' conviction that oil should not be mixed with policy. Rather, the Saudi leaders preferred to use oil as a "positive weapon" to build up the military and economic strength of the Arab world. Accordingly, the 1967 oil embargo had little impact and was largely ineffective.

In the aftermath of the 1967 war, several developments had drastically altered the environment under which the 1973 oil embargo was initiated and implemented. Internally, Saudi Arabia gradually expanded its control over Aramco, the main oil company in charge of exploring and developing Saudi oil. In 1973, the Saudi government took a 25 percent stake in Aramco. A year later, this share was increased to 60 percent, and in 1980 it was amicably agreed that Aramco should become 100 percent Saudi-owned, with the date of ownership backdated to 1976. Before this Saudi takeover of Aramco, the authorities in Riyadh had repeatedly sought Aramco's parent companies' aid to lobby the U.S. administration on the Arab-Israeli conflict. These efforts were not successful. The nationalization of Aramco made the Saudi government the determinant of its oil policies. Regionally, Sadat's assumption of the presidency in Egypt consolidated the rapprochement between Cairo and Riyadh, which started shortly after the 1967 war. The Arab world, dominated by the Cairo-Damascus-Riyadh axis, was very different from the polarization that characterized Arab policy in the 1960s. Internationally, Western dependency on oil supplies from the Persian Gulf reached one of the highest points in 1973. The global oil market was essentially a seller's market. The combined impact of these developments created the appropriate conditions to make the 1973 oil embargo effective.

After expelling the Soviet advisors from Egypt, King Faisal tried unsuccessfully to press the United States to adopt a balanced stand on the Arab-Israeli conflict and to use its leverage on Israel to relinquish its occupation of Arab lands. The lack of progress on the diplomatic path convinced the Egyptian president that the military option was the only way to break the diplomatic stalemate. Sadat coordinated his military plans with President Assad of Syria and King Faisal of Saudi Arabia, whom he visited shortly before hostilities broke out. Faisal endorsed the joint Egyptian/Syrian decision to go to war and promised to weigh in by using oil as a weapon.

On October 6, 1973, Yom Kippur, the Egyptian and Syrian armies launched a coordinated attack on Israeli positions across the Suez Canal and the Golan Heights. This was the first time that Arabs managed to mount a surprise attack on Israel. Initially they enjoyed strategic and military advantages and were able to inflict substantial losses on Israel's military capabilities in terms of both personnel and equipment. For the first few days, Israel was losing the war.

In response to these Israeli losses and Arab advances, the United States decided to move decisively to change the course of the war. On the fourth day, President Nixon ordered a massive airlift of American arms to Israel. Within a few days the United States was providing Israel with a thousand tons of war materiel a day. "All in all," writes George Lenczowski, "Israel received a total of more than 22,000 tons of equipment including forty F-4 Phantoms, thirty-eight A-4 Skyhawks, twelve C-I30 transports, tanks, spare parts, and ammunition."[21] In addition to these military supplies, Nixon asked Congress to appropriate $2.2 billion in emergency aid to Israel, including $1.5 billion in outright grants.

This massive American aid to Israel outraged the Arab public opinion and put unbearable pressure on the Arab oil producers to employ the oil weapon against the United States. Thus a few days after the Yom Kippur War began, Kuwait called for a conference of the Organization of Arab Petroleum Exporting Countries (OAPEC) to determine the Arab response to American support to Israel. The participants in the conference agreed to reduce their oil production by at least 5 percent from their average September output and to make further cuts of 5 percent every month thereafter until a total evacuation of Israeli forces from Arab territories was completed and the legitimate rights of the Palestinians were restored.[22] Meanwhile, states that supported the Arabs actively or took significant steps to pressure Israel to withdraw "would be exempted from the cuts and would receive their full supply based on September imports."[23]

This progressive cut in oil production resulted in a sharp reduction in oil supplies in the global markets. By December 1973, Saudi oil production had fallen by 30 percent from its level before the October war. Simultaneously, the price of oil was abruptly and considerably increased from $2.83 in 1973 to an average of $10.41 in 1974.[24] This massive increase in the price of oil was an unintended result of the embargo and resulted in substantial increases in Saudi Arabia's oil revenues. Within a matter of months, the kingdom became one of the richest countries in the world. Consequently, Riyadh occupied center stage on the international scene and played a significant role in the global economy. Furthermore, Saudi leaders used their financial muscle to strengthen their position on regional issues, particularly the Arab-Israeli conflict. In 1974 King Faisal took the initiative to establish an annual contribution of $2.5 billion from the oil-rich countries to the "frontline" states and the PLO. It is no wonder, then, that since 1973 most of the decisions related to this conflict have been made in consultation with Riyadh.

American response to this unprecedented oil embargo ranged from peace-

ful appeals to lift the embargo to threats to use military force to occupy oil
fields in the Persian Gulf. One month after the embargo was imposed, Secretary of State Henry Kissinger visited Riyadh and tried to persuade Saudi
leaders to resume oil shipments. His plea proved of no avail. A few weeks later,
Kissinger announced that the United States would not rule out the use of military force to secure oil supplies from the Persian Gulf region. Similar threats
were made by Senator J. William Fulbright, chairman of the Foreign Relations
Committee. According to a declassified British government document made
public in late 2003, "the United States considered launching airborne troops
to seize oil fields in Saudi Arabia, Kuwait, and Abu Dhabi (UAE)."[25] Eventually
Nixon sent a letter to King Faisal pledging his total commitment to a peaceful
solution to the Middle East conflict based on the implementation of United
Nations Security Council resolutions 242 and 338, both establishing the principle of exchanging territory for peace.

These American appeals, combined with heavy Egyptian lobbying as well as
some progress on separation of Israeli and Arab troops, eventually convinced
Saudi leaders to lift the embargo. Initially the Saudi position was that the oil
embargo should not be lifted until Israel withdrew from the territories occupied during the 1967 war. Saudi Arabia and other oil producers gradually
mollified their attitude by demanding that Israel begin its withdrawal. Disengagement agreements between Israel and both Egypt and Syria finally led to
the resumption of oil shipments. In January 1974, the United States brokered
a disengagement agreement between Egypt and Israel. Sadat tried to encourage an Arab consensus to end the oil sanctions, but King Faisal declined to lift
the oil embargo until a similar Syrian-Israeli disengagement agreement was
reached. When this was accomplished in 1974, all restrictions on oil exports
were removed.

The use of oil as a political weapon during and after the Yom Kippur War
has had a fundamental impact on the Saudi domestic and foreign policies.
In the 1970s and early 1980s, the Saudi government enjoyed unprecedented
wealth, which enabled it to embark on ambitious social and economic development. Riyadh rose to a new position of prominence in the Arab world. Due
to its massive financial resources, Saudi Arabia has become a central player in
the Arab-Israeli conflict and in the efforts to negotiate a peaceful settlement.
The embargo brought the kingdom into confrontation with its closest international ally, the United States. This confrontation probably was the biggest
setback in Saudi-American relations until the terrorist attacks in September
2001.

Saudi Arabia and the Peace Process

Saudi Arabia's attitude toward Israel can be described as cautious acceptance. Riyadh participated, in a symbolic way, in some of the fighting against Israel; endorsed the "no peace, no negotiations, and no recognition" resolutions of the Khartoum Summit in 1967; supported the Palestinian struggle against Israel; and gave billions of dollars to the frontline states. On the other hand, since the mid-1970s Saudi Arabia has backed American-brokered peace negotiations; allied itself with Arab states and leaders who advocated a peaceful settlement with Israel, such as Sadat of Egypt and King Hussein of Jordan; and opposed those who called for the destruction of Israel, like Saddam Hussein of Iraq and Gaddafi of Libya. Moreover, periodically the kingdom has hosted delegations of prominent American Jews in efforts to explain its position on Arab-Israeli issues and to improve its image in the United States. Finally, Saudi leaders openly sponsored two "peace plans" with Israel. The first one was introduced by Crown Prince Fahd in 1981, and the other one was initiated by Crown Prince Abdullah in 2002. The provisions of the two plans explicitly include a conditional recognition of Israel. These apparent Saudi policies suggest that since the mid-1970s the kingdom has been willing to recognize Israel without breaking Arab ranks.

After the Yom Kippur War, two characteristics shaped the Middle East conflict. First, given the military balance of power between Israel and its Arab adversaries as well as the strong and unquestionable American commitment to the security of Israel, the Arab strategic goal was very limited. The Egyptian and Syrian objectives were not to try to threaten or challenge the mere existence of Israel. Rather, the goal was to achieve a limited military victory that would break the diplomatic stalemate that dominated the region following the 1967 war. This goal was partially achieved. However, the diplomatic efforts to reach a peaceful settlement of the conflict went nowhere. By the mid-1970s it became clear that the outcome of the Yom Kippur War did not create the right conditions for a diplomatic breakthrough. Second, Saudi Arabia increasingly emerged as the main powerbroker in inter-Arab policy. The accumulation of unprecedented wealth enabled the kingdom to occupy center stage on the Middle East and the international scenes.

Frustrated by the fruitless efforts to reach a comprehensive peace, President Sadat embarked on a unilateral path to end the conflict with Israel. In November 1977, he announced his intention to visit Jerusalem and address the Israeli Knesset (parliament). This announcement was disturbing to the Saudi leadership for three reasons: First, since Sadat's rise to the presidency, Saudi leaders had cemented strong economic, political, and even personal relations with their Egyptian counterparts. Riyadh provided Cairo with billions of dollars in military and economic aid. Nevertheless, Sadat failed to consult with the Saudi leaders regarding his new strategy. Indeed, shortly before announcing his decision to go to Israel, Sadat visited the kingdom but kept his hosts in the dark. Second, Sadat's initiative shattered the near Arab consensus, which the Saudis had worked hard to create and maintain. Sadat's move was immediately and strongly denounced by Syria, the PLO, and even Jordan. Other Arab parties—notably Iraq, Libya, and Algeria—expressed similar fiery opposition. Third, the United States strongly welcomed and supported Sadat's initiative. Indeed, a proposed peace negotiation between Egypt and Israel would create a firm partnership between Cairo and Washington and would eliminate any opportunity for the Soviet influence to return to Egypt. This is exactly what the Saudis had sought to achieve since the mid-1950s.

Confronted with this sharp polarization of the Arab world, Riyadh had to take into consideration several factors in formulating its stand on the Egyptian move. The Saudis did not wish to further antagonize the radical Arab states that might facilitate and deepen Soviet penetration of the Middle East. At the same time the kingdom did not want to antagonize and isolate Egypt, the most populous Arab country. Finally, Saudi Arabia did not want to oppose its main international ally, the United States. Given these contradictory considerations, the Saudi leadership adopted a vague low-key position. Instead of clearly allying itself with one side or the other, the Saudis decided to wait and see.

This uncommitted stand was demonstrated in the kingdom's response to the Camp David accords signed by Egypt, Israel, and the United States. After intense negotiations that lasted almost two weeks, Anwar al-Sadat, Menachem Begin, and Jimmy Carter signed two documents. The first one outlined the framework of an Egyptian-Israeli peace treaty based on the return of Sinai to Egyptian sovereignty, security arrangements, and provisions for normalization of relations. The other document highlighted general principles for promoting a settlement of the Palestinian question. Essentially this second document was vague and deferred the main issues of contention to negotiations on the "final status."

The official Saudi reaction to the Camp David accords was phrased in such a way that it could be read by the radicals as condemnation of Sadat and seen by Egypt and the United States as an expression of understanding for Sadat's efforts. Riyadh declared that the Camp David accords could not be considered a final formula for peace because they did not state Israel's intention to withdraw from all the territories occupied in 1967, they failed to stipulate the right of the Palestinians to an independent state, and they ignored the role of the PLO. On the other hand, writes Jacob Goldberg, "The kingdom asserted that it has no right to interfere in the internal affairs of any Arab country nor to dispute its right to restore its occupied territory by armed struggle or through peaceful efforts, provided that does not violate Arab consensus."[26]

This mild and uncommitted Saudi stand did not satisfy Egypt's opponents, who called for an Arab summit to formulate a response to the Camp David accords. By the time the Baghdad summit convened in November 1978, the Saudis were under heavy pressure from other Arab countries to participate and endorse a strong Arab rejection of Sadat's move. Still, hoping for an Arab reconciliation, the Saudis sought an opportunity for Egypt to reconsider its course. Under heavy Saudi pressure, the summit rejected the calls for immediate sanctions against Egypt and condemnation of the United States. Instead, it decided not to endorse the Camp David accords and to appeal to Sadat to renounce his signature. A mission was to go to Cairo to try to persuade the Egyptian president to return to the Arab fold and join an all-Arab strategy and to inform him that the summit was "prepared to place a vast fund of up to $9 billion at the disposal of the 'frontline' countries to continue the struggle, $5 billion of which would be earmarked for Egypt."[27] Finally, the participants decided to expel Egypt from the Arab League if Sadat signed a peace treaty with Israel.

A few months after the Baghdad summit, an Egyptian-Israeli peace treaty was officially signed—the first ever between Israel and an Arab state. This successful conclusion of Sadat's strategy of pursuing a unilateral peace with Israel intensified the pressure on Saudi leaders to clarify where they stood. The time for an unspecified and uncommitted low-profile approach was over. Riyadh had to choose between supporting the Egyptian-Israeli peace plan, sponsored by the United States, or joining the bulk of Arab states led by Iraq, Syria, and the PLO. This moment of choice came when an Arab meeting at the ministerial level was held in Baghdad to give final approval for the sanctions on Egypt, which Arab heads of states agreed on, following the signing of the Camp David accords. After intense negotiations Riyadh decided to join the radical Arab states in imposing diplomatic and economic sanctions on Egypt. Thus the majority of Arab states agreed to the immediate withdrawal of Arab ambassadors from Cairo, the severance of political and diplomatic relations, and the cessation of all financial and technical aid.

A major reason for the Saudi decision to oppose Egypt, the most populous Arab state, and the United States, the kingdom's closest international ally, was the development in Iran. The signing of the Egyptian-Israeli peace treaty occurred almost simultaneously with the Iranian revolution. One lesson the Saudis learned from the ouster of the shah of Iran was that the United States had failed to protect one of its closest allies from internal opposition. The Saudi public was strongly opposed to any peace overture to Israel, and Saudi leaders did not want the experience of the shah to be repeated in their country. Furthermore, the fall of the Pahlavi regime and the chaos that accompanied it meant that Iraq had become a more powerful force in the region. The idea of antagonizing Baghdad did not appeal to the Saudis. This was further reinforced by the close cooperation between Iraq, Syria, and the PLO. In other words, Riyadh's vulnerability domestically and regionally dictated that it follow the Arab consensus, thereby decreasing its exposure to internal and external subversion by radical Arabs and the new threat posed by the Iranian revolution.

Despite the kingdom's participation in the diplomatic and economic sanctions on Egypt, the Saudi leaders were never enthusiastic about completely isolating Egypt. They did not want to sabotage their close ties with Cairo. Thus the flow of remittances to Egypt from Egyptian nationals working in the kingdom was allowed to continue unabated, and low-level contacts with Egyptian officials were maintained. The outbreak of the Iran-Iraq War in 1980 and the creation of new alliances in the Middle East drastically altered the strategic dynamics in the region. The Iraq-Syria-PLO axis was broken, and the importance of Egypt as a major regional power was felt. More contacts with Egypt were established, and by 1987 diplomatic ties between Cairo and Riyadh were officially resumed.

To sum up, Saudi opposition to Egyptian efforts to negotiate a treaty with Israel should not be seen as rejection of a peaceful settlement of the Arab-Israeli conflict. Rather, the Saudis, like other Arabs, refused the unilateral approach Sadat had adopted and preferred a comprehensive agreement that would guarantee Israeli withdrawal from all occupied Arab territories and the realization of Palestinian rights. The Saudis wanted to contain the polarization of the Arab world. Not surprisingly, the Saudis formulated their own peace plans. In 1981 and 2002, the kingdom presented its own vision of a peaceful end to the Arab-Israeli conflict.

Fahd Plan

The Saudis opposed both the Camp David accords of 1978 and the subsequent Egyptian-Israeli treaty of 1979. They believed that President Sadat had signed a separate peace with Israel in return for vague and unspecified promises of Palestinian autonomy. The unsuccessful negotiations on the issue of Palestinian national rights further reinforced this conviction and deepened the division within the Arab world. In the early 1980s, the Arab world was sharply polarized into the handful of countries who supported Egypt and the majority who opposed it. This polarization shattered the hope of Arab consensus, which the Saudis worked hard to create. Furthermore, the position of Saudi Arabia and other moderate Arab states, the allies of the United States, was closely watched. Under these conditions the Saudis felt they had to choose between two courses of action: either pursuing the policy of isolating and punishing Egypt or coming up with their own plan, which would call for a comprehensive peace between all the Arab countries and Israel. The problem with the first alternative was that it would further strengthen the Arab radicals, deepen the polarization of the Arab world, and add more fuel to the rift in the relations with the United States. The Saudis chose to formulate their own vision for a comprehensive peace in the Middle East. This Saudi proposal was announced in 1981 and became known as the Fahd Plan.

In addition to Riyadh's desire to overcome the deep division in the Arab world, several other developments encouraged the Saudis to formulate and pursue their own vision of a peaceful settlement of the Arab-Israeli conflict. First, the Egyptian-Israeli negotiation regarding the Palestinian national rights reached a deadlock. Egyptian negotiators could not succeed in getting their Israeli counterparts to agree on any concrete steps to grant the Palestinians what most Arabs saw as legitimate rights. Second, President Carter lost the election to Ronald Reagan. The two American presidents had different styles and interests in negotiating an Arab-Israeli peace agreement. Carter was personally involved and considered making peace in the Middle East as an almost religious mission. Accordingly, he played a crucial role in the Egyptian-Israeli negotiations that led to the signing of the Camp David accords and the peace treaty. Reagan, on the other hand, was less committed to this path of making peace between Israel and its Arab neighbors. Third, on October 6, 1981, Sadat was assassinated by Muslim fanatics in the midst of a parade celebrating the anniversary of the Yom Kippur War. Sadat was assassinated partly because of failure of his domestic policy and partly because of the foreign policy strategy he pursued. This violent removal of the architect of the Egyptian peace process raised strong doubts about the validity of the strategy and technique Sadat had chosen to make peace with Israel. It showed that the Arab masses, including the Egyptians, strongly rejected a unilateral approach to the Arab-Israeli peace process. The obvious alternative was a proposal that would outline a framework for a comprehensive peace between all the Arabs and Israel. This was the thrust of the Saudi proposal known as the Fahd Plan.

The Fahd Plan consisted of eight points for a "just peace," as the Saudis saw it. It called for Israel to withdraw from all Arab territory occupied in the 1967 war and to dismantle settlements. It also demanded the creation of an independent Palestinian state with Jerusalem as its capital and a guarantee of the right of Palestinian refugees to return to their homes or be compensated. The most striking part of the plan was an implicit recognition of Israel by confirming that all states in the region have the right to live in peace. This was a fundamental departure from traditional Saudi policy. Equally important, the plan marked Saudi Arabia's first public attempt to play an active role in resolving the Arab-Israeli conflict.

The reaction to the plan varied from one state to another. The Reagan administration described the proposal as a positive step. Israeli leaders acknowledged that the Saudi readiness to recognize Israel should be viewed as a positive development. Still, Tel Aviv summarily rejected the proposal. The establishment of an independent Palestinian state with Jerusalem as its capital, an Israeli withdrawal from all Arab territories occupied in the 1967 war, and the right of return to the millions of Palestinian refugees were conditions that Israeli leaders could not swallow.

The Arab response to the Fahd Plan was not monolithic. Naturally, the Egyptians saw the proposal as an alternative to their own course and showed no enthusiasm for it. Given his long history of secret negotiations with the Israelis, the close alliance with the United States, and shared domestic and foreign policy orientations with conservative Arab regimes, King Hussein of Jordan was the strongest supporter of the Saudi initiative. The PLO response was mixed. The Palestinians were reluctant to accept the idea of recognizing and making peace with Israel. The Fahd Plan, however, provided the potential to become a full-fledged Arab peace initiative. The staunch opposition came from Syria, which officially maintained that a settlement of the Arab-Israeli conflict under existing conditions of Arab weakness would not lead to peace but would simply constitute an Arab surrender.

Given these opposite reactions, the Arabs failed to endorse the Fahd Plan in their summit, held in Fez, Morocco, in November 1981. Several heads of states abstained, including the leaders of Algeria, Iraq, Libya, and Syria. Others had reservations on some provisions, and a few supported the plan. Accordingly, after a short session, the attending Arab leaders decided to suspend the meeting until a later date, thus shelving the plan while keeping the project alive. Less than a year later (September 1982) at the reconvened Arab summit, the Saudi proposal was accepted as a set of principles that constituted the Arab framework for peace with Israel. Despite this Arab endorsement, the plan went nowhere. Instead of focusing on searching for a peaceful settlement to the Arab-Israeli conflict, the whole region was preoccupied with the Iran-Iraq War (1980–88) and then the Gulf War (1990–91). Two decades after Crown Prince Fahd introduced his vision for a comprehensive peace in the Middle East, his brother Crown Prince Abdullah presented a similar plan to pursue the same goal. Ironically, the Abdullah Plan did not fare any better than Fahd Plan.

Abdullah Plan

Two recent developments have provided the Saudis with strong incentives to resume an active role in the Arab-Israeli conflict and present another peace proposal. First, violence between the Palestinians and Israelis has substantially escalated following the outbreak of al-Aqsa intifada (uprising), which began in September 2000 when the Israeli leader Ariel Sharon visited a Muslim holy site in Jerusalem. The growing number of victims created a sense of despair on both sides. Furthermore, the images of Israeli bulldozers demolishing Palestinian homes and American-built jet fighters or helicopters firing on Palestinians have inflamed the Arabs' hatred of Jews and the rage against the United States. Second, the September 11, 2001, terrorist attacks in the United States dealt a heavy blow to American-Saudi relations. Osama bin Laden was a Saudi citizen, and fifteen of the nineteen hijackers held Saudi passports. Thus the Saudi image was badly tarnished, and many influential members inside and outside the American administration called for a reassessment and an examination of the close relations between Washington and Riyadh. Feeling the pressure, the Saudi leaders thought a conciliatory gesture toward Israel could take some of the heat and improve their country's image.

Within this context, Crown Prince Abdullah formulated his proposal for a comprehensive peace in the Middle East. After a long consultation with Egypt and Jordan it was decided that Riyadh should take the initiative. In an interview published in the *New York Times* in February 2002, the Crown Prince talked about the need for a bold step to end the Arab-Israeli conflict. A few weeks later, the Saudi plan was debated and endorsed by the other Arab leaders in their fourteenth summit, held in Beirut in March 2002. The Abdullah Plan is similar to the Fahd Plan in calling for a complete Israeli withdrawal from Arab territories occupied since the 1967 war, including full withdrawal from the Syrian Golan Heights and the remaining occupied parts of southern Lebanon, the establishment of an independent Palestinian state in the West Bank and the Gaza Strip with Jerusalem as its capital, confirming the Palestinian refugees' right to return to their land in Israel. In return, the Abdullah Plan goes one step further than the Fahd Plan. Instead of a mere recognition of the Jewish state to exist in the Middle East, Crown Prince Abdullah offered Israel full peace, including political, economic, and cultural normalization. Based on this initiative, the Arabs agreed to give Israel a complete integration in the region. Zvi Bar'el of the Israeli newspaper *Haaretz* foresaw "falafel in Damascus and stalls in the international market of Dubai; an Israeli flag in Riyadh; programming engineers in Bahrain, and gas from Qatar to Israel."[28]

The Abdullah Plan received a mixed response from the Arab world. The initial reaction was positive. The Palestinians supported the proposal. For most Arab states—especially Qatar, Oman, Mauritania, Morocco, and Tunisia, which had had some level of relations with Israel—there was no reason to reject the plan. Israel posed a problem to them only inasmuch as it aroused passions among their people, and any solution that had a Saudi stamp of approval—and particularly that of Crown Prince Abdullah, who has a reputation as an Arab nationalist—was considered a significant development. Jordan and Egypt had a clear interest in the initiative, since it served to validate the agreements they had reached earlier with Israel and for which they had been excoriated by many Arabs. Syria and Iraq did not reject the plan, and Lebanon voiced its demand that the more than 300,000 Palestinians living in refugee camps there should move to Israel once an agreement was signed. Libyan leader Muammar Gaddafi rejected the plan, saying it was "shocking and entailed cheap bargaining."[29]

The United States was slow to accept the plan. The Bush administration's caution appeared to derive in part from its determination not to end up where former president Bill Clinton had, with high hopes for peace turning abruptly into a wave of violence. Moreover, there was a widespread presumption that the administration wanted to keep the Israeli-Palestinian conflict on a back burner while it weighed its options for ousting the Iraqi dictator, Saddam Hussein. After some hesitation, Washington decided that the Saudi plan had the potential to end the violence and, accordingly, praised Crown Prince Abdullah and urged other leaders to build on his initiative to address the cause of peace in the Middle East.

Finally, the Israelis tried not to be outmaneuvered by the Saudis. Israeli president Moshe Katzav, whose role is largely ceremonial, offered to travel to Riyadh or, alternatively, to receive Crown Prince Abdullah in Jerusalem in order to hear the details of his proposal firsthand. Similarly, Prime Minister Ariel Sharon was skeptical about the Saudi proposal. Sharon announced that he was not going to disregard the Saudi plan completely, even though he did not attach a lot of credence to it. Sharon stated that the Israeli government would not leave any stone unturned if there was a chance for peace. Furthermore,

Sharon expressed his desire to go to the Arab summit in Beirut to explain the Israeli position. Finally, Israeli officials noted that no formal proposal had been made, complaining that the Saudis had gone to the press instead of contacting Israel directly through established diplomatic channels. They also suggested that "the true goal was to throw Prime Minister Sharon on the defense diplomatically, by putting him in the position of rejecting a vague but seemingly innovative offer."[30]

With regard to the substance of the Saudi plan, the Israeli government viewed the Arabs' call for the return of refugees, the division of Jerusalem, and an Israeli withdrawal to the 1967 borders as a nonstarter. According to an official statement issued by the Israeli government, "A decision calling for a complete withdrawal to the 1967 lines makes negotiations superfluous. Withdrawal to the 1967 borders is an absolute blow to Israel's security."[31] Given these fundamental differences between the Israeli and Arab visions for peace in the Middle East, the Abdullah Plan, like the Fahd Plan two decades earlier, was gradually shelved.

Concluding Remarks

Several conclusions can be drawn from the above discussion of Saudi Arabia's stand on the Arab-Israeli conflict. First, Saudi leaders have advocated a peaceful settlement with Israel since the early 1970s. This peaceful settlement is conditioned on Israeli withdrawal from all Arab territories occupied in the 1967 war, the establishment of an independent Palestinian state with Jerusalem as its capital, and confirmation of the Palestinian refugees' right to return or to receive compensation. The Saudis are then willing to recognize and normalize relations with Israel.

Second, the Saudi contribution to the Arab-Israeli conflict has been mainly financial and diplomatic, not military. For several decades, Saudi Arabia has used its oil revenues to provide substantial financial aid to Palestinian organizations, particularly the PLO, and to frontline states. It is true that Riyadh funded arms deals, which enabled the Egyptians, Syrians, and Palestinians to fight Israel. But it is also true that the kingdom has used its financial leverage to reward moderation and punish extremism (as defined by Saudi officials). For example, Saudi money facilitated the shift in Egyptian policy in the early 1970s from a pro-Soviet to a pro-American approach. Similarly, Saudi money did not go to extremist Marxist Palestinian organizations. Instead, the PLO, which generally adopts a less extremist stand on the conflict with Israel, received the bulk of the Saudi funds. On the diplomatic front, the Saudis have always sought to pressure the United States to open dialogue with the PLO and to take a balanced and evenhanded approach.

Third, until the September 11 terrorist attacks in the United States, when Islamic fundamentalism became the main issue of contention between Washington and Riyadh, American support to Israel constituted the main obstacle in U.S.-Saudi relations. Since the 1945 meeting between President Roosevelt and King Ibn Saud, the Palestinian question has been discussed. The Saudis have sought to use their close relations with Washington to influence its policy in the Middle East. For the most part, the Saudis have not succeeded and have been frustrated by what they perceive as American bias for Israel and against the Arabs. Occasionally, the Saudis and other Arabs have sought to rely on European countries rather than the United States to promote their rights. This strategy, however, is restrained by the presumption that although the Europeans have a more balanced view of the Arab-Israeli conflict than the Americans, their capabilities are limited.

Fourth, Israeli officials have generally viewed Saudi Arabia as an Islamic fanatic state that uses its massive resources to promote and fund hate against the Jewish state. Israeli supporters in the United States have always sought to undermine the close cooperation the kingdom has had with the United States. Despite this animosity, Saudi Arabia is not Israel's number one enemy. On the Israeli list, countries such as Islamic Iran, Iraq before the 2003 war, and Syria are ahead of Saudi Arabia.

Fifth, the Saudis' opposition to Israel was not enough to ensure their wholehearted support for the Palestinians. Indeed, while the kingdom has always been a strong advocate of the Palestinian cause (the right of return for the Palestinian refugees and the need to establish a sovereign Palestinian state), the relationship with the Palestinian leadership has not been always smooth. Before the 1967 war, the Saudis were not deeply involved with the Palestinian movement. In part this was because the Palestinian activists of the day were typically either leftists or followers of Egypt's Nasser. Following the war, the kingdom emerged as a central player in the Middle East conflict and became increasingly involved with the Palestinians. Riyadh has always been concerned about Palestinian radicalism, particularly the strong leftist and nationalist tones in the 1960s and 1970s. Accordingly, the Saudis established strong ties with the mainstream group within the Palestinian movement led by Yasser Arafat. Despite the generous financial support the Saudis provided Arafat, they were suspicious of his intentions and policies. This Saudi suspicion proved true in the Gulf War, when the Palestinian leader supported the Iraqi invasion of

Kuwait. For the next several years the kingdom froze any relationship with the PLO. Indeed, for several years following the Gulf War Arafat was not welcomed in the kingdom. Nevertheless, Saudi Arabia has continued to lobby the international community and the United States on behalf of the Palestinian cause. Since the late 1990s, relations between Riyadh and the PLO/Palestinian Authority have been resumed.

Finally, despite the two Saudi peace plans and the kingdom's endorsement of peaceful negotiations between different Arab parties and Israel, Riyadh is likely to be slow in making peace with the Jewish state. The Israeli flag is likely to fly in many Arab capitals before it flies in Riyadh. The Saudi traditions of consensus building and their perception of their country as the guardian of Islam and Arabism are likely to make Riyadh very cautious in any recognition of and normalization with Tel Aviv. Other Gulf monarchies are under less restraint in formulating their policy toward Israel.

The Other Gulf Monarchies and Israel

The other Gulf monarchies that share the Persian Gulf with Saudi Arabia are Bahrain, Kuwait, Oman, Qatar, and the United Arab Emirates. In the 1950s and 1960s, these five small states played a limited role, if any, in the Arab-Israeli conflict. They were not fully independent and later became involved in what can be described as a process of nation building. Given their small size and population, they were mainly preoccupied with domestic issues, and their foreign policy interests were focused on the Persian Gulf. This limited involvement in the Arab-Israeli conflict was drastically altered by three regional developments that have shaped the Gulf monarchies' attitude toward Israel and the Palestinians.

The first turning point was the sharp rise in oil prices following the Yom Kippur War in 1973. Suddenly, most of these oil-producing countries enjoyed massive oil revenues and unprecedented wealth. These financial resources offered them substantial political leverage. Kuwait, Qatar, and the United Arab Emirates have given generous financial aid to Egypt, Syria, Jordan, Lebanon, and the Palestinians. Moreover, the remittances sent home by laborers working in these Gulf monarchies represented a significant proportion of the Egyptian, Syrian, Jordanian, and Lebanese economies. Accordingly, these frontline states felt obligated to consult with the rich Gulf states on important issues related to the Arab-Israeli conflict. The second regional development was Yasser Arafat's decision to support Saddam Hussein when Iraq invaded Kuwait in 1990. This meant that Kuwait and the other Gulf monarchies were on the same side with Israel against Iraq, which received Palestinian sympathy and support. The majority of the population in the Gulf monarchies felt betrayed by the Palestinians. Arafat, who was a frequent visitor to the Gulf states, was never forgiven for his decision to support the Iraqis and was not allowed to visit most of these countries. Their financial support to the Palestinians was substantially reduced. On the other hand, this bitterness toward the Palestinians meant more acceptance and tolerance to Israel. Following the Gulf War (1990–91), the Gulf monarchies became less critical of Israel.

The third interrelated development, which shaped the Gulf monarchies' approach to the Arab-Israeli conflict, was the signing of the Oslo agreement between Israel and the Palestinians. For the first time, the two sides recognized each other. This step opened the door for reconciliation between the Gulf monarchies and Israel. The Gulf states felt that they did not need to be more Palestinian than the Palestinians themselves. Thus, low-level diplomatic and commercial contacts have been established between some of the Gulf states and Israel.

In formulating their policy toward the Arab-Israeli conflict and their approach toward Israel, the five Gulf monarchies have had to reconcile pressure from different directions. First, large Palestinian communities have resided in the Gulf region for decades.[32] Given the small indigenous population and the large expatriate Palestinian communities, the Palestinians represent a big proportion of the overall Gulf populations. Furthermore, many Palestinians occupy key positions in the commercial, economic, and educational sectors as well as in the mass media. They lobby the Gulf governments to adopt a strong anti-Israel and pro-Palestine position. Second, the escalating violence between the Israelis and the Palestinians adds more pressure on the Gulf governments to adopt a hard-line attitude toward the Jewish state. The impact of this violence has been further intensified in the last several years due to the revolution in information technology. Satellite dishes and the Internet have tremendously increased the Gulf populations' exposure to regional and international affairs. Third, the hostile attitude adopted by the regional superpowers (Iran, Iraq, and Saudi Arabia) toward Israel further complicates any rapprochement between Israel and the small Gulf states. In formulating their stand on the Arab-Israeli conflict, the five Gulf monarchies have to take into consideration the Iranian, Iraqi, and Saudi reactions. These three countries are too big and too powerful to be ignored by the smaller Gulf states.

Fourth, geography and history play an important role in shaping the five Gulf monarchies' regional and international policy. These coastal states have developed traditions of relative tolerance established through centuries of contact with seafaring traders in the Persian Gulf. For example, the practice of Wahhabism is much less rigid in Qatar than in Saudi Arabia. In Oman, Hindu temples, Christian churches, and Muslim mosques can be seen side by side. Bahrain has a small Jewish minority. These traditions of relative tolerance and acceptance of foreign culture have facilitated Western and Israeli ties and contacts with the people and governments of the five Gulf monarchies. Additionally, none of these Gulf states shares a common border with Israel, so Israel does not represent a direct threat to their national security. Fifth, considering the huge technological gap between Israel and the five Gulf monarchies, cooperation with the Jewish state will have many benefits. Many officials in the Gulf states value Israel's technological advances and skills, particularly in the areas of solar energy, drip irrigation, and other agricultural techniques. The severe scarcity of water in the Gulf region makes Israel's know-how in water conservation of particular interest. Finally, the often-exaggerated Jewish influence on American society and policy adds more attraction to establishing good relations with Israel. In other words, for some officials in the Gulf states, the road to Washington goes through Tel Aviv. By recognizing the Jewish state and establishing commercial and diplomatic ties with it, some Gulf states hope to improve their image in the United States.

Taking all these factors into consideration, the five Gulf monarchies, with some variation, have always expressed strong solidarity with the Palestinians and condemnation for Israel. Along with Saudi Arabia, they have provided massive financial aid to the frontline states and to the Palestinians. Repeatedly they have voiced their support to the peace process and commitment to a comprehensive solution to the Arab-Israeli conflict based on the United Nations resolutions, which would guarantee an Israeli withdrawal from Arab territories in both Syria and Lebanon and the establishment of a Palestinian state. In return, the five Gulf monarchies are prepared to recognize Israel and normalize relations with it.

In addition to this common policy, each Gulf monarchy has formulated its own policy toward Israel. In September 2003, an official Israeli delegation was allowed into the United Arab Emirates to attend an International Monetary Fund conference. The Dubai crown prince, Sheikh Muhammad bin-Rashid, met with the head of the Israeli delegation, Meir Sheetrit, a minister-without-portfolio.[33] This was the first meeting at such a high level between the two countries. Similarly, the first ministerial meeting between Bahrain and Israel took place in October 1994, when the Bahraini foreign minister, Sheikh Mubarak, met the Israeli minister of the environment, Yossi Sarid. Another gesture of reconciliation took place in September 2000, when Emir Hamad Ibn-Isa al-Khalifa appointed a Jewish man to serve on the country's consultative council.

Before the 1990 Iraqi invasion of Kuwait, the emirate was a strong proponent of Palestinian rights and a harsh critic of Israeli policy. This stand was softened following the liberation of Kuwait in 1991 due to Yasser Arafat's support to Saddam Hussein. Some 450,000 Palestinians lived in Kuwait before the invasion. Most were expelled or pressured to leave after the country was liberated. The Kuwaiti government stopped renewing work permits to thousands of Palestinians.[34] Officially, Kuwait recognized Arafat as the chairman of the PLO but demanded that he publicly apologize for supporting Iraq. Arafat never complied. Contacts between Kuwait and the Palestinians have been renewed. In 2001, members of the country's parliament invited Faisal Husseini, the PLO's top representative in Jerusalem, to participate in a seminar on the Palestinian issue. The visit triggered an unprecedented wave of attacks against Husseini. During the visit, Husseini died of a heart attack, prompting many Palestinians to hold the Kuwaitis responsible for his death. In October 2004, a delegation from the Palestinian Authority Ministry of Information visited Kuwait, the first such high-level contact between the two sides since 1990. A few weeks after Arafat's death in November 2004, the Palestinian leader Mahmoud Abbas visited Kuwait, apologized for the Palestinian support for Saddam Hussein's invasion of Kuwait, and inaugurated a new beginning in the relations between the two sides.

The main denominator of the three monarchies' stand toward Israel is that the time is not yet appropriate for direct relations with the Jewish state. In contrast, the other two Gulf monarchies, Oman and Qatar, were willing to move from denouncing Israel to playing a role as mediator between Tel Aviv and its Arab neighbors. Following the signing of the Oslo agreement in 1993, both Oman and Qatar have developed low-level diplomatic and commercial ties with Israel.

Oman has taken the lead in supporting the Arab-Israeli peace process. As early as 1979, Muscat was among a handful of Arab states that supported Sadat's peace treaty with Israel and resisted pressure to isolate Egypt. Since the early 1990s, Oman has been an active participant in all aspects of the multilateral peace process working groups created by the Madrid Peace Conference of 1991. The sultanate was the first Gulf state to host an Israeli delegation to a conference on water resources, which created the Middle East Desalination Research Center in Muscat.[35] In December 1995, Oman welcomed Israeli prime minister Yitzhak Rabin on his first visit to a Gulf state, where he met with Sultan Qaboos Bin Said al-Said. Rabin's visit inaugurated a new period of relations between the two countries. According to Jacob Abadi, "The two leaders agreed to open interest sections, as a precursor to full diplomatic relations."[36]

These Omani initiatives to establish economic ties and political dialogue with Israel can be explained by three factors. First, they can be seen as an extension of Muscat's long tradition of pro-Western policy. The peace process has also been supported by other Arab countries with strong ties with the West, such as Egypt, Morocco, and Jordan. Second, Muscat's willingness to accept and deal with Israel reflects a deep sense of both pragmatism and independence. Over the years, the sultanate has cooperated closely with Israel in methods of desalination, drip irrigation, and other agricultural techniques. Third, "an opening to Israel can be seen in part as a reaction to the Palestinian support of and involvement in the Dhufar rebellion, which threatened political stability in the sultanate for most of the 1960s and early 1970s."[37]

Like Oman, Qatar hosted an Israeli delegation in the multilateral talks on arms control that were created by the Madrid Peace Conference of 1991. Doha's rapprochement with Tel Aviv is driven by both economic and political considerations. According to the Energy Information Administration, "With proven reserves of 509 trillion cubic feet, Qatar contains the third largest natural gas reserves in the world behind Russia and Iran."[38] Economic prosperity depends on the state's ability to export increasing volumes of this hydrocarbon resource to the rest of the world. Since the early 1990s Doha has invested heavily in creating and expanding huge and sophisticated infrastructure to extract, market, and sell its natural gas. Israel represents not only an attractive market to the Qatari gas but also a potential transit route to shipments to the lucrative European markets.

In addition to these economic imperatives, political considerations have played a significant role in formulating the Qatari approach toward Israel. Since 1995, the emirate has been ruled by Sheikh Hamad Bin Khalifa al-Thani, who overthrew his father in a palace coup. The emir has shown strong interest in allying his tiny state with Western powers, particularly the United States. This pro-Western stand has proven irresistible to Washington. The 2003 war in Iraq was largely conducted from Qatar, not Saudi Arabia. Indeed, shortly after the war, Qatar became the main hub to American troops in the Persian Gulf. This alliance with the United States reflects the emir's desire to "put Qatar on the map" and to show independence from Saudi patronage and influence. Finally, Sheikh Hamad has introduced and pursued aggressive political reform. This includes municipal and parliamentary elections, where women have the right to vote and run for office. Most notably, the Qatari government not only encourages a free press but also sponsors the satellite television station Al-Jazeera, the most popular in the Middle East.

This liberal pro-Western environment has encouraged the Qatari authority to adopt a reconciliatory stand on the Arab-Israeli conflict and to establish and maintain commercial and diplomatic ties with Israel. Thus in September 2000, Sheikh Hamad met the Israeli prime minister, Ehud Barak, in New York, where the two leaders attended the UN Millennium Summit. After the outbreak of the Palestinian intifada in September 2000, Egypt pulled its ambassador from Israel, Jordan left its vacant ambassadorship position in Tel Aviv unfilled, and Oman, Morocco, and Tunisia cut trade ties. Israel's interest section in Qatar remained open, albeit at a very low level and out of the public eye. More recently, the Israeli foreign minister met in Paris with his Qatari counterpart to discuss bilateral relations and regional issues. Following the May 2003 meeting, the Qatari foreign minister said, "We don't object to having a treaty with Israel, but we don't think it is necessary now."[39]

Despite these commercial and diplomatic ties between Israel and both Oman and Qatar, the Gulf states are not likely to pursue full diplomatic relations with the Jewish state without some kind of solution with Syria and a recognition of basic Palestinian rights. Both Muscat and Doha are likely to continue their low-level rapprochement with Tel Aviv and play the role of mediator in the Arab-Israeli conflict.

5

The Persian Gulf and the Levant

Interactions between the Persian Gulf states and Israel over more than half a century suggest two conclusions. First, the two Middle East subsystems are strongly interconnected; developments in one arena are echoed in the other. All eight countries that share the Gulf have been, directly or indirectly, involved in the Arab-Israeli conflict/peace process. Israel, on the other hand, has reacted and frequently taken the initiative to promote its own national interests. The policy implication for this strong link between the Gulf and the Levant is that there will not be peace in the Middle East without addressing the grievances in both regions. Put differently, instability and violence in one arena have a spillover effect in the other. Second, with the exception of Iran under the Pahlavi regime, most of the episodes between the Persian Gulf states and Israel were characterized by mutual antagonism. Oman and Qatar aside, the other Gulf states do not recognize Israel, and Tel Aviv perceives them as its sworn enemies, albeit in different degrees. The foreign policy orientation of post-Saddam Iraq is yet to be decided.

This bleak assessment of the interaction between the two sides, however, does not have to endure. A less hostile and more promising attitude can prevail. Instead of trying to predict specific changes in the Persian Gulf states' foreign policy behavior toward Israel, this final chapter will discuss the major interrelated forces that are likely to shape Iran's, Iraq's, and Saudi Arabia's attitudes toward the Jewish state in the foreseeable future. Israel's attitude and reaction are beyond the scope of this volume. The list includes progress in the Arab-Israeli peace process, weakening of transnational ideological appeals, changes in the structure of the international system, strategic outcomes of the 2003 war in Iraq, and domestic political and economic developments in the Persian Gulf states.

Progress in the Arab-Israeli Peace Process

The 2003 war in Iraq was followed by a series of important developments in the peace process between the Palestinians and the Israelis. The most dramatic among these was the official announcement of a peace plan known as the "Road Map." This plan was sponsored by the United States, the European Union, Russia, and the United Nations. In June 2003, President Bush went to Sharm el-Sheikh, Egypt, and Aqaba, Jordan, where he met with regional leaders. Bush's personal involvement represented a turning point in his administration's diplomacy toward the Middle East. Unlike his predecessor, Bill Clinton, Bush preferred not to be directly involved in the negotiations between Middle Eastern parties. These international efforts in the aftermath of the 2003 war in Iraq are similar to another push for peace that brought the major players in the Middle East conflict as well as representatives of global powers to the Madrid Peace Conference, held in 1991, several months after the Gulf War. Like the Madrid Peace Conference, there is no guarantee that the "Road Map" will succeed. Indeed, a few months after it was introduced, Israeli prime minister Ariel Sharon presented a unilateral disengagement plan. Regardless of which plan might succeed, these efforts to make peace between the Arabs and the Israelis following two major wars against Iraq underscore the strong connection between the two arenas.

Obviously, progress in the peace process between Israel and the Palestinians and Syria would substantially increase the chances of Israel's acceptance by the Gulf states and its full integration in the Middle East. Put differently, the continuing violence against the Palestinians in the West Bank and Gaza Strip, the lack of consensus on the fate of millions of Palestinian refugees, the persistent disagreement over the status of Jerusalem, and the expansion of Israeli settlements in the West Bank and the Golan Heights fuel Arab and Iranian anger at Israel. Persian Gulf states' acceptance and recognition of Israel are conditioned on reaching a fair compromise on these issues.

Weakening of Transnational Ideological Appeals

Realism theory explains foreign policy behavior as a state's response to chiefly external threats and opportunities. This assumption, however, downplays the role of transnational ideologies in shaping states' orientation to other countries. Indeed, as Gregory Gause argues, "Most of the conflicts in the Middle

East—Arab-Israeli, inter-Arab, and Arab-Iranian—can be understood only in the context of the incentive powerful local leaders have to appeal to such transnational platforms to advance their interests."[1] For a long time, frontline Arab states' behaviors toward Israel have been driven more by national interests and less by ideological orientations while those of the Gulf states can be explained more by ideology and less by national interest. Pan-Arabism and political Islam have long shaped Persian Gulf states' perception of and policy toward Israel. Despite some fundamental differences between the two ideological appeals, both pan-Arabism and political Islam share a common stand—hostility to Israel. The loss of Palestine and the creation of a Jewish state at the heart of the Middle East are seen as both an Arab and Muslim disaster.

The militant stand Baghdad had adopted since the creation of Israel until the fall of Saddam Hussein can be largely explained by pan-Arabism. Iraqi leaders had sought to champion the Arab world by adopting a hard-line stand on the most important Arab cause—Palestine. As the discussion in previous chapters indicates, the Iraqis long rejected the compromises the Egyptians, Syrians, Lebanese, Jordanians, and even Palestinians have accepted. Tehran's stand on the Arab-Israeli conflict is similar to Baghdad's (until the 2003 war) but for another ideological appeal—political Islam. The overall foreign policy of the Islamic Republic of Iran since the 1979 revolution can be seen as an accommodation of both national interests and political Islam (as interpreted by the ruling elites). The Saudi foreign orientation reflects the kingdom's national interests as well as a combination of pan-Arabism and political Islam.

The Arab defeat in the 1967 war and the death of the champion of pan-Arabism, Egyptian president Gamal Abd al-Nasser, in 1970 have dealt a heavy blow to pan-Arabism all over the region. Similarly, the demise of the founder of the Islamic Republic, Ayatollah Khomeini, in 1989 has weakened the ideological drive in Iranian domestic and foreign policy. This does not suggest that the two ideological appeals play no role in formulating foreign policy. Rather, the emphasis on ideology throughout the region has been fading for some time. Ideological orientations increasingly have been replaced by national interests. This rising predominance of national interests has been reinforced by the complicating socioeconomic problems the Gulf states face. Rhetoric aside, this fundamental transformation has gradually shifted the perception of Israel. Tel Aviv is seen by a growing number of Arabs and Iranians not as a Zionist entity that has to be eradicated but as a Middle Eastern state that they have to live with.

Changes in the Structure of the International System

The decline of ideological appeals and the rise of national interests in for-mulating foreign policy in the Persian Gulf states reflect a global trend. The collapse of the Soviet Union in the early 1990s not only weakened the socialist model but also fundamentally altered the structure of the international system and the external alliance map in the Middle East. The traditional polarization of the cold war is over. For most of the cold war years, the United States was the main supporter to Israel and conservative Middle Eastern states (Saudi Arabia and Pahlavi Iran), while the Soviet Union was the main patron of revolution-ary Arab states (Iraq).

Middle Eastern states' relations with Moscow and Washington today are fundamentally different from those of the 1960s and 1970s. No attempt is made here to thoroughly examine Russian or American policy in the Middle East. Still, a brief discussion would help to shed light on potential changes in the Persian Gulf states' attitude toward Israel. Two themes have characterized Moscow's approach to the Middle East since the early 1990s. First, strategically Moscow was once a superpower equal to Washington. This perception has not completely disappeared. According to Robert Freedman, "Some Russian lead-ers still aspire to regain this status."[2] Second, Russia's Middle Eastern policy aims at protecting and promoting the country's economic interests. Within this context, Moscow's relations with Tel Aviv, Tehran, Baghdad, and Riyadh can be explained.

The hostile relations between Moscow and Tel Aviv started to change even before the collapse of the Soviet Union. Under heavy American pressure, in-creasing numbers of Soviet Jews were allowed to immigrate to Israel shortly before the collapse of the Soviet Union. In the 1990s there were no restrictions on immigration to Israel, and consequently the number of Russian Jews who immigrated to Israel skyrocketed. It is estimated that among the 6 million Israeli citizens today, more than 1 million are Russian immigrants. In other words, one in every six Israelis was born in the former Soviet Union. This large Russian-speaking community in Israel has brought Moscow and Tel Aviv closer than they have ever been. In addition to this demographic factor, Rus-sia has become a major trade partner to Israel, and the two countries work together on several scientific and military projects.

Moscow's relations with the Gulf states have also experienced dramatic shifts. Following the ouster of Saddam Hussein's regime, two issues have dom-inated Russia's policy in Iraq—the debt Baghdad owes to Moscow and the oil deals Saddam Hussein's government signed with Russian oil companies.

Russia plays a much weaker role in shaping the future of Iraq than the United States or some European countries.

The hostile relations between Washington and Tehran since the early days of the 1979 revolution brought Tehran closer to Moscow. Indeed, since the mid-1990s Russia has emerged as the main arms supplier to Iran. By the end of the decade, according to Mark Katz, "Iran had become the third largest purchaser of Russian weaponry."[3] The cooperation between the two countries expands to nuclear technology. In 1995 Iran signed an $800 million deal with Russia to finish building a nuclear reactor at Bushehr. The two countries also worked together to ensure stability in Central Asia. Despite this strategic and military cooperation, Moscow and Tehran have different (even conflicting) views and interests in sharing the Caspian Sea. At the time of this writing (early 2005), the two countries and the other three coastal states (Azerbaijan, Kazakhstan, and Turkmenistan) have not reached an agreement on how to divide the Caspian Sea between them. Finally, Moscow and Tehran compete in constructing pipeline routes to export the Caspian oil and gas to international markets.

Finally, Russian-Saudi relations witnessed a dramatic shift in 2003 when the kingdom's de facto ruler, Crown Prince Abdullah, led a large delegation in a three-day visit to Russia. This visit was the first top-level contact between the two countries since 1932, when the future king Faisal visited Moscow. For most of the second half of the twentieth century the Soviet-Saudi relations were characterized by mutual suspicion and antagonism. Indeed, Moscow and Riyadh engaged in proxy wars in East Africa and Afghanistan. By the early 2000s the Saudi leaders felt the need to coordinate their oil policy with Russia, a major oil-producing country, and to distance their country from the rebellion in Chechnya. For several years Russia has attended meetings of the Organization of Arab Petroleum Exporting Countries (OAPEC), not as a member but as an observer. Another potential area of cooperation between Moscow and Riyadh is within the framework of the Islamic Conference Organization (ICO). With an estimated Muslim population of 20 million, Russia has expressed interest in consolidating relations with Muslim countries and has attended the ICO's meetings as an observer.

On the other hand, Washington's strong support and commitment to the security of Israel have remained solid. Since the late 1960s, American diplomacy has been based on a commitment to Israel's right to exist within secure and recognized boundaries to be achieved through direct negotiations with its Arab neighbors. Believing that a strong Israel is a sine qua non for attaining peace in the region, the United States committed itself to maintaining Israel's qualitative edge over Arab armies.

Washington's relations with the Gulf states have substantially adjusted in response to the September 11, 2001, terrorist attacks and the 2003 war in Iraq. The fact that Osama bin Laden and fifteen out of the nineteen hijackers in the 9/11 attacks came from Saudi Arabia contributed to one of the biggest crises in American-Saudi relations. Members of Congress and major media outlets have since accused Riyadh of funding and supporting terrorism against the United States or at least not doing enough to halt terrorism. Within this context most of the American troops stationed in the kingdom since the Gulf War of 1990/91 were redeployed in 2003 to a new military base in neighboring Qatar. Finally, several influential members of the political establishment in Washington have called for reducing dependence on oil supplies from the Middle East, particularly from Saudi Arabia. These developments do not indicate that the American and Saudi governments see each other as enemies. Rather, they suggest that Washington and Riyadh face one of their most serious challenges in decades.

Certainly, the most obvious change is in Washington's relations with Baghdad. As has been mentioned, since the overthrow of the monarchy and the establishment of a republican system in 1958, the United States has had rocky relations with the Iraqi regimes. The animosity between the two sides reached its peak under Saddam Hussein (1979–2003). The United States led an international coalition into two wars against Iraq and twelve years of comprehensive economic sanctions. The next section will deal with the war's potential impact on Iraqi domestic policy. The regional impact of the ouster of Hussein's regime will take some time to materialize. Still, three outcomes can be identified with some certainty. First, the 2003 war represents a unique experience in Middle Eastern history. This is the first time American troops have ousted an Arab regime and arrested its leader. As a result, the war has significantly increased U.S. military, economic, political, and strategic involvement in the Middle East. The rebuilding of Iraq cannot be addressed in isolation from other developments in the Middle East. Regional powers have to be involved in articulating and creating the new Iraq. Second, the decision to go to war and the conduct of the war itself have demonstrated not only American military might but also how far the United States is willing to go to punish adversaries even without international consensus. This is a lesson other adversaries will not miss. Third, the removal of Saddam Hussein's regime has eliminated one of the most militant adversaries of Israel. It is unlikely that an Iraqi regime friendly to Israel will arise in the near future. As Ephraim Kam points out, "The hostility toward Israel has deep roots that predate Hussein's regime."[4] Continued and prominent American influence in Iraq, however, will prevent any new regime in Baghdad from playing an active role in the struggle against Israel.

Finally, U.S. relations with the Islamic Republic of Iran continued to be characterized by mutual suspicion and hostility. However, the wars in Afghanistan and Iraq have presented the Iranian leaders with new facts. Iran is surrounded by American troops almost from all directions. It is hard to predict Tehran's reaction, but it is also hard to imagine that these heavy American military deployments next to the Iranian borders are not taken into consideration by strategists in Iran. Anoushiravan Ehteshami defines Tehran's options: "In this new environment, Iran faces a stark choice: either continue to resist U.S. penetration of the region by heavy investment in what has become a shrinking circle of allies or exploit its considerable tactical advantages to broaden its policy of détente and diplomacy for greater economic and political gains."[5]

To sum up, the fundamental changes in the international system since the early 1990s—the collapse of the Soviet Union, rapprochement between Moscow and Tel Aviv, and unprecedented American involvement in the Middle East—provide both threats and opportunities to the Persian Gulf states to reassess their approach to the Arab-Israeli conflict and attitude toward Israel. As realism argues, states respond to external threats and opportunities. It is likely that these changes in the international system will be reflected in the cautious evolution of interactions between the Persian Gulf and the Levant.

The 2003 War in Iraq

Iraq is a unique country in the Middle East in the sense that it has been a participant in the major Arab-Israeli wars (1948, 1967, and 1973) as well as the three Gulf wars (1980–88, 1990–91, and 2003). It can be argued that domestic instability was one reason for Baghdad's adventurous and aggressive foreign policy. It can also be argued that Iraqi leaders used foreign policy to legitimize their regimes at home. In short, there is a connection between domestic stability and foreign policy behavior. The ouster of Saddam Hussein's regime opened the door for a long process of reconstruction of the country's economic and political systems.

The war in Iraq and the process to rebuild the country had been presented in Washington and some European capitals as the first step to installing democracy in the Arab world. Installing democracy by a foreign power in a country with no democratic traditions seems a daunting task. What of immediate concern is achieving stability in Iraq? There is no question that after forty-five years of totalitarian regimes (1958–2003) and twelve years of comprehensive economic sanctions (1991–2003), it will take time to bring Iraq back to stability and normalcy.

A complicating factor in making the country stable is the makeup of the Iraqi population. Iraq is a religiously and ethnically diverse nation, with at best a limited sense of national unity. As earlier discussion indicated, the policies adopted by previous Iraqi regimes failed to assimilate these religious, sectarian, and ethnic communities. Indeed, it can be argued that trying to impose Arabism on the Kurds and excluding a large segment of the Shi'ias from the top political apparatus have further alienated these two communities and fueled domestic instability. A delicate process of reconciliation between these religious and ethnic groups will take some time. The outcome is far from certain.

Equally important, the process of rebuilding and updating Iraq's economic infrastructure is complicated. Wars and sanctions left few resources to modernize the country's economic and social infrastructure. Furthermore, the state dominated the economic system for most of Iraq's modern history. Finally, Iraq is far from offering the physical security, political stability, and legal environment that will make it attractive for major foreign investment in the near future.

Despite these huge obstacles to achieving domestic stability in Iraq, the future is not bleak. The international community is strongly committed to rebuilding the country. Different foreign powers have debated whether the decision to go to war was the right one. However, they generally agree that there is no alternative to success. As Daniel Byman argues, "Perhaps the best argument for a democratic (stable) Iraq is that the alternatives are worse. Widespread repression, civil war, massive refugee flows, or other calamities might occur if Iraq does not gain a stable and decent government."[6]

Domestic Political and Economic Developments

Liberalism suggests that increasing economic interdependence should "constrain states from risky foreign policies."[7] Put differently, the higher the level of interdependence, the lower the likelihood of interstate conflict. This increasing interdependence is not only among states but also between them and the outside world. In other words, when countries become more integrated in the international economic and political system, they are more likely to adhere to global norms in their foreign policy behavior (i.e., less likely to resort to war). Finally, it is worth repeating, governments with stable domestic political and economic structures "do not resort to revolutionary or adventurous foreign policies to restore or preserve domestic cohesion."[8] In short, there is an intimate and immediate relationship between domestic and regional order. As Michael Barnett argues, "So long as there is little domestic peace, there is unlikely to be regional peace."[9] These theoretical assertions suggest that the growing institutionalization of states in the Persian Gulf and the hesitant and slow process of economic and political reform are likely to contribute to regional peace.

Since the 9/11 terrorist attacks in the United States and the accusations that the Saudi government supports terrorism, the regime in Riyadh has been subjected to intense international scrutiny. Opposition to the royal family also has become more vocal. In response, Saudi leaders have acknowledged the need to accommodate the demands for public participation in the political process. In 2003 Crown Prince Abdullah received at least three petitions signed by Saudi intellectuals, academics, and business professionals outlining the rationale and details of a potentially far-reaching program of reform.[10] Partly in response to domestic pressure and partly in response to international scrutiny, the Saudi government announced in October 2003 that it would hold its first elections to create local councils. The elections were held in late 2004 and early 2005. The official announcement stated, "The council of ministers decided to widen participation of citizens in running local affairs through elections by activating municipal councils, with half the members of each council being elected." In 1975 Saudi authorities issued a law to form municipal councils, but they were never formed. The kingdom has had no political elections at any level since its creation in 1932.

These signs of political reform have been echoed by a similar movement to reform the economic system. In 1999 King Fahd stated that "the world is heading for globalization and that it is no longer possible for Saudi Arabia to make slow progress."[11] Crown Prince Abdullah confirmed that privatization is a "strategic choice" for the kingdom. In line with these announcements, a Supreme Economic Council was created in 1999 and charged with boosting investment, creating jobs for Saudi nationals, and promoting privatization. In addition, Riyadh started talks to join the World Trade Organization (WTO) in 1993. The negotiations stalled over Saudi resistance to economic and trade reforms that the kingdom claimed ran counter to Islamic law. These talks have been activated, reflecting a strong Saudi desire to join the organization. It is important to point out that in 2005 Saudi Arabia was the only one of the six Gulf monarchies that was still not a member of the WTO.

Despite these initiatives to introduce economic reform, the Saudi economy is still largely dominated by the state. Large state corporations such as Saudi Aramco and the Saudi Basic Industries Corporation (SABIC) dominate the economy. "At the end of 2003, there has not been a single sale of state assets to private control."[12]

Probably more than Saudi Arabia, the Iranian domestic scene has witnessed dramatic changes since the establishment of the Islamic Republic in 1979. Shortly after the end of the war with Iraq in 1988, there were signs of popular demands for political accountability and freedom. These calls found a voice in President Muhammad Khatami, who was elected by a large margin of votes in 1997 and again in 2001. Confronting strong resistance from powerful conservative elements within the religious/political establishment in Tehran, Khatami has chosen a cautious approach in implementing his reform agenda. This approach has alienated some of his followers and made him look weak in confronting the hard-liners. Three characteristics of the process of political reform in Iran can be identified. First, despite the tremendous power the conservative camp holds, Iran is freer, in relative terms, than most of its Arab neighbors. There are lively debates in the Iranian Majlis (parliament) and press (despite frequent closures). Generally, women in Iran enjoy more rights than women in the other Gulf states. Second, the deep polarization of the Iranian policy between moderates and conservatives has created a state of stagnation and ineffectiveness. Occasionally the Iranian government speaks with more than one voice in both domestic and foreign policies. Third, Khatami was "a product of the reform movement," not the other way around.[13] The reform movement started before Khatami took office and continued after he left, despite some anticipated setbacks.

The Iranian government's efforts to reform the economy have been hesitant and have achieved little success partly because of the divisions within the religious/political establishment. In 1999 Khatami announced an ambitious program to privatize several major industries as part of total restructuring of the Iranian economy. Significant steps in the economic reform program were the unification of exchange rates and the issuing of the "Law on the Attraction and Protection of Foreign Investment."[14] Finally, for several years Iran has sought to start negotiations to join the WTO and has been blocked by the

United States. On the other hand, the European Union has negotiated a Trade and Cooperation Agreement with Iran since the late 1990s.

The main reason for the Gulf states to introduce economic and political reforms is the growing number of young, ambitious people open to new ideas and eager for jobs. These political and economic reforms still have a long way to go, however, and there is no guarantee they will succeed. However, this growing institutionalization of the Gulf states and their incremental integration in the global economic system are likely to have a moderate impact on their foreign policy behavior in general, including their attitude toward the Arab-Israeli conflict and the Jewish state.

For a long time, the interactions between the two Middle Eastern subsystems have been seen in zero-sum perspective; the gains of one side were considered the losses of the other side. Domestic, regional, and international developments discussed in this chapter suggest a new framework. Two developments on the Israeli and Palestinian sides have enhanced their chances to bring a peaceful end to the Arab-Israeli conflict. On the Israeli side, demographic facts have persuaded the Israeli leaders to take measures to ensure that Israel will remain Jewish, democratic, and safe. According to Dennis Ross, demographic trends indicate that "as early as the year 2010, and certainly not later than 2015, there will be more Arabs than Jews between the Mediterranean Sea and the Jordan River."[15] This trend is the main drive for Ariel Sharon's "Disengagement Plan." Reaching the same conclusion, Shai Feldman, a prominent Israeli strategist, argues that Israel's strategic surroundings permit it to "disengage from the territories in which the majority of the Palestinian population are located."[16]

On the Palestinian side, Arafat's death in November 2004 means that an era of modern Palestinian history has come to an end and that a new one has begun. It will take some time to adequately assess Arafat's legacy and the implications of his departure, but a few propositions can be made. Arafat played a prominent role in presenting the Palestinian question as a struggle to achieve national identity and statehood, not merely as a search for a humanitarian solution to refugees. More than any other Arab leader, Arafat made it possible to legitimize Israel in the Arab and Islamic worlds. Despite all the shortcomings of the 1993 Oslo agreement, it legitimized negotiations with Israel. Finally, Arafat failed to make the transition from revolutionary to statesman. He could not become Nelson Mandela. In order to maintain his status as an embodiment and symbol of the Palestinian struggle, Arafat avoided making the hard decisions and compromises that were necessary to reach a final peace.

These developments on the Israeli and Palestinian sides indicate that there is a historical moment to bring a peaceful end to the Arab-Israeli conflict and that this moment should be seized. Most likely there will not be a breakthrough in diplomatic and economic relations between the Gulf states and Israel any time soon. Assuming progress in the Arab-Israeli peace process, the analysis in this volume points out that a more peaceful pattern of interaction between the Gulf and the Levant is emerging.

Notes

Chapter 1. Introduction

1. Michael Brecher, *The Foreign Policy System of Israel*, 39.

2. It is important to point out that even when Iraq was a monarchy and enjoyed good relations with Western countries, it opposed Israel. This suggests that good relations with Western countries should be seen as a contributing factor, not as a determining one.

3. These themes of realism are thoroughly outlined in Hans J. Morgenthau, *Politics among Nations: The Struggle for Power and Peace*, and Kenneth M. Waltz, *Theory of International Politics*.

4. Simon Bromley, *American Hegemony and World Oil: The Industry, the State System, and the World Economy*, 12.

5. Bruce E. Moon, "The State in Foreign and Domestic Policy," 191.

6. Raymond Hinnebusch and Anoushiravan Ehteshami, *The Foreign Policies of Middle East States*, 21.

7. Saudi Arabia shares small borders with Israel.

8. Shireen Hunter, "Iran's Pragmatic Regional Policy," 139.

9. It is important to point out that this increased national interest is restrained by a new surge of Arab nationalism due to the outbreak of the Palestinian uprising since 2000 and the American-led military operations in Iraq. Both have been extensively covered by Arab satellite TV stations and seen all over the Arab world.

10. Gregory Gause, "Systemic Approaches to Middle East International Relations," 31.

11. Ofra Bengio and Gabriel Ben-Dor, *Minorities and the State in the Arab World*, 1.

12. Michael C. Hudson, *Arab Politics: The Search for Legitimacy*, 271.

13. Philippe Fargues, "Demographic Islamization: Non-Muslim in Muslim Countries," 104.

14. Albert H. Hourani, *Minorities in the Arab World*, 17.

15. Ibid., 22.

16. Will H. Moore and David R. Davis, "Transnational Ethnic Ties and Foreign Policy," 101.

17. James E. Dougherty and Robert L. Pfaltzgraff, *Contending Theories of International Relations: A Comprehensive Survey*, 553.

18. Raymond Hinnebusch, *The International Politics of the Middle East*, 94.

19. Tareq Y. Ismael, *International Relations of the Contemporary Middle East*, 36.

Chapter 2. Iran and Israel

1. R. K. Ramazani, "Iran and the Arab-Israeli Conflict," 414.

2. Ibid.

3. The decision to partition Palestine was adopted in November 1947, after six months of discussion by the UN General Assembly. The majority of the countries voted for the decision. However, three months later, when the Palestine question was up again for discussion in the UN Security Council, only two delegations—the Soviet and the Ukrainian—insisted that the General Assembly's decision to divide Palestine into two states should be carried out.

4. Uri Bialer, "The Iranian Connection in Israel's Foreign Policy, 1948–1951," 296.

5. Central Intelligence Agency, *The World Fact Book* 2002.

6. Shireen T. Hunter, *Iran and the World: Continuity in a Revolutionary Decade*, 7.

7. Muhammad Reza Pahlavi, *Answer to History*, 12–13.

8. For a detailed analysis, see Martin Sicker, *The Bear and the Lion: Soviet Imperialism and Iran*.

9. John L. Esposito, "The Iranian Revolution: A Ten-Year Perspective," 17.

10. Ayatollah Khomeini, the founder of the 1979 Islamic Revolution, was not against nationalism in the sense of patriotism, but he opposed it as a superiority of a particular race. See Hunter, *Iran and the World*, 13.

11. R. K. Ramazani, "Reflections on Iran's Foreign Policy: Defining the 'National Interests,'" 214. Twelver is the branch of Shi'ia Islam that believes in twelve Imams (religious leaders), beginning with Ali and ending with Muhammad al-Mahdi. See E. van Donzel, B. Lewis, and Ch. Pellat, *Encyclopedia of Islam*, 277.

12. R. K. Ramazani, "Khomeini's Islam in Iran's Foreign Policy," 21.

13. Anoushiravan Ehteshami and Raymond A. Hinnebusch, *Syria and Iran: Middle Powers in a Penetrated Regional System*, 31.

14. Energy Information Administration, *Country Profile: Iran*.

15. For example, between 1945 and 1972, Iran spent $1.2 billion to import arms. With a fourfold increase in the price of oil, Iran spent $18 billion on arms purchases from 1972 to 1978. See Henry Paolucci, *Iran, Israel, and the United States*, 12.

16. Roger M. Savory, "Religious Dogma and the Economic and Political Imperatives of Iranian Foreign Policy," 49.

17. Anoushiravan Ehteshami, *After Khomeini*, 78.

18. Anoushiravan Ehteshami, "Iran," 219.

19. Hooshang Amirahmadi, "Iran's Development: Evaluation and Challenges," 123.

20. R. K. Ramazani, *Iran's Foreign Policy, 1941–1973: A Study of Foreign Policy in Modernizing Nations*, 273.

21. Although the "twin-pillar strategy" of the United States was based on cooperation with both Iran and Saudi Arabia, Iran was unquestionably the more important of the two.

22. Sohrab Sobhani, *The Pragmatic Entente: Israeli-Iranian Relations, 1948–1988*, 6.

23. E. A. Bayne, *Persian Kingship in Transition*, 212.

24. Gary Sick, "The Clouded Mirror: The United States and Iran, 1979–1999," 192.

25. For a discussion of the reasons for "dual containment," see Anthony Lake, "Confronting Backlash States," 45–56.

26. For a detailed discussion of the Iran-Libya Sanctions Act,, see Laurie Lande, "Second Thoughts," 44–49.

27. For a thorough analysis of the three islands dispute, see Hooshang Amirahmadi, *Small Islands, Big Politics: The Tonbs and Abu Musa in the Persian Gulf*, and Richard Schofield, *Territorial Foundations of the Gulf States*.

28. R. K. Ramazani, *The Persian Gulf: Iran's Role*, 41.

29. R. K. Ramazani, *Iran's Foreign Policy, 1941–1973: A Study of Foreign Policy in Modernizing Nations*, 397. Other members of the Baghdad Pact were Britain, Iraq, Pakistan, and Turkey.

30. Diplomatic relations did not resume until just before Nasser's death in the fall of 1970.

31. Central Intelligence Agency, *The World Fact Book* 2003.

32. The Jews, Armenians, and Zoroastrians are officially recognized by the state. Other religious minorities, such as the Baha'i, are not recognized.

33. Walter J. Fischel, "Israel in Iran: A Survey of Judeo-Persian Literature," 817.

34. Robert B. Reppa, *Israel and Iran: Bilateral Relationships and Effect on the Indian Ocean Basin*, 86.

35. Nicholas De Lange, *Atlas of the Jewish World*, 222.

36. Nadir Shah showed great tolerance toward non-Muslims and even invited Jews to come and settle in Mashhad, the holy city of Iranian Shi'ites.

37. The information in this section was drawn from publications listed on the Center for Iranian Jewish Oral History Web site at www.cijoh.org, particularly Payvand's Iran News, *A Brief History of Iranian Jews*, May 2000, at www.payvand.com/ny/jews.html.

38. The Baha'is were not recognized as a religious minority.

39. M. G. Weinbaum, "Iran and Israel: The Discreet Entente," 1072.

40. Payvand, *A Brief History of Iranian Jews*.

41. Eli Barnavi, *A Historical Atlas of the Jewish People*, 214.

42. Uri Bialer, "The Iranian Connection in Israel's Foreign Policy, 1948–1951," 295.

43. David Menashri, "Khomeini's Policy toward Ethnic and Religious Minorities," 226.

44. According to some sources, Israel privately admitted to Iran that the Iranian Jews were spying for Israel. See Douglas Davis, "Report: Israel Admitted Iranian Jews Were Spies."

45. Akiva Eldar, "Jewish Tattlers Led to Arrests in Iran."

46. Yair Sheleg, "Informer in Shiraz: Ahead of Verdict, Iranian Jews Are Targeting Each Other."

47. David Menashri, "Khomeini's Policy toward Ethnic and Religious Minorities," 229.

48. The Eisenhower Doctrine underscored American readiness to provide economic and military assistance to countries that are subject to aggression from any nation controlled by international communism. For more details, see George Lenczowski, *American Presidents and the Middle East*, 52–54.

49. Sohrab Sobhani, *The Pragmatic Entente: Israeli-Iranian Relations, 1948–1988*, 37.

50. Joseph Alpher, "Israel and the Iran-Iraq War," 157.

51. Iran's radicalization was demonstrated during the hostage crisis, when fifty-three American diplomats were held hostage for 444 days.

52. For a detailed discussion of the U.S. reasons to approach Iran, see James A. Bill, *The Eagle and the Lion: The Tragedy of American-Iranian Relations*, 306–15.

53. David Kimche, *The Last Option: After Nasser, Arafat, and Saddam Hussein: The Quest for Peace in the Middle East*, 213–14.

54. Joseph Alpher, "Israel and the Iran-Iraq War," 160.

55. John Tower, *The Tower Commission Report*, 52.

56. As early as 1981, Israel was selling Phantom jet tires to Iran.

57. Tower, *Tower Commission Report*, 23.

58. Aaron S. Klieman, *Israel's Global Reach: Arms Sales as Diplomacy*, 159.

59. Secretary of State Shultz and Secretary of Defense Weinberger opposed the idea of an arms-for-hostages swap.

60. William B. Quandt, *Peace Process: American Diplomacy and the Arab-Israeli Conflict since 1967*, 357.

61. George Lenczowski, *American Presidents and the Middle East*, 242.

62. Tower, *Tower Commission Report*, 84.

63. James A. Bill, *The Eagle and the Lion: The Tragedy of American-Iranian Relations*, 313.

64. Sohrab Sobhani, *The Pragmatic Entente: Israeli-Iranian Relations, 1948–1988*, 152.

65. Ibid., 26.

66. Bernard Reich, "Israel and the Iran-Iraq War," 77.

67. R. K. Ramazani, "Iran and the Arab-Israeli Conflict," 418.

68. Reich, "Israel and the Iran-Iraq War," 77.

69. Weinbaum, "Iran and Israel: The Discreet Entente," 1083.

70. Hunter, *Iran and the World*, 127.

71. When the PLO accepted UN Resolution 242, Iran declared that no organization had the right to give away "even an inch of the Islamic land of Palestine."

72. Shahram Chubin, *Iran's National Security Policy: Intentions, Capabilities, and Impact*, 15.

73. Augustus Richard Norton, "Hizballah and the Israeli Withdrawal from Southern Lebanon," 22.

74. Barbara Harff, "Minorities, Rebellion, and Repression in North Africa and the Middle East," 239.

75. Helena Cobban, "The Growth of Shi'i Power in Lebanon and Its Implications for the Future," 144.

76. After arriving in Libya in August 1978, Imam Musa al-Sadr disappeared. While Libya claims that al-Sadr left Libya on an Alitalia flight bound for Rome, only his luggage and an impostor arrived. Most AMAL leaders believe that the Libyan government is responsible for the disappearance of their leader.

77. Augustus Richard Norton, "Shi'ism and Social Protest in Lebanon," 172.

78. John L. Esposito, *The Oxford Encyclopedia of the Modern Islamic World*, 346.

79. Helena Cobban, "The Growth of Shi'i Power in Lebanon and Its Implications for the Future," 139.

80. Anoushiravan Ehteshami and Raymond A. Hinnebusch, *Syria and Iran: Middle Powers in a Penetrated Regional System*, 124.

81. Augustus Richard Norton, "Insecurity Zones in South Lebanon," 65.

82. As a result of this invasion, the PLO moved its operations to Tunis.

83. The gunmen who carried out the assassination attempt were followers of Abu Nidal, an extremist dissident who is a sworn enemy of the PLO.

84. U.S. Department of State, *Patterns of Global Terrorism 2003*, 121.

85. Alan Philps, "Barak Tries to Salvage Dignity for Shaken Israel."

86. Tony Allen-Mills, "Villagers Braced for the First Attack in Israeli Border Limbo."

87. For an Israeli prospective on the disputed land, see Asher Kaufman, "Who Owns the Shebaa Farms? Chronicle of a Territorial Dispute."

88. Anoushiravan Ehteshami, "Tehran's Tocsin," 172.

89. Shahram Chubin, "Does Iran Want Nuclear Weapon?" 91.

90. Wyn Q. Bowen and Joanna Kidd, "The Iranian Nuclear Challenge," 264.

91. Jacqueline Simon, "United States Non-Proliferation Policy and Iran: Constraints and Opportunities," 371.

92. Robert J. Einhorn, "A Transatlantic Strategy on Iran's Nuclear Program," 22.

93. Avner Cohen and Thomas Graham, "An NPT for Non-members," 42

94. In December 2003 Muhammad El-Baradei, the director general of the IAEA, called on Israel to relinquish its nuclear weapons as part of a general peace agreement in the Middle East. He said that in spite of Israel's policy of not acknowledging possession of nuclear weapons, "we operate under the assumption that Israel has nuclear arms." See Yossi Melman, "El-Baradei Calls on Israel to Give Up Nukes."

95. Nader Entessar, "Israel and Iran's National Security," 16.

96. Israel also received crucial assistance from Norway and South Africa.

97. Joseph Cirincione, *Deadly Arsenals: Tracking Weapons of Mass Destruction*, 225.

98. Avner Cohen, *Israel and the Bomb*, 44.

99. Douglas Frantz, "Israel Extends Nuclear Weapons Capability."

100. Avner Cohen and Thomas Graham, "WMD in the Middle East: A Diminishing Currency," 24.

101. Shai Feldman, *Nuclear Weapons and Arms Control in the Middle East*, 185.

102. Gerald M. Steinberg, "The IAEA and Israel: A Realistic Agenda," 8.

103. Zeev Maoz, "The Mixed Blessing of Israel's Nuclear Policy," 73.

104. "Israel to Retain Ambiguous Nuclear Policy," Ma'ariv.

105. Louis Rene Beres, "Israel's Strategic Future: The Final Report of Project Daniel."

Chapter 3. Iraq and Israel

1. Simon Henderson, *Instant Empire: Saddam Hussein's Ambition for Iraq*, 94.

2. For a thorough analysis of military coups in contemporary Arab politics, see Eliezer Be'eri, *Army Officers in Arab Politics and Society*.

3. Tim Niblock, "Introduction," 4.

4. Ahmad Yousef Ahmad, "The Dialectics of Domestic Environment and Role Performance: The Foreign Policy of Iraq," 149.

5. Mark N. Katz, "Iraq and the Superpowers," 86.

6. Meanwhile, the Soviet Union continued and expanded its close ties to Syria.

7. Barry Rubin, "United States–Iraq Relations: A Spring Thaw?" 116.

8. Barry Rubin, "The United States and Iraq: From Appeasement to War," 257.

9. Simon Henderson, *Instant Empire: Saddam Hussein's Ambition for Iraq*, 184.

10. Zachary Karabell, "Backfire: U.S. Policy toward Iraq, 1988–2 August 1990," 35.

11. Paul A. Gigot, "A Great American Screw-Up: The U.S. and Iraq, 1980–1990," 8.

12. Edmund Ghareeb, *The Kurdish Question in Iraq*, 45.

13. Saddam Hussein participated in this failed operation and was wounded.

14. Helen Chapin Metz, *Iraq: A Country Study*, 189.

15. Marion Farouk Sluglett and Peter Sluglett, *Iraq since 1958: From Revolution to Dictatorship*, 108.

16. Ofra Bengio, *Saddam's Word: Political Discourse in Iraq*, 33.

17. John F. Devlin, *The Ba'ath Party: A History from Its Origins to 1966*, 31.

18. Ofra Bengio, *Saddam's Word: Political Discourse in Iraq*, 44.

19. Charles Tripp, "The Foreign Policy of Iraq," 169.

20. Charles G. MacDonald, "The Kurdish Question," 234.

21. Monte Palmer, *The Politics of the Middle East*, 276.

22. R. D. McLaurin, Mohammed Mughisuddin, and Abraham R. Wagner, *Foreign Policy Making in the Middle East: Domestic Influences on Policy in Egypt, Iraq, Israel, and Syria*, 130.

23. Graham E. Fuller, *Iraq in the Next Decade: Will Iraq Survive until 2002?* 6.

24. Indeed, possession of Mosul province became a key source of contention between Turkey and the British authorities in Iraq, only resolved after intense negotiations in 1926 when it was agreed that the province should go to Iraq.

25. J. M. Abdulghani, *Iraq and Iran: The Years of Crisis*, 133.

26. Aliya, literally meaning "going up," is the standard Israeli term to denote immigration.

27. Simon Henderson, *Instant Empire: Saddam Hussein's Ambition for Iraq*, 92.

28. Abbas Shiblak, *The Lure of Zion: The Case of the Iraqi Jews*, 14.

29. Ibid., 23.

30. Moshe Gat, *The Jewish Exodus from Iraq, 1948–1951*, 7.

31. Daphne Tsimhoni, "Jewish-Muslim Relations in Modern Iraq," 98.

32. Moshe Gat, *The Jewish Exodus from Iraq, 1948–1951*, 37.

33. Yehouda Shenhav, "The Jews of Iraq, Zionist Ideology, and the Property of the Palestinian Refugees of 1948: An Anomaly of National Accounting," 610.

34. Eli Barnavi, *A Historical Atlas of the Jewish People From the Time of the Patriarchs to the Present*, 212.

35. Avner Yaniv, "Israel Faces Iraq: The Politics of Confrontation," 233.

36. Given its large Jewish community and its pro-Western foreign policy orientation, Morocco has always been friendlier to Israel than the other North African states.

37. Avner Yaniv, "Israel Faces Iraq: The Politics of Confrontation," 237.

38. Benny Morris, *Righteous Victims: A History of the Zionist-Arab Conflict, 1881–1999*, 251.

39. Marion Farouk-Sluglett and Peter Sluglett, *Iraq since 1958: From Revolution to Dictatorship*, 132.

40. Charles Tripp, *A History of Iraq*, 210.

41. Farouk-Sluglett and Sluglett, *Iraq since 1958*, 203.

42. R. D. McLaurin, Mohammed Mughisuddin, and Abraham R. Wagner, *Foreign Policy Making in the Middle East: Domestic Influences on Policy in Egypt, Iraq, Israel, and Syria*, 145.

43. Avner Yaniv, "Israel Faces Iraq: The Politics of Confrontation," 248.

44. Phebe Marr, "Iraq: Balancing Foreign and Domestic Realities," 196.

45. The Israeli Labor Party advocated this approach.

46. Joseph Alpher, "Israel and the Iran-Iraq War," 159.

47. Bernard Reich, "Israel and the Iran-Iraq War," 83.

48. Yair Evron, "The Invasion of Kuwait and the Gulf War: Dilemmas Facing the Israeli-Iraqi-U.S. Relationship," 314.

49. Reich, "Israel and the Iran-Iraq War," 82.

50. Kamran Mofid, "Economic Reconstruction of Iraq: Financing the Peace," 53.

51. Saddam Hussein also mentioned that Syria should agree to withdraw its troops from Lebanon.

52. A few days after Saddam Hussein was arrested in December 2003, Israeli media revealed that the Israeli government had developed a plan in 1992 to assassinate Saddam Hussein to punish him for his missile attacks. The operation, however, was called off after a training accident.

53. Joseph Alpher, *War in the Gulf: Implications for Israel*, 41.

54. Shai Feldman, "Israeli Deterrence and the Gulf War," 191.

55. Avner Yaniv, "Israel Faces Iraq: The Politics of Confrontation," 247.

56. R. D. McLaurin, Mohammed Mughisuddin, and Abraham K. Wagner, *Foreign Policy Making in the Middle East: Domestic Influences on Policy in Egypt, Iraq, Israel, and Syria*, 108.

57. Shahram Chubin and Sepehr Zabih, *The Foreign Relations of Iran*, 184.

58. Graham E. Fuller, *Iraq in the Next Decade: Will Iraq Survive Until 2002?* 10.

59. J. M. Abdulghani, *Iraq and Iran: The Years of Crisis*, 139.

60. George Lenczowski, *American Presidents and the Middle East*, 119.

61. Abdulghani, *Iraq and Iran*, 145.

62. Jonathan C. Randal, *After Such Knowledge, What Forgiveness? My Encounters with Kurdistan*, 191.

63. Ibid., 197.

64. Nader Entessar, "Kurdish Conflict in a Regional Perspective," 52.

65. Since the Shat al-Arab was Iraq's only major outlet to the Persian Gulf, the Iraqi regime had always insisted on total control of this river, claiming that Iraq's economic survival depended on total sovereignty over the Shat al-Arab. Iran, on the other hand, had insisted that the waterway was crucial to its economy and navigation and that international law had clearly recognized the Thalweg Line as the boundary between countries sharing a body of water such as the Shat al-Arab.

66. Sa'ad Jawad, "Recent Developments in the Kurdish Issue," 58.

67. Charles Tripp, A History of Iraq, 213.

68. Jed C. Snyder, "The Road to Osiraq: Baghdad's Quest for the Bomb," 578.

69. Amos Perlmutter, "The Israeli Raid on Iraq: A New Proliferation Landscape," 40.

70. Snyder, "The Road to Osiraq," 583.

71. Shai Feldman, "The Bombing of Osiraq—Revisited," 136.

72. Ghassan Bishara, "The Political Repercussions of the Israeli Raid on the Iraqi Nuclear Reactor," 69.

73. Ibid., 60.

74. In December 2003, following long negotiations with Washington and London, Libya announced its complete cooperation with the IAEA in disclosing its WMD programs.

75. Rosemary Hollis, *Iraq in Transition: Vortex or Catalyst?* 21.

76. Gal Luft, *All Quiet on the Eastern Front? Israel's National Security Doctrine after the Fall of Saddam*, 17.

Chapter 4. The Gulf Monarchies and Israel

1. Bahgat Korany, "Defending the Faith: The Foreign Policy of Saudi Arabia," 250.

2. William B. Quandt, *Saudi Arabia in the 1980s: Foreign Policy, Security, and Oil*, 31.

3. Monte Palmer, *The Politics of the Middle East*, 221.

4. M. Th. Houtsma, A. J. Wensinck, H. A. R. Gibb, W. Heffening, and E. Levi-Provencal, *The Encyclopedia of Islam*, 1089.

5. Palmer, *The Politics of the Middle East*, 226.

6. David E. Long, *The Kingdom of Saudi Arabia*, 108.

7. Gregory Gause III, "The Foreign Policy of Saudi Arabia," 205.

8. J. E. Peterson, *Saudi Arabia and the Illusion of Security*, 33.

9. Hermann Frederick Eilts, "Saudi Arabia's Foreign Policy," 221.

10. Palmer, *The Politics of the Middle East*, 229.

11. The official reasoning for the withdrawal of U.S. troops from Saudi Arabia was that they were stationed there to reinforce the "no-fly zones" in Iraq under Saddam Hussein. With his toppling, there is no need to maintain American troops in the kingdom.

12. Quandt, *Saudi Arabia in the 1980s*, 143.

13. John Marlowe, *The Persian Gulf in the Twentieth Century*, 94.

14. George Lenczowski, *Oil and State in the Middle East*, 17.

15. Energy Information Administration, *OPEC Revenues Fact Sheet*.

16. Energy Information Administration, *OPEC Revenues: Country Details*.

17. Hermann Frederick Eilts, "Saudi Arabia's Foreign Policy," 229.

18. Itamar Rabinovich and Jehuda Reinharz, eds., *Israel in the Middle East: Documents and Readings on Society, Politics, and Foreign Relations, 1948–Present*, 222.

19. Adeed Dawisha, "Saudi Arabia and the Arab-Israeli Conflict: The Ups and Downs of Pragmatic Moderation," 677.

20. George Lenczowski, *American Presidents and the Middle East*, 135.

21. Ibid., 130.

22. The conference included representatives of Abu Dhabi, Algeria, Bahrain, Egypt, Iraq, Kuwait, Libya, Qatar, Saudi Arabia, and Syria.

23. Nadav Safran, *Saudi Arabia: The Ceaseless Quest for Security*, 157.

24. British Petroleum, *BP Statistical Review of World Energy*, 14.

25. Lizette Alvarez, "Britain Says U.S. Planned to Seize Oil in 1973 Crisis."

26. Jacob Goldberg, "Saudi Arabia and the Egyptian-Israeli Peace Process, 1977–1981," 28.

27. Nadav Safran, *Saudi Arabia: The Ceaseless Quest for Security*, 263.

28. Zvi Bar'el, "Prince of Peace."

29. Gil Hoffman, "Sharon Warns Saudi Plan May Be Arab Plot."

30. Serge Schmemann, "A Saudi Peace Idea, Suddenly in the Spotlight."

31. Aluf Benn, "Official Government Response: Saudi Plan Endangers Israel's Security."

32. No accurate data are available, but it is estimated that hundreds of thousands of Palestinians have lived in the Gulf states since the early 1950s.

33. Dan Gerstenfeld, "Dubai's Crown Prince Invites Israelis to Visit."

34. Jacob Abadi, "Israel's Relations with Oman and the Persian Gulf States," 69.

35. For more information, see the center's website at www.medrc.org.

36. Jacob Abadi, "Israel's Relations with Oman and the Persian Gulf States," 50.

37. Gawdat Bahgat, "Security in the Gulf: The View from Oman," 450.

38. Energy Information Administration, *Country Profile: Qatar*.

39. Herb Keinon, "Israel Holds Talks with Qatar."

Chapter 5. The Persian Gulf and the Levant

1. Gregory Gause III, "Systemic Approaches to Middle East International Relations," 26.

2. Robert O. Freedman, "Russian Policy toward the Middle East under Putin: The Impact of 9/11 and the War in Iraq," 67.

3. Mark N. Katz, "Losing Balance: Russian Foreign Policy toward Iraq and Iran," 343.

4. Ephraim Kam, "The War in Iraq: Regional Implications," 114.

5. Anoushiravan Ehteshami, "Iran-Iraq Relations after Saddam," 127.

6. Daniel Byman, "Constructing a Democratic Iraq: Challenges and Opportunities," 48.

7. Will H. Moore and David R. Davis, "Transnational Ethnic Ties and Foreign Policy," 103. For a detailed explanation of liberalism, see Robert O. Keohane and Joseph S. Nye, *Power and Interdependence: World Politics in Transition*.

8. James E. Dougherty and Robert L. Pfaltzgraff, *Contending Theories of International Relations: A Comprehensive Survey*, 116.

9. Michael N. Barnett, "Regional Security after the Gulf War," 618.

10. One of these petitions was presented by the leaders of the Shi'ia minority in the kingdom, who demanded more equal treatment in public employment and religious

rights. For a detailed discussion of these petitions, see Richard Dekmejian, "The Liberal Impulse in Saudi Arabia."

11. Energy Information Administration, *Country Profile: Saudi Arabia*, June 2004.

12. Ibid.

13. Ali M. Ansari, "Continuous Regime Change from Within," 61.

14. Energy Information Administration, *Country Profile: Iran*.

15. Dennis Ross, *The Missing Peace: The Inside Story of the Fight for Middle East Peace*, 797.

16. Shai Feldman, "A National Moment of Truth?"

Bibliography

Abadi, Jacob. "Israel's Relations with Oman and the Persian Gulf States." *Journal of South Asian and Middle Eastern Studies* 20, no. 1 (Fall 1996): 46–73.

Abdulghani, J. M. *Iraq and Iran: The Years of Crisis*. Baltimore: Johns Hopkins University Press, 1984.

Ahmad, Ahmad Yousef. "The Dialectics of Domestic Environment and Role Performance: The Foreign Policy of Iraq." In *The Foreign Policies of Arab States*, ed. Bahgat Korany and Ali E. Hillal Dessouki, 147–73. Boulder: Westview Press, 1984.

Allen-Mills, Tony. "Villagers Braced for the First Attack in Israeli Border Limbo." *Sunday Times* (May 28, 2000).

Alpher, Joseph, ed. *War in the Gulf: Implications for Israel*. Boulder: Westview Press, 1992.

———. "Israel and the Iran-Iraq War." In *The Iran-Iraq War: Impact and Implications*, ed. Efraim Karsh, 154–68. New York: St. Martin's Press, 1989.

Alvarez, Lizette. "Britain Says U.S. Planned to Seize Oil in 1973 Crisis." *New York Times* (January 2, 2004).

Amirahmadi, Hooshang, ed. *Small Islands, Big Politics: The Tonbs and Abu Musa in the Persian Gulf*. New York: St. Martin's Press, 1996.

———. "Iran's Development: Evaluation and Challenges." *Third World Quarterly* 17, no. 1 (March 1996): 123–47.

Ansari, Ali M. "Continuous Regime Change from Within." *Washington Quarterly* 26, no. 4 (Fall 2003): 53–67.

Bahgat, Gawdat. "Security in the Gulf: The View from Oman." *Security Dialogue* 30, no. 4 (December 1999): 445–58.

Bar'el, Zvi. "Prince of Peace." *Ha'aretz* (February 28, 2002).

Barnavi, Eli. *A Historical Atlas of the Jewish People from the Time of the Patriarchs to the Present*. New York: Alfred A. Knopf, 1992.

Barnett, Michael N. "Regional Security after the Gulf War." *Political Science Quarterly* 111, no. 4 (Winter 1996–97): 597–618.

Bayne, E. A. *Persian Kingship in Transition*. New York: American Universities Field Staff, 1968.

Be'eri, Eliezer. *Army Officers in Arab Politics and Society*. New York: Praeger, 1970.

Bengio, Ofra. *Saddam's Word: Political Discourse in Iraq*. New York: Oxford University Press, 1998.

Bengio, Ofra, and Gabriel Ben-Dor. *Minorities and the State in the Arab World*. Boulder: Lynne Rienner, 1991.

Benn, Aluf. "Official Government Response: Saudi Plan Endangers Israel's Security." *Ha'aretz* (March 3, 2002).

Beres, Louis Rene. "Israel's Strategic Future: The Final Report of Project Daniel." *NATIV Online* 3, no. 2 (April 2004) online at www.acpr.org.il.

Bialer, Uri. "The Iranian Connection in Israel's Foreign Policy, 1948–1951." *Middle East Journal* 39, no. 2 (Spring 1985): 292–315.

Bill, James A. *The Eagle and the Lion: The Tragedy of American-Iranian Relations.* New Haven: Yale University Press, 1988.

Bishara, Ghassan. "The Political Repercussions of the Israeli Raid on the Iraqi Nuclear Reactor." *Journal of Palestine Studies* 11, no. 3 (Spring 1982): 58–76.

Bowen, Wyn Q., and Joanna Kidd. "The Iranian Nuclear Challenge." *International Affairs* 80, no. 2 (March 2004): 257–76.

Brecher, Michael. *The Foreign Policy System of Israel.* New Haven: Yale University Press, 1972.

British Petroleum. *BP Statistical Review of World Energy.* London, 2003.

Bromley, Simon. *American Hegemony and World Oil: The Industry, the State System, and the World Economy.* University Park: Pennsylvania State University Press, 1991.

Byman, Daniel. "Constructing a Democratic Iraq: Challenges and Opportunities." *International Security* 28, no. 1 (Summer 2003): 47–78.

Central Intelligence Agency. *World Fact Book 2002.* Online at www.cia.gov/cia/publications.

———. *World Fact Book 2003.* Online at www.cia.gov/cia/publications.

Chubin, Shahram. *Iran's National Security Policy: Intentions, Capabilities, and Impact.* Washington, D.C.: Carnegie Endowment for International Peace, 1994.

———. "Does Iran Want Nuclear Weapon?" *Survival* 37, no. 1 (Spring 1995): 86–104.

Chubin, Shahram, and Sepehr Zabih. *The Foreign Relations of Iran.* Berkeley: University of California Press, 1974.

Cirincione, Joseph. *Deadly Arsenals: Tracking Weapons of Mass Destruction.* Washington, D.C.: Carnegie Endowment for International Peace, 2002.

Cobban, Helena. "The Growth of Shi'i Power in Lebanon and Its Implications for the Future." In *Shi'ism and Social Protest,* ed. Juan R. I. Cole and Nikki R. Keddie, 137–55. New Haven: Yale University Press, 1986.

Cohen, Avner. *Israel and the Bomb.* New York: Columbia University Press, 1998.

Cohen, Avner, and Thomas Graham. "An NPT for Non-members." *Bulletin of the Atomic Scientists* 60, no. 3 (May/June 2004): 40–44.

———. "WMD in the Middle East: A Diminishing Currency." *Disarmament Diplomacy,* no. 76 (March/April 2004): 22–26.

Davis, Douglas. "Report: Israel Admitted Iranian Jews Were Spies." Jerusalem Post (August 10, 2000).

Dawisha, Adeed. "Saudi Arabia and the Arab-Israeli Conflict: The Ups and Downs of Pragmatic Moderation." *International Journal* 38, no. 4 (Fall 1983): 674–89.

De Lange, Nicholas. *Atlas of the Jewish World.* New York: Facts on File, 1984.

Dekmejian, Richard. "The Liberal Impulse in Saudi Arabia." *Middle East Journal* 57, no. 3 (Summer 2003): 400–413.

Devlin, John F. *The Ba'ath Party: A History from Its Origins to 1966.* Stanford, Calif.: Hoover Institution Press, 1976.

Donzel, E. van, B. Lewis, and Ch. Pellat. *Encyclopedia of Islam.* Leiden: E. J. Brill, 1978.

Dougherty, James E., and Robert L. Pfaltzgraff. *Contending Theories of International Relations: A Comprehensive Survey*. London: Longman, 2001.

Ehteshami, Anoushiravan. *After Khomeini*. London: Routledge, 1995.

———. "Iran." In *Economic and Political Liberalization in the Middle East*, ed. Tim Niblock and Emma Murphy, 214–36. London: British Academic Press, 1993.

———. "Tehran's Tocsin." *Washington Quarterly* 23, no. 3 (Summer 2000): 171–76.

———. "Iran-Iraq Relations after Saddam." *Washington Quarterly* 26, no. 4 (August 2003): 115–29.

Ehteshami, Anoushiravan, and Raymond A. Hinnebusch. *Syria and Iran: Middle Powers in a Penetrated Regional System*. London: Routledge, 1998.

Eilts, Hermann Frederick. "Saudi Arabia's Foreign Policy." In *Diplomacy in the Middle East: The International Relations of Regional and Outside Powers*, ed. L. Carl Brown, 219–44. London: I. B. Tauris, 2001.

Einhorn, Robert J. "A Transatlantic Strategy on Iran's Nuclear Program." *Washington Quarterly* 27, no. 4 (Fall 2004): 21–32.

Eldar, Akiva. "Jewish Tattlers Led to Arrests in Iran." *Ha'aretz* (July 16, 1999).

Energy Information Administration. *Country Profile: Iran*. November 2003. Online at www.eia.doe.gov.

———. *Country Profile: Qatar*. October 2002. Online at www.eia.doe.gov.

———. *Country Profile: Saudi Arabia*. June 2004. Online at www.eia.doe.gov.

———. *Country Profile: Saudi Arabia*. December 2003. Online at www.eia.doe.gov.

———. *OPEC Revenues: Country Details*. June 2002. Online at www.eia.doe.gov.

———. *OPEC Revenues Fact Sheet*. December 2002. Online at www.eia.doe.gov.

Entessar, Nader. "Israel and Iran's National Security." *Journal of South Asian and Middle Eastern Studies* 27, no. 4 (Summer 2004): 1–19.

———. "Kurdish Conflict in a Regional Perspective." In *Change and Continuity in the Middle East: Conflict Resolution and Prospects for Peace*, ed. M. E. Ahrari, 47–73. London: Macmillan Press, 1996.

Esposito, John L. *Oxford Encyclopedia of the Modern Islamic World*. New York: Oxford University Press, 1995.

———. "The Iranian Revolution: A Ten-Year Perspective." In *The Iranian Revolution: Its Global Impact*, ed. John L. Esposito, 17–39. Miami: Florida International University Press, 1990.

Evron, Yair. "The Invasion of Kuwait and the Gulf War: Dilemmas Facing the Israeli-Iraqi-U.S. Relationship." In *The Middle East and the United States: A Historical and Political Reassessment*, ed. David W. Lesch, 313–23. Boulder: Westview Press, 1996.

Fargues, Philippe. "Demographic Islamization: Non-Muslim in Muslim Countries." *SAIS Review* 21, no. 2 (Summer/Fall 2001): 103–16.

Feldman, Shai. *Nuclear Weapons and Arms Control in the Middle East*. Cambridge: MIT Press, 1997.

———. "Israeli Deterrence and the Gulf War." In *War in the Gulf: Implications for Israel*, ed. Joseph Alpher, 184–208. Boulder: Westview Press, 1992.

———. "The Bombing of Osiraq—Revisited." *International Security* 7, no. 2 (Fall 1982): 114–42.

———. "A National Moment of Truth?" *Strategic Assessment* 6, no. 4 (February 2004). Online at www.tau.ac.il.

Fischel, Walter J. "Israel in Iran: A Survey of Judeo-Persian Literature." In *The Jews: Their*

History, Culture, and Religion, ed. Louis Finkelstein, 817–58. New York: Harper and Brothers, 1955.

Frantz, Douglas. "Israel Extends Nuclear Weapons Capability." *Los Angeles Times* (October 11, 2003).

Freedman, Robert O. "Russian Policy toward the Middle East under Putin: The Impact of 9/11 and the War in Iraq." *Alternatives* 2, no. 2 (Summer 2003): 66–97.

Fuller, Graham E. *Iraq in the Next Decade: Will Iraq Survive until 2002?* Santa Monica, Calif.: RAND, 1993.

Gat, Moshe. *The Jewish Exodus from Iraq, 1948–1951*. London: Frank Cass, 1997.

Gause, Gregory, III. "The Foreign Policy of Saudi Arabia." In *The Foreign Policies of Middle East States*, ed. Raymond Hinnebusch and Anoushiravan Ehteshami, 193–211. Boulder: Lynne Rienner, 2002.

———. "Systemic Approaches to Middle East International Relations." *International Studies Review* 1, no. 1 (Spring 1999): 11–31.

Gerstenfeld, Dan. "Dubai's Crown Prince Invites Israelis to Visit." *Jerusalem Post* (September 24, 2003).

Ghareeb, Edmund. *The Kurdish Question in Iraq*. Syracuse, N.Y.: Syracuse University Press, 1981.

Gigot, Paul A. "A Great American Screw-up: The U.S. and Iraq, 1980–1990." *National Interest*, no. 22 (Winter 1990/91): 3–10.

Goldberg, Jacob. "Saudi Arabia and the Egyptian-Israeli Peace Process, 1977–1981." *Middle East Review* 18, no. 4 (Summer 1986): 25–33.

Harff, Barbara. "Minorities, Rebellion, and Repression in North Africa and the Middle East." In *Minorities at Risk: A Global View of Ethnopolitical Conflicts*, ed. Ted Robert Gurr, 216–51. Washington, D.C.: United States Institute of Peace Press, 1993.

Henderson, Simon. *Instant Empire: Saddam Hussein's Ambition for Iraq*. San Francisco: Mercury House, 1991.

Hinnebusch, Raymond. *The International Politics of the Middle East*. Manchester: Manchester University Press, 2003.

Hinnebusch, Raymond, and Anoushiravan Ehteshami. *The Foreign Policies of Middle East States*. Boulder: Lynne Rienner, 2002.

Hoffman, Gil. "Sharon Warns Saudi Plan May Be Arab Plot." *Jerusalem Post* (March 3, 2002).

Hollis, Rosemary. *Iraq in Transition: Vortex or Catalyst?* London: Chatham House, 2004.

Hourani, Albert H. *Minorities in the Arab World*. London: Oxford University Press, 1947.

Houtsma, M. Th., A. J. Wensinck, H. A. R. Gibb, W. Heffening, and E. Levi-Provencal, eds. *Encyclopedia of Islam*. London: Luzac, 1934.

Hudson, Michael C. *Arab Politics: The Search for Legitimacy*. New Haven: Yale University Press, 1977.

Hunter, Shireen T. *Iran and the World: Continuity in a Revolutionary Decade*. Bloomington: Indiana University Press, 1990.

———. "Iran's Pragmatic Regional Policy." *Journal of International Affairs* 56, no. 2 (Spring 2003): 133–47.

Ismael, Tareq Y. *International Relations of the Contemporary Middle East*. New York: Syracuse University Press, 1986.

"Israel to Retain Ambiguous Nuclear Policy." *Ma'ariv* (July 6, 2004).

Jawad, Sa'ad. "Recent Developments in the Kurdish Issue." In *Iraq: the Contemporary State*, ed. Tim Niblock, 47–61. London: Croom Helm, 1982.

Kam, Ephraim. "The War in Iraq: Regional Implications." In *After the War in Iraq*, ed. Shai ' Feldman, 101–14. Brighton: Sussex Academic Press, 2003.

Karabell, Zachary. "Backfire: U.S. Policy toward Iraq, 1988–2 August 1990." *Middle East Journal* 49, no. 1 (Winter 1995): 28–47.

Katz, Mark N. "Iraq and the Superpowers." In *Iraq in Transition: A Political Economic and Strategic Perspective*, ed. Frederick W. Axelgard, 85–96. Boulder: Westview Press, 1986.

———. "Losing Balance: Russian Foreign Policy toward Iraq and Iran." *Current History* 102, no. 666 (October 2003): 341–45.

Kaufman, Asher. "Who Owns the Shebaa Farms? Chronicle of a Territorial Dispute." *Middle East Journal* 56, no. 4 (Fall 2002): 576–95.

Keinon, Herb. "Israel Holds Talks with Qatar." *Jerusalem Post* (May 14, 2002).

Keohane, Robert O., and Joseph S. Nye. *Power and Interdependence: World Politics in Transition*. Boston: Little, Brown, 1977.

Kimche, David. *The Last Option: After Nasser, Arafat, and Saddam Hussein: The Quest for Peace in the Middle East*. New York: Charles Scribner's Sons, 1991.

Klieman, Aaron S. *Israel's Global Reach: Arms Sales as Diplomacy*. Washington, D.C.: Pergamon, 1985.

Korany, Bahgat. "Defending the Faith: The Foreign Policy of Saudi Arabia." In *The Foreign Policies of Arab States*, ed. Bahgat Korany and Ali E. Hillal Dessouki, 241–82. Boulder: Westview Press, 1984.

Lake, Anthony. "Confronting Backlash States." *Foreign Affairs* 73, no. 2 (March/April 1994): 45–56.

Lande, Laurie. "Second Thoughts." *International Economy* 11, no. 3 (May/June 1997): 44–49.

Lenczowski, George. *American Presidents and the Middle East*. Durham, N.C.: Duke University Press, 1990.

———. *Oil and State in the Middle East*. New York: Cornell University Press, 1960.

Long, David E. *The Kingdom of Saudi Arabia*. Gainesville: University Press of Florida, 1997.

Luft, Gal. *All Quiet on the Eastern Front? Israel's National Security Doctrine after the Fall of Saddam*. Washington, D.C.: Brookings Institution, 2004.

MacDonald, Charles G. "The Kurdish Question." In *Ethnicity, Pluralism, and the State in the Middle East*, ed. Milton J. Esman and Itamar Rabinovich, 233–52. Ithaca, N.Y.: Cornell University Press, 1988.

Maoz, Zeev. "The Mixed Blessing of Israel's Nuclear Policy." *International Security* 28, no. 2 (Fall 2003): 44–77.

Marlowe, John. *The Persian Gulf in the Twentieth Century*. New York: Frederick A. Praeger, 1962.

Marr, Phebe. "Iraq: Balancing Foreign and Domestic Realities." In *Diplomacy in the Middle East: The International Relations of Regional and Outside Powers*, ed. L. Carl Brown, 181–205. London: I. B. Tauris, 2001.

McLaurin, R. D., Mohammed Mughisuddin, and Abraham R. Wagner. *Foreign Policy Making in the Middle East: Domestic Influences on Policy in Egypt, Iraq, Israel, and Syria*. New York: Praeger, 1977.

Melman, Yossi. "El-Baradei Calls on Israel to Give Up Nukes." *Ha'aretz* (December 12, 2003).

Menashri, David. "Khomeini's Policy toward Ethnic and Religious Minorities." In *Ethnicity, Pluralism, and the State in the Middle East*, ed. Milton J. Esman and Itamar Rabinovich, 215–29. Ithaca, N.Y.: Cornell University Press, 1988.

Metz, Helen Chapin. *Iraq: A Country Study*. Washington, D.C.: Government Printing Office, 1990.

Mofid, Kamran. "Economic Reconstruction of Iraq: Financing the Peace." *Third World Quarterly* 12, no. 1 (January 1990): 48–61.

Moon, Bruce E. "The State in Foreign and Domestic Policy." In *Foreign Policy Analysis: Continuity and Change in Its Second Generation*, ed. Laura Neack, Jeanne A. K. Hey, and Patrick J. Haney, 187–200. Englewood Cliffs, N.J.: Prentice Hall, 1991.

Moore, Will H., and David R. Davis. "Transnational Ethnic Ties and Foreign Policy." In *The International Spread of Ethnic Conflict*, ed. David A. Lake and Donald Rothchild, 89–103. Princeton: Princeton University Press, 1998.

Morgenthau, Hans J. *Politics among Nations: The Struggle for Power and Peace*. New York: Knopf, 1948.

Morris, Benny. *Righteous Victims: A History of the Zionist-Arab Conflict, 1881–1999*. London: John Murray, 2000.

Niblock, Tim. "Introduction." In *Iraq: The Contemporary State*, ed. Tim Niblock, 1–6. London: Croom Helm, 1982.

Norton, Augustus Richard. "Hizballah and the Israeli Withdrawal from Southern Lebanon." *Journal of Palestine Studies* 30, no. 1 (Fall 2000): 22–35.

———. "Shi'ism and Social Protest in Lebanon." In *Shi'ism and Social Protest*, ed. Juan R. I. Cole and Nikki R. Keddie, 156–77. New Haven: Yale University Press, 1986.

———. "Insecurity Zones in South Lebanon." *Journal of Palestine Studies* 23, no. 1 (Fall 1993): 61–79.

Pahlavi, Muhammad Reza. *Answer to History*. New York: Stein and Day, 1980.

Palmer, Monte. *The Politics of the Middle East*. Itasca, Ill.: F. E. Peacock, 2002.

Paolucci, Henry. *Iran, Israel, and the United States*. Naples: Press Marketing Services, 1991.

Payvand's Iran News. *A Brief History of Iranian Jews* (May 2000). Online at www.payvand.com/ny/jews.html.

Perlmutter, Amos. "The Israeli Raid on Iraq: A New Proliferation Landscape." *Strategic Review* 10, no. 1 (Winter 1982): 34–43.

Peterson, J. E. *Saudi Arabia and the Illusion of Security*. Adelphi Paper # 348, London: Oxford University Press, 2002.

Philps, Alan. "Barak Tries to Salvage Dignity for Shaken Israel." *Daily Telegraph* (May 28, 2002).

Quandt, William B. *Peace Process: American Diplomacy and the Arab-Israeli Conflict since 1967*. Washington, D.C.: Brookings Institution, 1993.

———. *Saudi Arabia in the 1980s: Foreign Policy, Security and Oil*. Washington, D.C.: Brookings Institution, 1981.

Rabinovich, Itamar, and Jehuda Reinharz, eds. *Israel in the Middle East: Documents and Readings on Society, Politics, and Foreign Relations, 1948–Present*. New York: Oxford University Press, 1984.

Ramazani, R. K. *Iran's Foreign Policy, 1941–1973: A Study of Foreign Policy in Modernizing Nations*. Charlottesville: University Press of Virginia, 1975.

———. *The Persian Gulf: Iran's Role*. Charlottesville: University Press of Virginia, 1972.

———. "Iran and the Arab-Israeli Conflict." *Middle East Journal* 32, no. 4 (Fall 1978): 413–28.

———. "Reflections on Iran's Foreign Policy: Defining the 'National Interests.'" In *Iran at the Crossroads*, ed. John L. Esposito and R. K. Ramazani, 211–37. New York: Palgrave, 2001.

———. "Khomeini's Islam in Iran's Foreign Policy." In *Islam in Foreign Policy*, ed. Adeed Dawisha, 9–33. Cambridge: Cambridge University Press, 1983

Randal, Jonathan C. *After Such Knowledge, What Forgiveness? My Encounters with Kurdistan*. New York: Farrar, Straus and Giroux, 1997.

Reich, Bernard. "Israel and the Iran-Iraq War." In *The Persian Gulf War: Lessons for Strategy, Law, and Diplomacy*, ed. Christopher C. Joyner, 75–90. New York: Greenwood Press, 1990.

Reppa, Robert B. *Israel and Iran: Bilateral Relationships and Effect on the Indian Ocean Basin*. New York: Praeger, 1974.

Ross, Dennis. *The Missing Peace: The Inside Story of the Fight for Middle East Peace*. New York: Farrar, Straus and Giroux, 2004.

Rubin, Barry. "United States–Iraq Relations: A Spring Thaw?" In *Iraq: The Contemporary State*, ed. Tim Niblock, 109–24. London: Croom Helm, 1982.

———. "The United States and Iraq: From Appeasement to War." In *Iraq's Road to War*, ed. Amatzia Baram and Barry Rubin, 255–72. New York: St. Martin's Press, 1993.

Safran, Nadav. *Saudi Arabia: The Ceaseless Quest for Security*. Cambridge: Harvard University Press, 1985.

Savory, Roger M. "Religious Dogma and the Economic and Political Imperatives of Iranian Foreign Policy." In *Iran at the Crossroads*, ed. Miron Rezun, 35–67. Boulder: Westview Press, 1989.

Schmemann, Serge. "A Saudi Peace Idea, Suddenly in the Spotlight." *New York Times* (March 3, 2002).

Schofield, Richard, ed. *Territorial Foundations of the Gulf States*. London: UCL Press, 1994.

Sheleg, Yair. "Informer in Shiraz: Ahead of Verdict, Iranian Jews Are Targeting Each Other." *Ha'aretz* (June 29, 2000).

Shenhav, Yehouda. "The Jews of Iraq, Zionist Ideology, and the Property of the Palestinian Refugees of 1948: An Anomaly of National Accounting." *International Journal of Middle East Studies* 31, no. 4 (November 1999): 605–30.

Shiblak, Abbas. *The Lure of Zion: The Case of the Iraqi Jews*. London: Al Saqi Books, 1986.

Sick, Gary. "The Clouded Mirror: The United States and Iran, 1979–1999." In *Iran at the Crossroads*, ed. John L. Esposito and R. K. Ramazani, 191–210. New York: Palgrave, 2001.

Sicker, Martin. *The Bear and the Lion: Soviet Imperialism and Iran*. New York: Praeger, 1988.

Simon, Jacqueline. "United States Non-Proliferation Policy and Iran: Constraints and Opportunities." *Contemporary Security Policy* 17, no. 3 (December 1996): 365–94.

Sluglett, Marion Farouk, and Peter Sluglett. *Iraq since 1958: From Revolution to Dictatorship*. London: KPI, 1987.

Snyder, Jed C. "The Road to Osiraq: Baghdad's Quest for the Bomb." *Middle East Journal* 37, no. 4 (Fall 1983): 565–93.

Sobhani, Sohrab. *The Pragmatic Entente: Israeli-Iranian Relations, 1948–1988*. New York: Praeger, 1989.

Steinberg, Gerald M. "The IAEA and Israel: A Realistic Agenda." *Jerusalem Issue Brief* 3, no. 27 (July 2004): 8–10.

Tower, John. *The Tower Commission Report*. New York: Bantam Books and Times Books, 1987.

Tripp, Charles. *A History of Iraq*. Cambridge: Cambridge University Press, 2002.

———. "The Foreign Policy of Iraq." In *The Foreign Policies of Middle East States*, ed. Raymond Hinnebusch and Anoushiravan Ehteshami, 167–92. Boulder: Lynne Rienner, 2002.

Tsimhoni, Daphne. "Jewish-Muslim Relations in Modern Iraq." In *Nationalism, Minorities, and Diasporas: Identities and Rights in the Middle East*, ed. Kirsten E. Schulze, Martin Stokes, and Colm Campbell, 95–116. London: I. B. Tauris, 1996.

U.S. Department of State. *Patterns of Global Terrorism 2003*. Washington, D.C.: Government Printing Office, 2004.

Waltz, Kenneth M. *Theory of International Politics*. Reading, Mass: Addison-Wesley, 1979.

Weinbaum, M. G. "Iran and Israel: The Discreet Entente." *Orbis* 18, no. 1 (Winter 1975): 1070–87.

Yaniv, Avner. "Israel Faces Iraq: The Politics of Confrontation." In Iraq's *Road to War*, ed. Amatzia Baram and Barry Rubin, 233–351. New York: St. Martin's Press, 1993.

Index

References to notes are indicated by "n" after the page number.

Gawdat Bahgat is professor of political science and director of the Center for Middle Eastern Studies at Indiana University of Pennsylvania. He is the author of *The Gulf Monarchies: New Economic and Political Realities* (1997), *The Future of the Gulf* (1997), *The Persian Gulf at the Dawn of the New Millennium* (1999), and *American Oil Diplomacy in the Persian Gulf and the Caspian Sea* (UPF, 2003). He has also published numerous articles on the Persian Gulf and the Caspian Sea in scholarly journals. His work has been translated into Arabic, Russian, German, and Italian.